AWESOME GAME CREATION: NO PROGRAMMING REQUIRED

AWESOME GAME CREATION: NO PROGRAMMING REQUIRED

Luke Ahearn

CHARLES RIVER MEDIA, INC.
Rockland, Massachusetts

Publisher: Jenifer Niles
Production: Electro-Publishing
Cover Design: The Printed Image
Cover Image: Luke Ahearn
Printer: Inter City Press, Inc.

CHARLES RIVER MEDIA, INC.
P.O. Box 417
403 VFW Drive
Rockland, Massachusetts 02370
781-871-4184
781-871-4376(FAX)
chrivmedia@aol.com
http://www.charlesriver.com

This book is printed on acid-free paper.

Awesome Game Creation: No Programming Required
by Luke Ahearn
   ISBN 1-886801-48-7
   Printed in the United States of America

00 01 02 03 7 6 5 4 3 2 1

CHARLES RIVER MEDIA, INC. titles are available for site license
or bulk purchase by institutions, user groups, corporations, etc. For
additional information, please contact the Special Sales Department
at 781-871-4184.

DEDICATION

Julie, Ellen, and Cooper

- Luke Ahearn

ACKNOWLEDGMENTS

As you have no doubt read a million times, no book is the sole creation of one person. This book is no exception. *Awesome Game Creation* was made possible by the following individuals and companies who bent over backwards to help us pull it together. Their contributions to this book were enormous and invaluable.

Mike Whalen (www.blitz.simplenet.com) for writing the History of Games in chapter four.

Clickteam (www.clickteam.com) for providing The Games Factory and Install Maker; François Lionet, Yves Lamoureux, and *The Games Factory Manual* writers Ian Young, assisted by Philip Chapman, Richard Vanner, and Lee Bamber.

Pie in the Sky Software (www.pieskysoft.com) for The Pie 3D Game Creation System; and the user-created site GCS Games (www.gcsgames.com). I suggest you visit GCS Games, if you get serious about using GCS, and join the mailing list.

Nick Marks (www.nickmarks.com) for access to his free textures on the FreeTextures site (www.freetextures.com). I mention when a texture of his is in use.

3D RAD (www.3drad.com) for the latest and greatest version of 3D RAD (v2.5.6) and the complete documentation of 3D RAD.

GoldWave (www.goldwave.com) for the shareware version of the GoldWave digital editor.

Jasc Software (www.jasc.com) for the demo of Paint Shop Pro.

Jenifer Niles at Charles River Media Inc., for being a writer's dream.

And as always, the past and present employees and associates of Goldtree who made this book possible by hunkering down and staying in the trenches.

CONTENTS

PREFACE

"I must not fear. Fear is the mind-killer.
Fear is the little-death that brings total obliteration.
I will face my fear.
I will permit it to pass over me and through me. And when it has gone
past I will turn the inner eye to see its path.
Where the fear has gone there will be nothing.
Only I will remain."

—Frank Herbert, *Dune*

Since starting in game development eight years ago, I have asked a million questions and fought hard to get the answers. And a funny thing happened: After a few years, people began to ask *me* questions, and I never forgot the time I was that wide-eyed, "wanna-be" gamer, ready to lay waste to all of the established developers and claim my fortune — after sheepishly asking how they did it. Well, I don't drive a Ferrari, but a Mustang GT isn't too bad.

As a game developer, I've discovered that the up-and-coming developers always ask the same questions and tend to make the same mistakes — the same ones I made along the way. Unfortunately, this is not a "self-help" book, so it won't address the worst and most glaring mistakes, which are those concerning attitude, self-esteem, and ability. But it can help with the same old questions about the generation of design documents, how to design, and the important steps of developing a game. Even these answers, however, without the benefit of some advice on approaching your subject, would be useless. Game development is actually similar to most things in life; if you really want to do something, the answers are available, and there are people out there to help you. This is especially true as it relates to game development.

In my experience, there has never been a question that has gone unanswered or a need that hasn't been met. So if you want to write a novel, have a body like The Hulk, or have a game that you developed under your belt — you simply must have the desire to do it, enjoy the process of doing it(not just the end result), and then, you must *do* it. The next step is to overcome the "demons" of self-doubt and fear.

The genesis of this book started when I was combing through my e-mail archives in preparation for a workshop at the local university. Having answered the same questions so many times about the numerous aspects of game design and development, I thought it would be useful to go through all of the accumulated e-mail to prepare my course material. Realizing that these same questions had been answered over and over again, I probably had enough organized material for a book on game design and development (as it turned out enough for two books — this one and *Designing 3D Games That Sell* which will be published later this year).

Since it was important for the book to cover game design completely, I spent months researching the Web, visiting the newsgroups, looking at other books, and e-mailing fellow developers for their ideas, tips and design techniques. My suspicions were confirmed and validated — most developers run into the same types of problems — so doing a book like this seemed to make sense.

I wrote the book for the following reasons:

1) Ideally, so novice game developers won't waste the same amount of time and money getting to the point I'm at now. There are many individuals who wanted to be game developers — and possessed more innate talent than I had at the beginning — but they quit while on the cusp of success. It is important to remember that in order to finish a game and get somewhere with it, you can't give up.

2) It's discouraging to see extremely talented individuals and teams fail in the game development industry due to stupid mistakes — whether their own or those they were subjected to because of the inexperience to recognize them. Let's face it, most of us aren't good at everything. We have our strengths and weaknesses that help us to soar or crash and burn, depending on the situation. It is common in business and in life to see the talented and deserving turned away (or never show up at all),

while the motivated, go-getters bask in the glory of their spoils. This frequently occurs because the go-getters, simply *go and get*, while too many of us are "thinkers" and "creators" — content to sit back and watch the others seize the opportunities. Among many other topics in the book I also included aspects that up-and-coming developers often neglect: the market, the publisher, and the product design.

3) Finally, discouragement in any form bothers me, especially when one person discourages another from seizing a great opportunity or from completing an important task. Therefore, my primary purpose for writing this book is to encourage you to try your hand at game development. I've attempted to provide you with all of the tools and the necessary skills to develop games that are substantial as well as fun.

Stick with it and become a game developer, and good luck in whatever you decide to do.

Luke Ahearn
New Orleans
May, 2000

INTRODUCTION

**Basic Game
Development 101**

Anyone can develop a game. Despite the common opinion that game development is beyond the grasp of the ordinary mortal, game development is very easy — especially today. The tools and techniques needed are readily accessible and, in fact, are on the CD-ROM in the back of this book.

To make a great game, or even a good game, takes a lot of hard work, talent, and intelligence, but we won't let that get in our way right now. Seriously, this book is meant to be fun and informative, so don't worry about how your work compares to the games at Comp USA. Just have fun and learn the basics. Once you know your way around the tools and terminology of game development, you will be able to focus on your "production values" and produce the game you've always dreamed of.

NOTE

Production values refer to the quality, polish, and professionalism of your product. Often you will hear people talk about "tweaking," tightening up their work, or "God is in the details" — these are all hallmarks of a professional adding high production values to their work.

This brings me to an important point. You must resist the common belief that, "The days of the small developer are gone!" or other such nonsense. I personally hate to hear this sentiment mindlessly parroted and used as a bludgeon to discourage newcomers to game development. There always has and always will be room for the small guy, the pioneer, the independent.

Sure, you almost certainly can't develop a massive game all by your lonesome, and even if you were technically able, you would probably be pretty old and very far behind the cutting edge when you finished. But you can develop a small game or interactive product by yourself that is of high quality, useful, original, and entertaining. You will see that by the end of this book, you will have the vocabulary of a game developer, a working knowledge of a 2D and 3D game development tool, and hopefully a greater sense of empowerment to become an actual game developer.

In fact, by the end of this book, you will see that garage developers have never been more powerful. This is due to the availability of easy-to-use, affordable tools, and access to the knowledge of game development, thanks to the Internet.

So how is it that anyone can develop a game? Well, one of the main reasons is the advent of the drag-and-drop application. This application allows users to click an image, sound, or other file type, drag it into their application, and then drop it there. This makes game creation possible without programming.

Let's face it, there are a lot more of us that can do artwork for games than can actually program games. So when the first programmer wrote an application that allowed us to do our art, and simply make menu selections that visually built a game rather than having to actually program it, the doors blew wide open. It must be pointed out that this happened in all areas of computing; Web site creation, word processing, and even sound editing all became increasingly easy to use due to drag-and-drop editing. No longer do you have to type in cryptic codes and program everything you see on the screen. Now, for the most part, all you need is your creativity to make a game.

As game developers started giving the tools, and even the code and art resources of their games to the audience, gamers started making their own levels with them. Now almost every game, primarily the top sellers, have entire online communities that support the game. A typical game will have numerous fan sites, a news site that posts user screen shots and tournaments, updates and patches, and news on the developers. When you buy a computer game today, you are seldom in the dark and alone anymore. Most games have user forums and mailing lists, hint and cheats sections, and, of course, the editing tools and tutorials. If you buy Quake 3 or Delta Force 2 and you like the game, but have some ideas of your own you would like to see enacted, you can do it. Download the level editors and make or modify the levels to your liking.

Of course, professionals use advanced applications like NEMO (www.nemo.com), Director (www.macromedia.com), and the editors and tools that come with commercial games, like the Lith Tech editor or the Q3Radiant editor, to create their games, game worlds, and interactive applications. The only problem with these tools and systems is that they are very expensive and/or overwhelming even to an experienced software user.

In this book, I assembled some excellent game systems and tools that will give you a very easy introduction to game design and development. When you are comfortable with these systems and concepts, you will have a good foundation to use as you move on to the more complex systems and tools.

While you generally won't get the same level of performance from a shareware or freeware product that you will from Quake 3 or Macromedia Director, you can still make some pretty stunning creations and even make some money. Remember, tweaking is often the missing factor in most beginner productions. A well-tweaked production using a shareware tool will almost always outsell a poorly developed production in any other tool.

NOTE

Shareware products may be used with limits: limited features, limited amount of time, or frequent reminder screens to register. Freeware products may be used at no charge and are typically distributed freely. The freeware product is still owned by the creator and their rights are protected by law. Typically, anything created by a freeware application is owned by you, the creator.

There are actually a lot of companies that create and sell productions made with these lower-end tools. And they are quality productions and profitable companies. The work done with these lower-end tools can be powerful and successful for the following reasons:

1) Not everyone runs a system that can handle Quake 3 or the latest greatest application. There are large groups of people out there with older machines, slower chips, and not much RAM, etc. Some of the newer games and applications require some pretty high system specifications.

2) Not everyone *wants* to play Quake 3. Believe it or not, there are actually people who don't think it is relaxing to rush through dark halls trying not to get killed. Some people like card games, quiz games, and more mellow pursuits. (There are a lot of these *mellow* people, too. We look at the game market later in Part 1.)

There are other applications that can be created with the lower-end tools as well. For example, there are real estate companies, colleges, and businesses that may need a 3D scene of a location or building to use as a 3D simulation for proposed development. Other examples include interactive tests that deliver questions and record answers automatically, screen savers, or some type of novelty to attract attention to Web sites and businesses.

Remember, to most people, 3D is still a hot buzzword and they cannot distinguish between DOOM technology or Quake 3 technology.

But if you can learn the fundamentals of game creation, with the demand requiring these types of skills and the demand for interactive content growing daily as businesses flock to the Web, you will have a tremendous edge.

What This Book Will Cover:

PART 1 – AWESOME GAME CREATION

In Part 1 we will look at the things you need to know before you begin to develop games and interactive applications. We will look at the equipment needed for game development and the process for designing a game.

Game development and game design are two separate things that are often confused. Design comes first, then development.

Designing is planning the game.

Development is making the game.

This distinction is critical and I will refer to it often. We will focus a lot on design in Part 1, and then spend a good portion of the rest of the book on development.

PART 2 – AWESOME 2D GAME CREATION

In this part of the book, we will actually make a 2D game, thanks to the wonderful people at Clickteam who supported this book with its product.

On the CD-ROM in the back of this book, you will find a copy of TGF, and you need to install it before we get started. Don't worry if you have trouble installing it. The following section will walk you through the installation:

TGF is a very easy-to-use games creator. It represents state-of-the-art animated graphics and sound, multimedia functions, and fabulous game-structuring routines that make it very quick and easy to produce your own games with no programming.

NOTE

You can also make slide shows, interactive tests, presentation, and screen savers with the full version of TGF!

With TGF, you can create platform games, maze games, and many other graphic adventures. You don't even have to make the characters or assets for your games, since TGF has huge graphics libraries containing many different characters and backdrops. After you learn the basics, you can make your own animated characters and backdrop, and even record your own sound effects, making a completely unique game.

In this section of the book, we will make a few simple games that will introduce you to TGF.

PART 3 – AWESOME 3D GAME CREATION

In Part 3, we will actually make a 3D game using The Pie 3D Game Creation System. The Pie GCS is an integrated software package for non-programmers. With this program, the user can create a 3D action game which is comparable to DOOM, Wolfenstein 3D, Terminator, and others. The GCS is a DOS application that requires a 386 or better computer, with a VGA graphics card. This product has been designed from the ground up with the intent of making an easy-to-use program for nonprogrammers to use. Hence the program is very much mouse- and graphics-based.

If you are new to the subject of game development, I encourage you to read this book from beginning to end and work through the exercises. You will need to understand the terms and technology reviewed in Part 1, and the skills you learn in Part 2 will be applied in Part 3.

Who This Book is For

THE COMPLETE NEWCOMER

Totally lost in the terms and technology of today's computerized world? This book will help you get up to speed on things going on behind the scenes of your computer. You may even make a few dollars along the way.

THE GAME DEVELOPER WANNA-BE

Want to be a game developer and haven't a clue as to where to start? Start here. This book will introduce you to the design, development, terminology, and even the history of games. And by the end of the book, you will be able to make your first game.

THE BUSINESS PROFESSIONAL

A game is the epitome of what many of you are used to hearing referred to as "interactivity." When designing and developing a game, you are designing and developing "interactive content." With this book, you can gain the edge in whatever market or business you are in by creating screen savers, presentations, Web content, 3D environments, interactive tests, and promotional games with any theme you desire.

KEEP IN TOUCH

I would love to see the games or other applications you create with the skills you learn here and the tools provided on the CD-ROM. Please send links to your creations to awesome@goldtree.com, and I will post or link to the best ones.

    Please, links only and no attachments.

1

SETTING UP
YOUR GAME
STUDIO

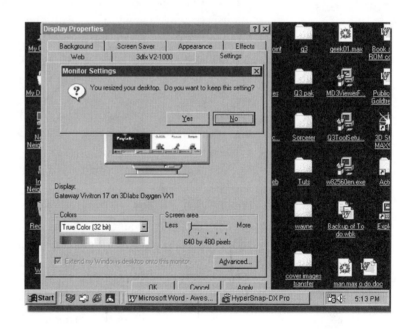

etting up a game development studio sounds expensive, but it doesn't have to be. Not only are computers cheaper and more powerful than ever, there are also more tools and information available to develop games. When setting up your game studio, there are several factors that determine what kind of equipment you need to have. You most likely have the essentials of a game studio already — a computer and this book — however, we will look closer at how to determine if what you have is enough and the best way to determine what more you may need.

In this chapter, we will also look at the basic elements of the game development studio and tips on how to buy them. We will look at the hardware you will need if you are to progress to a full-fledged game developer.

What System Do You Need?

If you were driving six kids to school, driving in a road race, or driving into combat, what vehicle would you choose? Computers are similar to vehicles in this respect. While a minivan, a race car, and a jeep all have four wheels, they are all designed for very different purposes. So the big question for you is, what will you be doing with your computer? You may not be able to adequately answer this question until you have worked through this book and tried the different types of things you will have to do on your computer as a game developer. Once you have worked a bit in the various applications and learned their specific needs, as well as your needs as a user, you will know what kind of a system you will need to buy.

Some things to consider while working on your currently available system are:

What are the system requirements for the applications you will be using or intend to use? These requirements are usually clearly stated on the box, in ads, and on the home pages of the product. Usually the system requirements are broken down into Minimum and Recommended.

CAUTION

Warning! Usually the Minimum System Requirements are just that — the bare minimum to run the application. The minimum system will usually not be the most comfortable or even the most usable system to run the application and does not take into account other applications that you may be running at the same time. Let's say that the minimum RAM requirements for your art application are 16 MB, but you plan on running other applications at the same time (and you will as a game developer), such as a level editor, game engine, word processor, and 3D application. Your system will be severely taxed and may run poorly, if at all. And the minimum system does not usually take into account the files you will be working with. For example, if you are using an art program like Paint Shop Pro or Photoshop to lay out art images, laying out images for the Internet and for print are drastically different. While a Web image has to be small for quick transfer over the Internet, print images are huge by comparison. The cover image for this book on my Web site is a 5-by-5-inch JPEG and is only 50K, while the actual print image of higher resolution reached 30 megabytes in size as I was working on it.

Of course, you can open and close applications that are not in use, but this takes time (especially with slow, RAM-deficient machines) and will severely cut into your productivity and work flow.

Other things to watch for are recommended hard drive space, which does not include the assets you will create with the application, only the application itself, and processor speed, which only includes the speed to run the application and does not take into account larger files.

SYSTEM AND EQUIPMENT

The equipment you will need to create a computer game depends on the type and scope of your game. The right setup can range from a very minimal investment to tens of thousands of dollars for the latest and most powerful computer setup. To get started, you need to own a basic computer setup with a few important peripherals.

Computer

Owning a computer would be a good place to start since you are interested in computer game development. Great deals can be had these days for a minimal investment (See "Tips for buying your equipment" on page 10). And for general purposes, you can buy a median, off-the-shelf system and get all (or most of) the following items in this chapter.

When purchasing your system, you should take into account the work and applications you will run. The operating system is important (Windows 95/98 for the tools in this book), and new systems usually ship with the latest version of the biggest OS on the market at the time. The minimal system today usually has a 17-inch monitor, lots of RAM, and fairly large hard drives. You should have no problem with an off-the-shelf system or a mail-order system from a reputable company.

How Fast Should My Processor Be?

Simply put, as fast as you can afford it to be. The processor is the hardest and most expensive part of a computer to upgrade. Most of the other components can be more easily upgraded when needed. Getting the fastest chip possible not only makes sense in general, but as a game developer, you will be pushing your system harder than most other users and will have a need for the speed.

But don't worry if your system is not the latest and greatest, you can still design and develop games with a minimal system, as long as it can run the applications you are using.

Graphic (Video) Cards and 3D Cards

A graphic (video) card is what allows images to appear on your monitor. A video card usually controls how big the image is on your screen, how much detail it can have, and how many colors are displayed (in the next chapter, we will discuss the specific elements of an image).

There are also 3D video cards or hardware accelerated cards. While most applications only require the drawing of simple pictures, such as your Windows desktop, a game or 3D application like 3D Studio MAX needs a lot of help with the intense 3D calculations used to draw a 3D scene. With 3D, the computer is literally building each image many times a second as you play the game or work in the 3D application. This uses a lot of processor power. A 3D card is specifically designed to take the tasks of 3D rendering from the computer by handling textures, effects, and geometric calculations.

How Much RAM Should I Get?

Again, as much as possible. RAM is the most important thing you can have. It is often the best and cheapest (and easiest) thing to upgrade in a computer. More RAM usually makes a bigger, or more noticeable, performance difference than a faster chip will. If you have 16 or 32 MB of RAM and a fairly decent chip (at this point, a P200 is pretty minimal but fairly decent), then going to 120 MB of RAM or more will be cheaper than a new computer, and you will see a huge performance boost.

A Quickie on RAM

RAM means Random Access Memory and is measured in Megabytes, or MB, or the slang term "MEGs." RAM is used by the computer as *temporary* storage for the applications in use. This is why the 30-page paper you were writing disappeared when the power went out. It was in RAM, which only functions when the computer is on. A surge protector would have saved that paper by keeping the computer running on a battery, while beeping to let you know it is running on battery power. (You would have thought Nedry would have put this feature into the Jurassic Park system, huh? More on surge protectors on page 10).

Other Peripherals

Other peripherals that you will need are standard on most computers: a modem, a zip drive, and a sound system.

Advanced peripherals that you will eventually want to have if you are to continue on into a game development/content creation career include the following:

Scanner. Basically this works like a copy machine from the user point of view. A scanner converts your flat document or image into a digital image that can be manipulated in the computer, as we describe in the next chapter. This can be very useful for creating game art, Web sites, logos, and simply getting your picture on the Quake guy's face.

Digital Camera. Works like a camera, but instead of film you get a digital image like the scanner produces. The major difference is that a scanner is good for high-resolution scans of flat images while a digital camera is great for real-life 3D image capture. A digital camera can be used to capture a cracked-stone driveway for use in the computer, whereas a scanner could not do this.

High-Speed Internet Access

Most computers still come with a 56K modem. This is adequate for most uses, but if you are serious you should try to get high-speed Internet access. The Internet is such an invaluable resource, especially to game developers, that it is worth the investment. Some of the large downloads you will be making are images, game demos, sound files, development tools, and animation files.

Following is a download time comparison for a 3.75 MB file:

Modem	Min:Sec
14.4 Kbps dial-up modem:	35:33
28.8 Kbps dial-up modem:	17:47
33.6 Kbps dial-up modem:	15:14
56 Kbps dial-up modem:	09:09
1.5 Mbps ADSL:	00:20

CD-ROM Burner

This is almost a necessity now and it comes on many new systems. When you start serious asset creation, you will want to back up those assets for safety.

When you have a demo due, you will want to deliver it on a CD-ROM instead of 50 floppy disks. When you do an interactive project, most people expect to get a nice gold CD-ROM they can send to the replication plant. There are other large-capacity storage disks, such as the 250 megabyte disks, and even removable drives that hold many gigabytes of information, but the 100 MB zip and the CD-ROM are the most common.

- A floppy holds 1.3 MB of data. You can erase and recopy data on a floppy.
- A zip disk holds 100 MB of data. You can erase and recopy data on a zip disk.
- A CD-ROM holds 650 MB of data. On some burners, you can rewrite data. You can also burn multi-session CDs that allow the laying down of more data to empty parts of the disk. Usually you can write data only once.

There are also drives that operate like the zip drive that have larger data capacity, such as 250 MBs or more. There are many companies working on many types and sizes of storage, and one Boulder, Colorado, company is working on a 500 MB optical disk that is about an inch square. These are write-only disks, like CDs, and will cost about $5 a piece.

Digital Art Pen and/or Digitizer

The artist especially will like this. These are pen-like devices that allow you to draw more naturally into the computer. This is far from a necessity and very expensive. The less expensive digital pens are good for recording signatures and basic sketching, but they lack the fine control an artist needs.

A SOHO Network

A network means that your computers can communicate with each other. While this sounds like an expensive proposition and a complex undertaking, it is a very achievable goal today. A top-notch SOHO (Small Office Home Office) network system can cost about $150 and comes in a kit with everything you need, extending your computing abilities dramatically.

A few of the benefits of a home network are shared peripherals and resources. You can have one scanner, printer, or device on the network that other people on the system can use from their computers. This can be useful since most computers (especially older PCs) have a limited number of devices they can have installed. Also, having many devices installed on a system tends to bog down the system's boot up and response times. You can also back up data on multiple PCs easily. During development of a title, having a network is almost essential since multiple team members are updating code and resources constantly.

There are several types of home networks available.

Ethernet

Ethernet is the most common home-networking system and the most easy to have friends hook into. A typical system for two computers uses two cards, called Ethernet cards, and a crossover cable, a special cable designed for connecting only two computers. If you have three or more computers, you need what is called a hub, a device you plug all the computers into that routes, or directs, the traffic. The actual software portion of a network can range from simply finding the other computers on the network and accessing the data on their drives, to setting up special software that operates peripherals, and adds security, chatting, and other advanced functions.

Wireless

Wireless networks obviously mean you don't need to string wires between each computer, but wireless networks tend to be more expensive, are susceptible to data corruption, and are limited in distance between computers.

Phone Wire

Some networks use the phone wires in your house. These are quickly becoming the best option for home users.

AC Wire

These network systems use the electrical wiring in your home as the network wires and tend to be slower and prone to interference. They also have a security problem since they use the transformer (the big thing on the telephone pole outside) as the common link for data traveling through your power lines. The transformer may be shared by 20 or more houses on the street, and it is possible for anyone with the same network system to pry into your computers.

A Good Chair

Buy a good chair. You will be sitting a lot.

TIPS FOR BUYING YOUR EQUIPMENT

1. Use a Credit Card

Or find someone to do this for you, especially when buying online. With a credit card, you have the credit card company and The Fair Credit Billing Act behind you. This rule allows you 60 days in which to report a billing error or vendor dispute.

2. Don't Get Cheap

Avoid the "under a thousand dollar" computers unless you *really* know what you are getting into. In some cases these systems may not include all of the components (larger hard drive, quality monitor, etc). Expect to pay about $2,000 for a computer with all the fixins'. It is probably a good idea to get the extended warranty at the time of purchase.

3. Protect Everything!

Buy the CD-ROM burner and Zip drives. I usually back up data daily to a Zip (or another computer on my network) and monthly to a CD-ROM. You can never be too safe.

Buy a battery-supported surge protector or UPS (Uninterruptible Power Source). For about a $100 you can get one that will protect several components, including your modems and phone lines. The surge protector will allow you plenty of time to save your work and shut down your computer if the power goes out.

Surge protectors are easy to use — you just plug them in, and they protect your computer from power spikes and shutdowns. The surge protector will actually blow a fuse or circuit if it gets hit by a surge of electricity from lightening or bad wiring, in order to protect your computer's innards from being damaged.

Of course the best protection is to turn off your computer and unplug it during thunderstorms.

4. Research

Above all, learn about computers for yourself. If possible, try the applications you expect to run on a few systems first. See how those systems handle massive graphic files and huge levels. And remember, most people are very biased about their own systems, so be careful when opinion-hunting for computer systems among individuals.

Once you have assembled your game development studio and have it up and running, whether it is an off-the-shelf special or the latest and greatest system money can buy, you will have made a huge step towards becoming a game developer. The next step is to learn the basic building blocks of a game — sights and sounds.

2

THE BASIC BUILDING BLOCKS OF A GAME

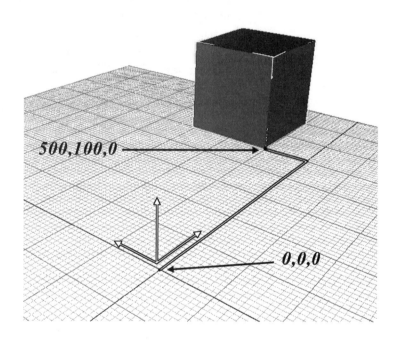

In order to start making games, you will need to learn and eventually master the fundamental elements of a game — sights, sounds, and interactivity. Although interactivity (or the ability to interact with a computer to play a game) is important, the basics of interactivity are dependent on game type and the application you are using to develop the game. We will learn more about interactivity in the tutorials later in the book as we make the different types of games. In this chapter, we will concern ourselves with the core building blocks that exist in virtually all games — sights and sounds.

This simple approach is to help you break down and understand a game in your mind at it's most fundamental level. This knowledge can be applied to many areas beyond game development as well, since this is the core of graphic design, Web layout, and almost all of interactive computing.

Sights are obviously what you see on the screen. In any major production, from a Web site to a game, these sites are very important and are usually determined by a number of people: the designer, producer, art director, and others. Even in your one- or two-person development efforts, you will need to wear several hats and think like the designer, producer, and artist. 2D art assets need to look good, but also fit in with the audience, technology, and atmosphere for which you are designing. This is actually the marketing mindset we talk about later in this book.

When the assets are finally created, many tools and techniques are used. Assets are often sketched on paper or mocked up on the computer before they are created. Some of the tools used are 2D paint programs that work only with flat images, 3D programs that allow you to build and render objects that look lit and solid, and even digital photographs and scans are used. But there is always present a core of basic knowledge that even the best artist relies on — the knowledge of technology or what is actually happening to the image they are working on.

2D Art assets include (by are not limited to) the following:

Menu screens. Look at the toolbar in your word processor, browser, or even your favorite game, and you will see art that was created by an artist.

Credit screens. These screens often contain art such as logos, images, and even "fonts" or special letters from the product, people, and company they represent.

Logos for companies, products, and services. Logos can be simple letters, 2D masterpieces, or fully rendered 3D scenes. Look around on the Net and you will see logos that range from clipart to actual pieces of art.

User interfaces. These are broken down into background images, buttons, cursors, and other art objects a user must click on or interact with.

In-game assets. In the game, the sights are the textures on the walls, the floors, and the characters. Even the 3D models and objects have 2D art applied to them.

What you hear in a game can range from recorded (or sampled) sounds such as voices and music, menu sounds like beeps and button clicks, and other effects in the game such as explosions, weapon's fire, footsteps, and a long list of other in-game sound effects, both subtle and deafening. We will look at why sound can be very important to a game or any production.

Sights

The very first computers did not have graphics. They only displayed text — letters and numbers. But games were still made on these primitive machines. Once the first graphics cards were made, we were able to have the colorful games we see today. It is argued that games have pushed the development of the computer as the gamers demanded (and were willing to pay for) faster chips, better video cards, and better sound.

But even as the technology advanced, it was common for the artist on any given project to primarily be a programmer. This was because it was still demanding to get decent art into a computer format, and an understanding of technology was necessary to do so. Today (thank the gods of digital art) we are almost able to ignore the technology we are working with, though not quite totally yet.

Artists, think about this. Imagine you just got a new job as an artist, and your first assignment is to design and paint the company logo. So you get a big piece of white paper and your favorite set of colors — hundreds of colors in every shade. You sit down to work and up comes your boss. "Sorry," he says, "for this project you need to work in a *new* medium. "He chuckles as he takes all your colors and tosses them into the "round file," as he so likes to call the garbage can. He replaces all your colors with 16 big square stamps.

"Cool dude," you say, but in reality you are a bit taken aback. You think Zen thoughts to get you through. Because you are so creative, you are already stamping away like a mad man — you manage to make some cool effects and shades by twisting, overlapping, and smudging the stamps. You realize your boss is still standing over your shoulder chuckling. "What are you doing?" he asks incredulously. And suddenly up comes your paper, ripped away in the middle of your creative exploration. The boss chuckles, "I wasn't finished." He tosses your paper aside. He pulls a new sheet out that is smaller and has a grid penciled across it.

"Here, let me show you how this works," the boss says in the most anal manner, as he stamps one color precisely in each square. At the end of an hour or two he wakes you up. "Look," he says as he holds up a red page with white blocky letters that reads, "The Logo." He makes you hold it and steps back admiringly. "I like it. I think we will use that."

That's what computer art was like for a while. Very limited. All this technology will be explained in this chapter so you can see how we have advanced. You still need to understand the technology underlying the art since there will be (in the immediate future, at least) times where you will have to make formats compatible, and adapt to screen sizes and color limitations. In other words, you are still a slave to the technology.

Let's look at the core technology a computer artist deals with everday.

In computer graphics today, there is 2D and 3D art. 2D, or two dimensional, art is a flat image with no depth. 3D art, on the other hand, shows depth, as illustrated in Figure 2.1.

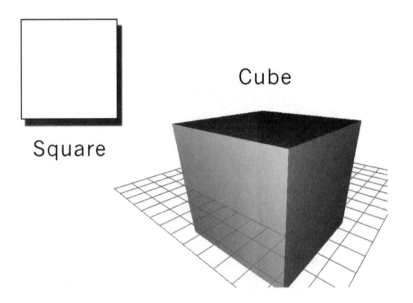

FIGURE *A square is 2D while a cube is 3D.*
2.1

The three dimensions are described as X, Y, and Z coordinates. Yes, the Cartesian Coordinate System. In fact, making a game requires a lot of the stuff you hated in high school — geometry, physics, reading, writing, etc. The Cartesian Coordinate System, at its simplest, is X being a horizontal line (or axis), Y being a vertical line, and Z being the distance backward and forward (See Figures 2.2, 2.3, and 2.4).

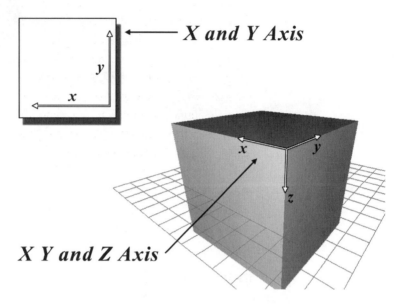

FIGURE *The Cartesian coordinate system. The X axis, Y axis, and Z axis.*
2.2

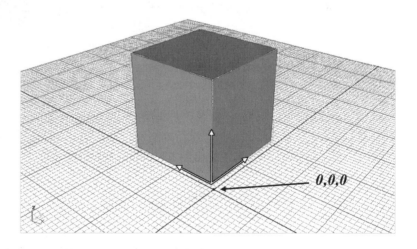

FIGURE *A cube and the xyz value of its location in space.*
2.3

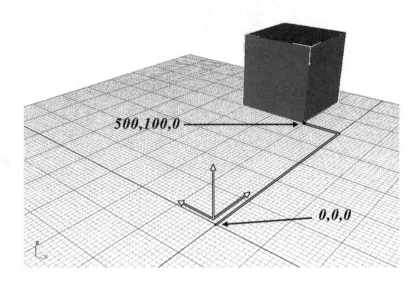

FIGURE *Another cube in a different xyz position.*
2.4

PIXEL

To begin with, we will look at the most fundamental of fundamentals —the most basic element of an image — which is the pixel, or a picture element. A pixel is a colored dot on the screen. A computer image is made up of pixels arranged in rows and columns. See Figure 2.5 for an illustration of a pixel. No matter how big and fancy a computer image is or what has been done to it, it is all just a bunch of pixels.

Once an image is in a computer, the maximum detail is set and cannot be increased. The image can be enlarged and the number of pixels can be increased by a mathematical process called interpolation, which is illustrated in Figures 2.6 and 2.7, but this does not increase the detail. It simply adds extra pixels to smooth the transition between the original pixels.

RESOLUTION

Resolution is the number of pixels displayed (width x height) in an image.

NOTE

Dots per inch, or dpi, refers to the number of pixels per inch in an image. A typical computer monitor displays 75 to 90 dpi. A printed image usually needs to be 300 dpi or more if it is to look good in print. Often a computer-based person requesting an image from a person used to working in print is surprised when the one-inch

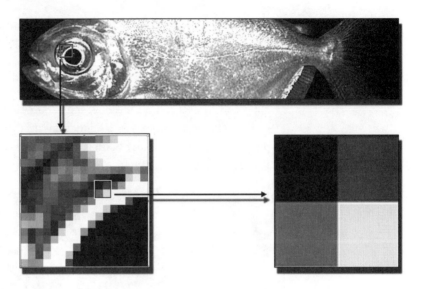

FIGURE *A pixel is the smallest unit of a computer image — simply colored dots.*
2.5

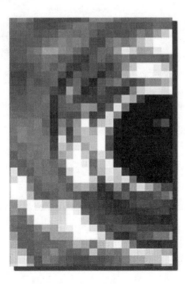

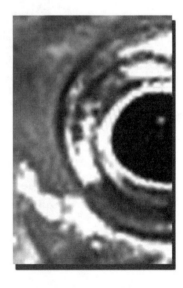

FIGURE *Here is an area of the fish*
2.6   *image before enlarging.*

FIGURE *Here is the same area enlarged*
2.7   *with pixels interpolated.*

icon they requested is HUGE, but the image attributes still read one inch by one inch. The reason for the enormous size is that the print person saved the file at a higher dpi.

Some of the most common screen resolutions are 320 x 200, 640 x 480, 800 x 600, 1024 x 768, 1152 x 864, and 1280 x 1024.

For example, an 800 x 600 resolution means that your screen will be 800 pixels wide (horizontal) and 600 pixels high (vertical). (See the examples in Figures 2.8, 2.9, and 2.10.)

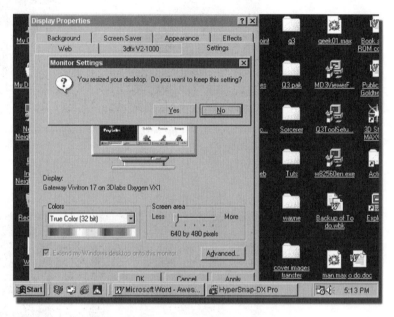

FIGURE *Here is the Windows Desktop at 640 x 480 dots per inch.*
2.8

Aspect Ratio

Another important component of resolution is aspect ratio, or the ratio of the pixel's width to the pixel's height. Not all pixels are square.

In 640 x 480, 800 x 600, and 1024 x 768 mode, the aspect ratio is 1:1 or 1, meaning the pixels are perfectly square.

In 320 x 200 mode, the aspect ratio is 1.21:1 or .82, meaning the pixels are higher than they are wide.

If you create an image in 320 x 200 mode and display it in 640 x 480 mode, it will appear slightly squashed, since the pixels are about 20% shorter. See Figures 2.11 and 2.12 and notice the distortion in the image.

FIGURE   *Here is the Windows Desktop at 800 x 600 dots per inch.*
2.9

FIGURE   *Here is the Windows Desktop at 1024 x 768 dots per inch.*
2.10

Image created by Nick Marks 1999-2000

FIGURE *Here is an image created at 320 x 200 dots per inch.*
2.11

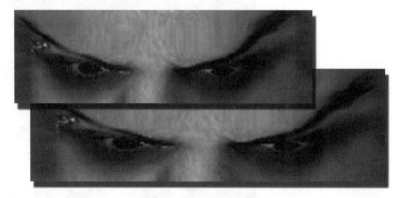

Image created by Nick Marks 1999-2000

FIGURE *Here is the same image displayed in 640 x 480 mode.*
2.12

COLORS

"Yo, I be flashing my colors with pride. What is the RGB value of your gang? 255,0,0 or 0,0,255?"

When working with most interactive content, you need to understand how color works in the computer. You will have to have precise control over your colors in certain situations in order to achieve certain effects and accomplish some jobs. In games and Web sites, you often have to set precise color information to achieve certain effects. Often other computer artists will give you the number of a color to use in an image.

An RGB value is the mixture of Red, Green, and Blue to make other colors — like in art class when you mixed red and yellow paint to make orange.

So 255,0,0 means you have all Red and no Green or Blue. Black would be 0,0,0 and white would be 256,256,256. In Figures 2.13 through 2.17, you can see the RGB values of the color, and (even though the images are in 0,0,0 and 256,256,256 — excuse me, black and white) you can see the position of the marker in the color palette.

You will also hear color referred to as CMYK. CMYK is a mode used by traditional printing processes and stands for Cyan, Magenta, Yellow, and Black. You will almost certainly never use CMYK color in game and computer content creation and will always deal in RGB or indexed color.

NOTE

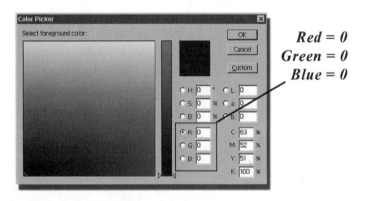

Red = 0
Green = 0
Blue = 0

FIGURE *This is the RGB color palette for black.*
2.13

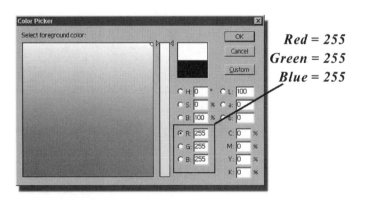

Red = 255
Green = 255
Blue = 255

FIGURE *This is the RGB color palette for white.*
2.14

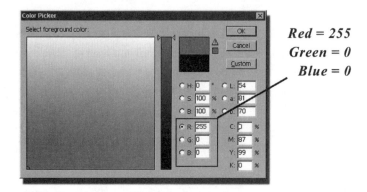

Red = 255
Green = 0
Blue = 0

FIGURE *This is the RGB color palette for red.*
2.15

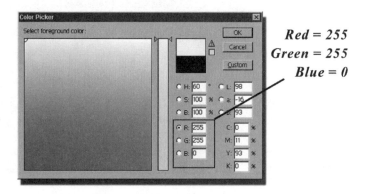

Red = 255
Green = 255
Blue = 0

FIGURE *This is the RGB color palette for yellow.*
2.16

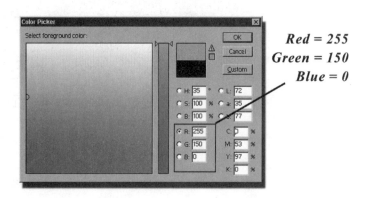

Red = 255
Green = 150
Blue = 0

FIGURE *This is the RGB color palette for orange.*
2.17

NUMBER OF COLORS

A computer video card can display a certain number of colors at a time —
16, 256, thousands, million (See Figures 2.18, 2.19, 2.20, and 2.21).

FIGURE *This is an image in 16 colors. See the color gallery for the color version of this*
2.18 *image.*

FIGURE *This is an image in 256 colors. See the color gallery for the color version of this*
2.19 *image.*

FIGURE *This is an image in thousands of colors. See the color gallery for the color*
2.20 *version of this image.*

FIGURE *This is an image in millions of colors. See the color gallery for the color version*
2.21 *of this image.*

The number of colors is called color depth, which describes how many colors can be displayed on your screen at once. Color depth is described in terms
of bits, and refers to the amount of memory used to represent a single pixel.
The most common values are 8-bit, 16-bit, 24-bit, and 32-bit color. The more
bits correspond to a wider range of colors that can be displayed.

True-Color (24-bit color) is capable of displaying 16.8 million colors for each pixel on the screen at the same time. The human eye cannot distinguish the difference between that many colors.

High-Color only displays 32,000 or 64,000 colors, but is still a very impressive range of colors, enough colors for most work.

256-Color is the most limited in colors. It stores its color information in a palette. Each palette can be set to any of thousands or millions of different color values, but the screen can't show more than 256 different colors at once. Some games still use these because, like resolution, more colors means more data pumped to the screen. So if you can get away with only 256 colors, you can render (or draw) the game pictures to the screen faster. More recently, games are starting to use thousands of colors as the hardware permits.

NOTE

The word render *is used in games, especially Real Time 3D games, as the computer and software literally renders or builds an image instantly, based on where you are in the 3D world. Hence the term* interactive. *In a movie, you watch each frame as it was created by the movie maker. The frame is unchangeable. In a 3D game, you control how each frame looks by where you choose to go in the world and what you do. Each frame of your gaming experience is made for you "on the fly," or as your experience is happening.*

256 palettes explained

Hopefully, you will never need to know this, but here it goes. Each pixel can have a numerical value from 0-255 (a total of 256!). Now the screen knows only where to get the color from, but it does not know the color. Figure 2.22 shows the 256 color palette.

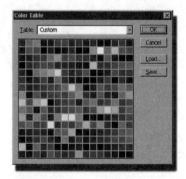

FIGURE *A 256 color palette. You can only see shades of gray here, but those squares are*
2.22 *256 different colors.*

So follow me here. Say you have a picture and you open the color palette to have a look. If you note that a certain color is assigned to the number 3 place on the color palette and then decide to reassign another color to the number 3 position, your image will now display that new color where the original color used to be.

Even if you have that original color in the palette, it will not be displayed where the number 3 position is being displayed. What this means is that a computer can't distinguish color; it sees numbers. You will have to be aware of this for later tutorials. In Figures 2.23 and 2.24, you can see how the changing of one color affects the image.

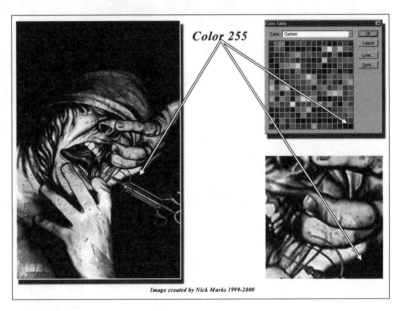

Color 255

Image created by Nick Marks 1999-2000

FIGURE *This is a 256-color image.*
2.23

Now that we understand the basics of images, we can move onto the basics of manipulating images.

MANIPULATING IMAGES

During the development of your project, you will have to manipulate images in order to get them to fit your needs. The basics of image manipulation are similar to the text editing you may have done in your word processor. Commands such as Cut, Copy, and Paste are common. We will also look at Skew, Rotate, Resize, Crop, and Flip.

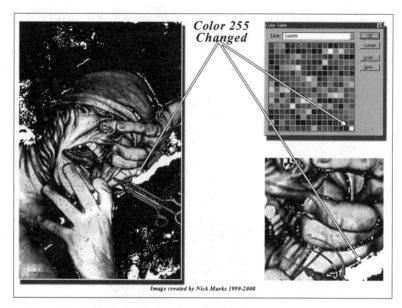

Image created by Nick Marks 1999-2000

FIGURE **2.24** *This is the same image after changing the palette colors. The computer sees the number, not the color.*

Cut. If you cut an image, you remove it from the scene. But do not worry — you can paste it back in or undo your action.

Copy. Copy does not alter your image, but creates a copy in the memory of your computer that you can paste in somewhere else, as shown in Figure 2.25.

FIGURE **2.25** *Cutting and copying sections of an image. **Note:** Copying does not affect the image.*

Paste. As mentioned above, after cutting or copying an image, you can paste it in somewhere else, as shown in Figure 2.26.

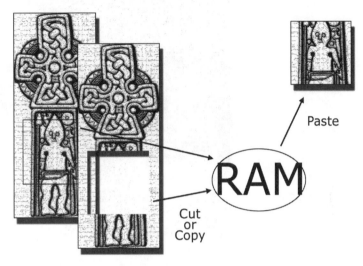

FIGURE   *Pasting a section of an image.*
2.26

Skew. Some image manipulation programs allow you to skew (slant, deform, or distort) an image, as shown in Figure 2.27.

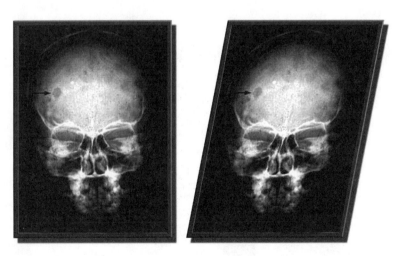

FIGURE   *Skewing an image.*
2.27

Rotate. Rotating is pretty self-explanatory. You can free rotate an image or rotate it precisely a certain amount, as shown in Figure 2.28.

FIGURE *Rotating an image.*
2.28

Resize. Resizing an image is useful, but be careful. Any severe manipulation of an image degrades it, and resizing does a lot of damage. Caution: If you reduce an image and then enlarge it again, you will seriously degrade it. This is because, in effect, you are enlarging a small image. The degradation takes place going down as well as going up in scale. This is illustrated in Figures 2.29, 2.30, and 2.31.

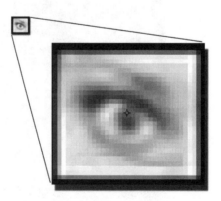

FIGURE *A smaller image blown up; pixel rip.*
2.29

FIGURE *An image reduced.*
2.30

FIGURE *The same image enlarged to its original size. Notice what this has done.*
2.31

Crop. Cropping actually cuts an image smaller to a defined area, as shown in Figures 2.32 and 2.33.

Image created by Jennifer Meyer 1999-2000

Image created by Jennifer Meyer 1999-2000

FIGURE **2.32** *Cropping an image. The crop outline.*

FIGURE **2.33** *The image cropped. Everything outside the crop outline is now gone.*

Flip (horizontal and vertical). Finally, you can flip images horizontally and vertically (See Figures 2.34, 2.35, and 2.36).

The image

Flipped horizontally

Flipped vertically

FIGURE **2.34** *The image.*

FIGURE **2.35** *The image flipped horizontally.*

FIGURE **2.36** *The image flipped vertically.*

ADVANCED MANIPULATION

No, this is not what my five-year-old does to get what he wants. This is the more complex form of dealing with an image.

Sprites

Sprites are small pictures of things that move around — characters, buttons, and items in your games. Sprites can be animated as well. A sprite is a graphic image that can move within a larger image. Notice that the sprite image in Figure 2.37 has a solid border around it, and in Figure 2.38, the solid part is not seen.

FIGURE   *A sprite image. Notice the solid part surrounding the image.*
2.37

Sprite animation is done just like cartoon animation. A series of images is played in sequence to make it appear that a character is walking or a logo is spinning, for instance. Examples of sprite frames can be seen in Figures 2.39 and 2.40.

Masking

A mask is a special image that is used to "mask" off portions of another image. A mask works like a stencil. Since an image is square or rectangular, the mask allows the edges to be any shape — it renders the masked portions invisible (See Figures 2.41, 2.42, and 2.43)

FIGURE *A sprite image in a game. Notice the solid part is not displayed. You can see the*
2.38 *background.*

FIGURE *A series of sprite images for a game animation.*
2.39

FIGURE *A series of sprite images for a spinning logo.*
2.40

FIGURE *An image of a ghost.*
2.41

FIGURE *The mask for the ghost image.*
2.42

FIGURE *The mask and image combined in a scene.*
2.43

Color Masking

Masking can also be achieved by dedicating a specific color to be rendered as clear or transparent. This color is usually an ugly green or purple that most likely will not be used any other time in the game art.

Palette or Positional Masking

Finally, some games use a specific position on the color palette to determine what color will not render or be clear. Remember, the computer cannot see color, only the numbers. This method for masking has the computer looking at the position on the palette, not the color, to determine transparency.

Usually the last color place on the palette is used, so instead of rendering a certain color as transparent, it will render whatever color is in the designated position of the color palette as clear.

Opacity

Images can also be displayed in games as opaque — halfway between solid and clear (like our ghost image). This is done by looking at each pixel in the image and the pixel directly under it, and creating a new pixel that is a blended value of the original pixels (See Figures 2.44 and 2.45).

FIGURE *The masked ghost image with opacity set at 50%.*
2.44

FIGURE   *A close-up detail of the ghost image.*
2.45

ANTI-ALIASING

Look really close at a computer-generated image. Wait! Don't go boot up your system, just look at Figures 2.46, 2.47, and 2.48. See those jagged edges on the letters? Those are actually the pixels we have been talking about. They look really jagged if made from a solid color. But using various shades of that color and gradually blending the edge color with the background color will make the transition smooth and will fool the eye from a distance. Yes, this is similar to opacity.

This technique is called anti-aliasing. This is also the reason more colors look better in an image since you can blend more gradually. This is also the reason high resolution (more pixels) makes an image look better—the blending is smoother between pixels.

FIGURE **2.46** *This image has no anti-aliasing.*

FIGURE **2.47** *This image has anti-aliasing.*

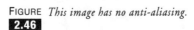

FIGURE **2.48** *Here is a close-up of both of the image's edges.*

GRAPHIC FORMATS

Graphic images are stored in many formats for many reasons. In business, this may be for technical support and product design reasons, competitive reasons, and security reasons. But the main reason is image quality and usefulness. Some image formats are quite large since they retain a lot of image data, whereas some formats allow compression and strip out data for a smaller file size. Still others degrade the image so they can be really small for uses like Web sites. You will see in Figures 2.49 and 2.50 two versions of an image. The degradation is not that bad (See Figure 2.51), considering the file size of the BMP is almost 20 times the size of the JPG image.

FIGURE
2.49
This 640 x 480 image is in the BMP format. It is 900K.

FIGURE
2.50
This 640 x 480 image is a compressed JPEG and is only 40K.

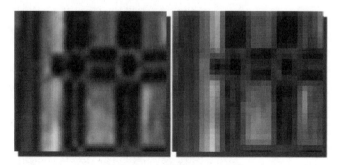

FIGURE
2.51
Here is a close-up of the same area of both images.

The specifics you need to know about graphics formats are discussed more later in this book and in the documentation of any applications you will be working with.

Sounds

Sound and music can be very important to a game, for atmospheric reasons alone. You can really get immersed in a game with the lights off and the sound turned up. Sound and music can set the mood, as well as change it (think of the *Indiana Jones* score or Darth Vader theme). Sound can deliver a strong message to the players about the quality of your game and even your company, the threat of the enemies, and the overall level of satisfaction they get from the game.

And sound is more immersive than graphics. That's right. Sound is more immersive than graphics. While graphics will draw you into a scene, the sound going on in the background and all around you will have a mental effect on a player that can never be done with graphics alone. I think this is probably because we can reproduce sounds on a computer much better than we can reproduce visuals. We can make a sound system on a computer sound like a real dinosaur roar, whereas we can't make the visual of that dinosaur nearly as real.

Visually, we are looking into another world through a tiny window and therefore, can feel safe from that world. But when we hear that world all around us (in the dark), we are really in that world in an auditory sense.

A good example of sound effectiveness is *Jaws*. Who can forget that sound? In gaming, I found the game Trespasser to be incredible. The sound makes the game a terribly tense and scary experience. I turned the sound off to play (didn't want to scare the dog) and started laughing. Without the sound, the game looked just like that — a game. Puppet-like raptors stumbled about and floated like balloons. The tension was gone.

I got interested in this effect and started playing the game with and without sound to analyze what was happening. I began to consciously pull out the sound effects, ambient noises, and music that made the game scary. Those raptor's footfalls topped the list. There was also the "distraction factor." With the sound off, I could actually play better because I wasn't hearing those footfalls or raptor screams.

Sound can reinforce a physical feeling and can actually create a physical sensation. Ever hit a roll over button with your speakers all the way up? You feel it roll, baby! Sound can be important even in the menu buttons. Sound in the menu can convey a solid feeling like steel switches being moved, or a light feeling like paper pages turning with a ruffle. This adds a lot to your production values. This is the same principle that car manufacturers are aware of. The sensation you get when slamming a car door is important. If the door gives a solid *thunk* when closed and produces no rattles, the car must be safe and built really solid, right?

The best way to get sound effects is to buy them or go to a free sound site on the Internet and download them. In reality, it is hard to record a lion's roar, an explosion or gunshot, or a head getting cut off. There are ways to sample, create, and record sounds, and usually the guy who is into music has the gear to do it. Be careful, though. Making music and recording voices is very different from making sound effects, and it requires different skills. It may require two or three people with different talents.

To begin with, you will have no problem getting sounds for your games. The Game Factory comes with plenty of sounds to use.

Now that you are familiar with the building blocks of a game, you are almost ready to start the blind, headlong rush into developing it. Before you go running off into unexplored territory, let's first look at some of the facts and fables that surround game design and development. It is important that you are not hindered by some of the misinformation surrounding game development and design.

CHAPTER

3

THE FACTS ABOUT GAME DESIGN AND DEVELOPMENT

Everything you have ever read about game design and development is wrong!

Pretty conclusive statement, huh? And it's wrong too. It can't be true, since I don't know what you have read, what you will do with the knowledge you have gained, or even what you are trying to develop.

My point is that a lot of the game design and development information available (especially on the Internet) is presented as conclusive end-all statements. "A game MUST have this," or "a game must have that!" People argue about this stuff incessantly on the Internet. These conclusive statements also make things confusing, since they make everything you read contradictory.

Don't get me wrong. There are a lot of great sites and individuals on the Internet that are invaluable: The Inspiracy, Lupine Games, G.O.D.'s Oracle, and Gamastura, just to name a few. Many of the newsgroups and discussion forums on the Internet have the nicest people who will help you out no matter who you are. In the back of this book, I assembled a list of links that I find useful, but they are by no means the only links. Hopefully, they will give you a running start in your journey as a game developer.

NOTE

The Links List in the back of this book is also on my Web site at www.goldtree.com. Please visit and let me know if there are dead links or links that you feel should be added.

But you must learn to sift through all the good and bad content so it does not overwhelm you, discourage you, or lead you into a place you don't want to be. This is fairly easy to do, however. When getting advice on your development, ask yourself: Who is writing what am I reading? Did they ever make a game? How long ago, and in what situation? What types of games do they like and develop?

Some people have only worked for either a very large or very small developer all of their career and that will skew their outlook on the development process. Also, keep the job of the developer in mind when reading their advice or opinions.

Others have simply never made a game in any sense of the word, and these people fall into the following two general categories:

The Pompous Poison Pen — These people will tell you what you should and should not do in specific terms and argue the point violently, with absolutely no credibility and only the desire to be right. They are generally very negative.

The Constructive Critic — These people will tell you the good and the bad of something and use examples and comparisons to other games. They will be intelligent and open-minded. They may disagree with you, but they will engage in a civilized debate. And that debate is where true progress originates. I seek out people like this as beta testers. Generally, they are positive, encouraging, and helpful. These are the people that will help you improve your product.

You have to step back and decide what is right for you, your situation, and your game. What do *you* want to accomplish? Do you want to make a game out of collecting business cards? Go ahead — there are probably a lot of people who would love it. Not everyone has to make the world's most cutting edge and spectacular game to be a game developer.

A Few Conclusive Statements Examined	*"You must design a game in a certain order or a certain way."*

Some folks maintain that you must write the entire game story first; another says you have to draw all the characters first; still another suggests coding it completely using dummy assets, and then hiring an artist.

It really depends on what type of game you are developing. What if you are doing a puzzle game, a technology driven shooter, a Role Playing Game, or simply a company screen saver? Are you using a preexisting technology? Are you an artist who has to generate the interest of a programmer? Then you have to do conceptual art first.

What you should do first can only be answered by you.

"You can no longer publish using the shareware model."

How absurd! It has never been an easier thing to do. More people are doing it now than ever. The Internet is easier to access, and now individuals can set up online stores.

Of course, the most well-known game success is by id with Castle Wolfenstein. Other large shareware successes are ICQ, Win Zip, MP3 players, and other utilities and viewers.

ICQ (I Seek You) was a piece of shareware developed by a handful of twenty-something developers in Israel who saw an unexplored niche, an unfilled need.

"They observed the fast deployment of the World Wide Web, which was propelled by the mounting popularity of surfing and browsing . . ."

"They realized, however, that something more profound was evolving under the surface. Millions of people have been connected to one huge worldwide

network — the Internet. They noticed that those people were connected —
but not interconnected."

"They realized that if one missing component would be added, all these
people, in addition to interacting with Web servers, would be able to interact
with each other. The missing link was the technology which would enable the
Internet users to locate each other online on the Internet, and to create peer-to-
peer communication channels, in a straight-forward, easy, and simple manner."

"They pioneered this technology, opening a whole new industry."

— www.icq.com

Pretty impressive for a few 20-year-olds. They are huge now, having been
bought by AOL, and they have more than a million subscribers.

"You need (or don't need) a college degree to get a job game developing."

You will also read a lot of professional game designers giving their opinions
of game development too. While these opinions should be taken seriously,
don't take them as end-all statements either — read between the lines. Some
will say that you can no longer get a job in the game industry without a college
degree, while others will say a degree is not a factor. In fact, most people in the
industry were never asked for a degree and will never ask the people they hire
for a degree. The industry generally looks at ability and personality.

Let's consider two professionals from the "Real World." Professional Number One works for a successful and very huge game development company that
has offices worldwide and a personnel department; whereas Professional Number Two works for a very small, but very successful, game development company where hiring is done by the team as a whole after seeing the persons work
and meeting them face-to-face.

"You must play games A LOT to be a game developer."

While this is certainly a lot more true than false, realize that even this is not
always true. I am sure it helps a lot, but often people who play a lot of games
don't take the time to master the tools of the game developer — many are not
even capable of developing games in any capacity. Some developers play games
incessantly and attribute that to their success, while still other very successful
developers play hardly any games. They watch movies, read books, and work,
work, work.

Basically, it is a safe bet that you do need to play enough games to understand the technology, no matter what aspect you are working on — art, code, design, or sound. And if you are designing the next great game of a certain type, you may want to know what has already been done and what has yet to be attempted. Besides, if you aren't playing a lot of games, that may indicate that you are not really all that hot on them, and passion is important in anything you want to do well.

What Makes A Great Game?

"When you go hunting for information on game design, the first thing you probably come across is someone's top-ten list (or any number) of "Things you must have in a game," or "What is a Game," or "The x Elements of a Successful Game," and the list goes on. It's difficult to identify the "most important" component of a good game, because it varies from game to game. In one, it could be the graphics; in another it could be the action or story.

Games are like films and novels in many ways. For a film to be successful, must it always have great special effects, the biggest budget, or the biggest star?

A movie can be successful or successfully attract attention at the box office for many reasons:

- A top-name star like Arnold Schwarzenegger
- A top-name director or producer like Steven Spielberg or George Lucas
- A unique idea like *The Blair Witch Project*
- A well-known character like James Bond
- It is based on a great book like *Jurassic Park*
- It has great special effects like *Jurassic Park*
- It has dinosaurs like . . .

You get the idea. There are many different reasons for a person to go see a film: word of mouth, good story, etc. Movies can also have many of the above elements and still fail. Remember *The Last Action Hero*? It had Arnold, a big budget, special effects, the works — and it still bombed.

The same is true for computer games.

- A top-name star would be like John Carmack of id software or Sid Meier of *Civilization* fame
- A top-name producer would be a company like G.O.D. or Activision
- A unique idea like *Deer Hunter*
- A well-known character like Lara Croft or Duke Nukem'
- It is based on a great book like *Jurassic Park*

- It has great special effects like *Jurassic Park*
- It has dinosaurs like . . .

Trespasser is a game mentioned a few times. I really liked it for what it was, but I knew what to expect. Despite the fact that it had a lot of very strong elements going for it, it didn't sell as well as anticipated, and did not fare well among critics. This game had going for it the following;

- A *very* hot license — *Jurassic Park*!
- Top-name stars did the voices: Minnie Driver and Richard Attenborough (John Hammond in the movie)
- It had a top producer — DreamWorks Interactive
- A unique idea — We discuss this below
- It had a very talented team working on it — lead by Seamus Blackley and Austin Grossman
- It had a huge marketing and publicity push

So What Happened to Trespasser?

First off, the team should be applauded for doing what people are always asking for — they tried something different. What happened, in my opinion (which is based on playing the game through many times, reading the book, watching the movies, reading the online reviews and forums, and developing games — but is still *only* an opinion, but an opinion validated by the Postmortem published on the Gamasutra site), was that not enough up-front design was done on the game. This affected the entire development and resulted in the failure of the game, as documented by the team.

Here are some quotes on the development of Trespasser from the Gamasutra Postmortem. They state in the beginning of this Postmortem that the original plans for Trespasser were very ambitious, and compromises were made from day one. From what I read, the game they wanted to make was awesome and their ideas were fresh, they just were not allowed to develop them properly.

"The biggest indication that Trespasser had game design problems was the fact that it never had a proper design spec."

"When the game had a complete team and had essentially entered production… the project artists had been building assets for nearly a year and programmers had been implementing code for even longer."

"They developed half a game with no design in place."

"Our experiences on Trespasser made it clear that it is worse to not have a design spec at all than to have one which becomes out of date and is frequently rewritten. Design should really set the direction for all other development of a game, as no amount of programming or art can suffice for a lack of gameplay, but Trespasser started and finished weak in the game design, and this affected every other part of the project."

— Gamasutra.com
(www.gamasutra.com)

It appears the *Trespasser* team was not allowed a proper design phase and was not allowed to redesign when they needed to — they were forced to compromise and *hack* solutions. The point here is that even with all the right stuff, projects like *Trespasser*, *The Last Action Hero*, and many other projects go sour. On the other hand, we will always have the *Deer Hunters* and *Blair Witches* popping up. At first, id was a small developer that went the shareware route with Wolfenstien, then DOOM, and then hit it big.

So What Makes a Great Game?

Depends.

What are your strengths and weaknesses? What is your passion? What kind of games do you like and, more important, what are you good at or passionate about away from computer games?

It is interesting that some of the top-selling authors didn't set out to be writers:

- John Grisham was an attorney and now writes legal thrillers.
- Ann Rule was a crime reporter for years in Seattle and now writes crime fiction and nonfiction.
- Michael Crichton was an M.D. and now writes high-technology and medical thrillers.
- Jeff Deaver was an attorney as well.
- Stephen King . . . well he was always a writer, actually born to be a writer — the exception and not the rule.

The list goes on and on. You will notice in life that many people combine a previous career with a new one — or even a hobby with a career — and come out with a successful product or business.

So you should expand your abilities as a game developer and designer by playing games, reading books, going to movies, and educating yourself in any area. But keep in mind that many game developers don't even play a lot of games. Even John Carmack admits to not playing a lot of games. He attributes his success to his focus on programming, and that is pretty much all he does.

But I imagine most of the successful designers and producers do play a lot of games.

What makes a great game depends on you; what you want to accomplish and what you are able to accomplish this moment. You don't have to make Quake 4 if, in fact, you would be better suited to making Putt-Putt Loses Big in Vegas. A small production that is well done and completed is better than a barely started game that frustrated and discouraged you before you even got rolling.

What makes a great game is satisfying the audience you define. If you make the next leap in action games and unseat id, that is pretty great. But so is making the next quiz game like You Don't Know Jack or making the next low-production giant like *Deer Hunter*. Even if all you do is make a screen saver or cheesy shoot em' up that makes people laugh and remember your company, then that is great too.

DESIGNING A GAME AS A PRODUCT

It usually doesn't occur to most people when they begin to design and develop games that a game is simply a product. They realize it when they see other games advertised in magazines and when they pay for those games at the store. But when working on their own title, that fact seems to go out the window. This brings me to the first concrete lesson of successful game design.

Realize that your game, no matter how small or what the circumstances are, is a product intended to be played by someone.

Now by a product, I don't necessarily mean your goal is to sell it to a mass audience or even a small audience. You need to step back from your myopic enthusiasm to start making the game immediately and plan the game somewhat.

Even if all you are doing is a simple company screen saver, you still have a little planning to do. You have to acquire the assets, learn the application, and assemble and test the screen saver. After all that, you may discover that the boss does not like the colors, the lawyer insists on the (TM) or Copyright notice on the product, the secretary noticed you misspelled a word, and you have to redo it and then reinstall it on every system.

Something that you may have considered a small deal has suddenly turned into a real pain. If you had handled it like a real project, you would have gone through a testing and beta phase that not only would have caught those mistakes, but also may have expanded the usefulness of the screen saver.

Often, during a product test, great ideas come about from the objective tester. In this case, maybe the simple suggestion of adding the phone number or Web address to the screen image would allow the company to offer the screen saver for download to its customers who, in turn, could more easily call the company.

Some people are tapped into gaming and know the development process so well that they can just start making a game, but most can't. On a small scale, if you use TGF to make a one-level game all by yourself, you can just start anywhere and make changes as you go.

A game has to be designed for you to be successful. Now, what you want to be successful at is another question. There are many definitions and areas for success.

DESIGNING A GAME FOR AN AUDIENCE

A game designer is akin to an architect. A designer must have a basic working knowledge of all aspects of making a game, including both the technical elements (art, programming, sound, and game play issues), and the business components (marketing, budgets, and schedules). A designer needs to know who they are developing a game for and what that game is supposed to accomplish.

When Designing Your Game Ask Yourself, "Why Am I Doing My Game?"

If you are doing a game for educational purposes or learning the basics of the tools, etc., then just do it. Follow the tutorials in this book so you can gain a working knowledge of TGF and game development technology.

If it is for pure enjoyment, you can ignore the marketing and business aspects of game design. Go hog-wild with your creativity. Make a game you and your friends will enjoy.

If you are designing a game that you want to sell, get published, or give away in a professional capacity, then you need to start learning about the marketing and distribution of a game.

So, ultimately, a game is designed for someone — either you or a larger group of people. Your design will be decided by what you intend to do with the game. Are you designing a screen saver for your business? Then what will your customers like and what can they handle technologically? If you intend to sell your game, then how will you distribute it and to whom?

What to Design and Develop and for Whom

Don't make mistake number two — looking at Quake 3 and thinking you can recreate it and catch their sales — or thinking that you *have* to recreate Quake 3 to be successful.

Not only is it most likely beyond your abilities to create a Quake 3-level game at this point, you won't get the sales you think you will. Why?

- Because Quake 3 has already been done,
- Produced by a company with a big name;
- If you set out now to recreate Quake 3, you will be up against Quake 4 when you are finished.

Quite simply, even if you could do a game technologically, artistically, and comparable to Quake 3, the simple fact is that you won't sell as well because most people will prefer id's Quake 3 over your modification of Quake 3. This idea eludes many people.

So what's the answer? Do something else with your time and talents.

To address the "So what do I do?" question, let's look at the market for games. It will surprise you.

THE GAME MARKET

Women (and girls) are making interactive entertainment part of their lives. For example, my wife went from being indifferent to computer games to being the oracle of the neighborhood, especially when it comes to Mario64. My eight-year-old daughter can put most adults to shame with her prowess on the computer, Gameboy, and Nintendo 64.

But don't trust this microcosm of the market — let's look at some facts.

IDSA's fourth annual Video and PC Game Industry Trends Survey reports that more women than ever are playing games. Thirty-five percent of console game players and more than 43 percent of PC gamers are women. The March 2000 edition of *Yahoo Internet Life* features a cover with a few bullet points stating:

- More women than men
- More adults than kids
- More bingo than Quake

They back up this claim with a well-researched article.

Contrary to popular belief that games are only for kids, nine out of ten purchasers of video game software are over 18 years of age.

The genre of interactive games is as diverse as those who play them. The survey suggests that Americans are most likely to purchase the following types of PC games:

1) Puzzle/Board/Card/Learning games

2) Action games and Strategy games,

3) Driving/Racing and Adventure/Role Play games

Entertainment software users are well-educated. Three-quarters (74 percent) have attended some college, earned a bachelor's degree, and/or completed post-graduate work.

More than half (51.2 percent) of households that own both a PC and a dedicated game console earn more than $50,000 a year.

All this tells us that we don't have to make Quake 3 to make money. We can make all manner of games in many different genres and of differing levels of technology and artistry. There is a lot of room for new game and interactive products.

Quite simply, you must be able to sift through all the game development information that you will come across and take it for what it is worth so it does not discourage you or lead you to disaster. Then you have to set out to design your game with an eye for an audience and try to innovate what your are designing.

Finally, in order to innovate or change something, you must understand what you are trying to change. Our understanding of game design and development takes us into the next chapter, where we look at the history of game development and the genres (or classifications) of games — or how our one-celled games mutated into the monsters we have now.

Let's take a look at where we came from.

4

THE HISTORY OF GAME DEVELOPMENT AND GAME GENRES

L et's look at the history of computer game development. No, not the "history of computer games" or the "history of computers," — the history of computer game development.

Understanding the history of something helps you appreciate where you are and what you are working with. Ours is truly a great industry to be in. In this chapter, you will see the evolution of computer games (See Figure 4.1).

FIGURE *The evolution of man.*
4.1

Think about all that we can do now with a computer and our creativity. Pop in the CD-ROM from the back of this book and you can launch The Games Factory or The Pie 3D GCS and, with a little planning, you can create games almost as good as the stuff at your local computer store (even better in many cases).

By now you may say, "Naturally! Computers make it easy." Not many years ago, such game systems would be difficult to create. Twenty years ago? Impossible.

The game and interactive developer has come a long way from the days when one had to memorize codes and numbers — every bit as opaque and complicated as an alien language — to even work on a game. Basically, you had to be a programmer, and the focus was on the code and not the art. Currently, anyone can make a game — 2D and 3D. The doors have been opened for great artists to contribute to a game and even for the lowliest newcomers to try their hands at game design and development.

Let's take a look at how far we have come.

Solid-State Stone Knives and Micro Bearskins

In 1959, Jack St. Kirby at Texas Instruments, and Robert Noyce and Jean Hoerni at Fairchild Semiconductor Corporation independently devised a way to shrink much of the redundant and sluggish elements on an electronic circuit board and place them all onto a tiny square of silicon. It was called the integrated circuit; you know it as the microchip.

Remember those names: Kirby, Noyce, Hoerni. They are the folks that really jump-started the computer game revolution. The microchip led to the microprocessor; the microprocessor led to high-level computer languages; high-level computer languages led to death matches and 3D worlds!

The year 1959 laid the track and path to follow for the computer as we know it today, but there were a number of hurdles to jump before there was a PC on every desk. When the microchip appeared, it was hampered by high prices and very small stock, much like when any technology debuts. Until such time, programmers would simply have to content themselves with the electric equivalent of stone knives and bearskins.

Did this stop the advent and evolution of computer games? Of course not. The computer had already been invented. "How," you may ask, "did they do it?"

Before the microprocessor, everything was "solid-state."

Solid-state is, basically, a circuit board full of electrical components which provide a system of computing power and temporary memory. The capacitor played the lead to this troupe. A capacitor could hold electric charges, negative or positive, for a variety of purposes. It was, in a room-sized nutshell, the world's first RAM. Indeed, it was on a "solid-state digital computer" that the first computer game would be written.

We of the PDP, Declare SPACEWAR!

In November of 1960, Digital Equipment Corporation (DEC) debuted the first of a widely successful computer line, the Programmed Data Processor (PDP). The first PDP, PDP-1, showed up at The Hingham Institute in Cambridge, Massachusetts, where J. Martin Graetz and a bunch of his buddies waited for it. Everything the group had read about the PDP-1 told them it would be the world's first useful computer, the world's first "toy computer," as Graetz put it in a 1981 issue of *Creative Computing* magazine.

"The PDP-1 would be faster than the Tixo, more compact, and *available*. (The Tixo, a nickname for TX-0, was an earlier computer, also at Hingham.) It was the first computer that did not require one to have an E.E. degree and the patience of Buddha to start it up in the morning; you could turn it on any time by flipping one switch, and when you were finished you could turn it off. We had never seen anything like that before." The PDP-1 is shown in Figure 4.2.

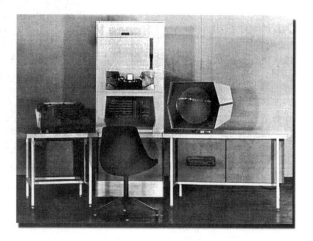

FIGURE *The Programmed Data Processor (PDP-1) by DEC.*
4.2

It was in the Institute's "kludge room," next to the Tixo, that the PDP-1 resided. Graetz, a published author, along with Stephen R. "Slug" Russell, an artificial intelligence specialist, and Wayne Witanen, a mathematician, had all experimented with coding on the Tixo for months, showing off such things as "Bouncing Ball." (Heady stuff for the late 1950s.) When they sat around the PDP-1, they transferred Tixo code and rewrote it for the PDP to get a feel for the new "toy."

They wrote and rewrote, trying new experiments. (Lines intersecting one another – or the "Minskytron" – was a particular favorite.) Soon enough, two spaceships appeared, a sun, then a star field – images fueled by a recent, healthy dose of 1950s pulp science fiction in the form of E.E. "Doc" Smith's Lensman novels. More coding – a way to rotate the ships, a thrust, torpedoes.... .

Spacewar! On the PDP's so-called "Precision CRT Type 40" monitor, two spaceships drifted against a backdrop of silent stars. In the middle, a larger star grew and shrank, tugging the ships toward it, as seen in Figure 4.3.

Players flipped console switches to control their spacecraft – one for clockwise rotation, another for counterclockwise, one to shoot "torpedoes," and the last for thrust (See Figure 4.4). The game looked very much like the arcade game Asteroids; white outlines and dots made up the figures against a "black"

FIGURE *This is a screen from the original Spacewar on the PDP-1.*
4.3

FIGURE *The controller for Spacewar (a while away from Force Feedback Joysticks!)*
4.4

background. (This graphics style would come to be known as "Vector Graphics.") The PDP-1 also allowed two users to operate the computer simultaneously. That's right — the world's first death match!

Immediately, Institute dwellers and students from nearby MIT took a liking to Spacewar. And as more computers showed up on campuses around the country, Spacewar was copied.

NOTE

You can still find Spacewar on the Internet. It has been ported (or re-coded) to other computer languages, such as Java, and can be played in your Web browser. How's that for evolution (See figure 4.5)?

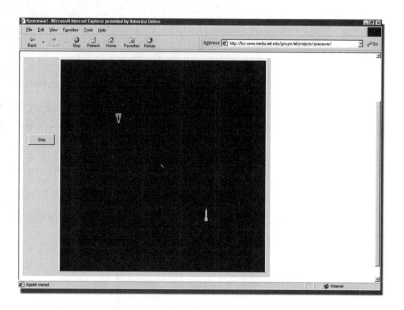

FIGURE *The same old Spacewar, but now in a browser near you.*
4.5

It wasn't soon after Spacewar that new and different games started to appear. Adventure, the world's first computer text adventure, was created shortly thereafter, as was, Lunar Lander, Hammurabi (the first simulated (sim) world), and a bunch of others. Spacewar had made a single, clear point: Computer games were fun – and cool.

Speaking Processor-eese!

But however cool Spacewar was, it was difficult to program – at least by today's standards. The guys had to write the game in a proprietary code —one that only the PDP-1 could understand. Indeed, this language could be called a form of *assembly language.*

NOTE

Machine language speaks directly to the computer hardware and tells it what to do. Assembly language is a level above this in ease of use, and above that is the current crop of high-level languages such as C, PASCAL, and FORTRAN (See Figure 4.6).

Hierarchy of Languages

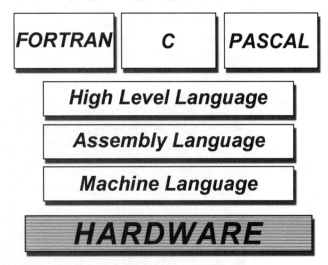

FIGURE   *The hierarchy of computer languages.*
4.6

Computers speak what's typically known as machine language. All computers understand machine language, but humans? Forget about it. It consists entirely of numbers.

Assembly language is one step toward what are known as "human-readable" languages. Instead of numbers, you have labels, or codes, that perform different processor functions. Assembly is "readable" in the sense that the different codes have a structure and format that is easily committed to memory. Well, at least that's the way the theory goes.

Following is an example of the assembler code:

```
.$13e3   [26 61    ]   rol $61
.$13e5   [26 62    ]   rol $62
.$13e7   [26 63    ]   rol $63
.$13e9   [26 52    ]   rol $52
.$13eb   [26 53    ]   rol $53
.$13ed   [26 54    ]   rol $54
.$13ef   [a5 54    ]   lda $54
.$13f1   [d0 0a    ]   bne $13fd
```

Assembly was, and is, difficult to master and is about the closest a programmer can come to understanding a processor's native tongue. Master Assembly and you can speak to your processor. But remember: Your processor can only understand one particular dialect. A different processor? A 6502, for instance? Another dialect.

Spacewar had been written in Assembly – many early games were – and it remained a staple of game programming for nearly 20 years. As long as there was a "processor" involved, there would be an assembly for it. This stays true today. But it became especially important in the early 70s, as another invention changed everything.

NOTE

Using TGF, you can create a drag-and-drop game in minutes that is technically far beyond Spacewar, with textures, sounds, and a whole lot more (See Figure 4.7). You will see that once you are able to drag and drop instead of hand-coding everything, your creativity can really take off.

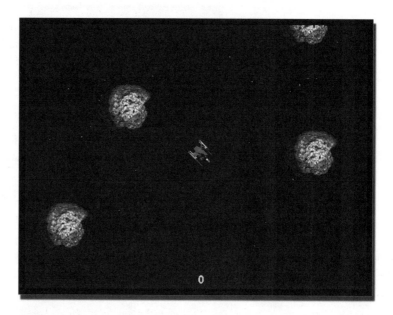

FIGURE *A TGF game that is similar to Spacewar and technically superior due to*
4.7 *modern tools.*

A Computer On A Chip

In the late 60s, science writers in various trade and consumer science magazines theorized about a so-called computer-on-a-chip. The microchip was still fresh in many scientists' minds, and many wondered about that next step. But everyone concluded that integrated circuits weren't where they needed to be. Certainly, many more experiments would have to be conducted. It would take years! In fact, don't hold your breath.

What was that saying about necessity being the mother of invention?

Intel had recently invented a so-called "MOS technology" (Metal Oxide Semiconductor), which used the inherent properties of silicon to create gates that insulated conducting channels from nonconducting ones. This, theorized Ted Hoff, Stanley Mazor, and Federico Faggin, would make a single-chip CPU possible.

Theory no more. In 1971, Intel officially announced the first microprocessor, the Intel 4004, a single chip as powerful as ENIAC, the first electronic computer that filled an entire room.

The 4004 was more of a technological curiosity than anything. But what it did was spur development of other microprocessors. Rockwell introduced the 6502 microprocessor series in the mid-1970s, which would power the Atari 2600 and the Commodore 64. General Instruments developed the 1610, which Mattel used in the Intellivision. And, of course, Intel developed the 8088, 80286, x386, x486, Pentium, etc. Not to mention Motorola's achievements with their 68000 and PowerPC series of chips.

And throughout the life span of each processor, games were developed – some of them simple, some bad, some ingenious. Each one tried to squeeze just a little more out of each processor. That squeezing continues today.

But at some point, the microprocessor, while certainly remaining at the forefront of developers' minds, became just a little less important. The speed was there and it continued to accelerate as new and better processors came out. Many developers turned their attention to graphics. How do we make better pictures?

A Vector Sprite? Uuuh, No Thanks, I'm Not Thirsty

It's a perpetual battle: Gamers want better graphics. They see the games in the arcade and they want to bring all that color and explosive sound home. Developers want to give consumers all of that and more. Developers like the same graphics the gamers do. In the middle lies the hardware, pulled at from both ends. The developer forges a compromise.

The first compromise: vector graphics. Vector simply consists of light; light stretched into lines or squeezed into points. Remember the original Asteroids? Tempest? Battlezone? All vector. In its earliest days, colored gels were physically placed on the screen to color the light.

But vector didn't appear outside of the arcade all that often. The world's only vector video game console, the Vectrex, is a highly sought after collector's item. But for the millions of people who owned Atari 2600s, Apple //e's, and Commodore 64s, the developer/processor/gamer compromise was sprites.

You will remember from Part 1 that the basic definition of a sprite is: A graphic image that can move within a larger image. Remember Pac-Man? Ol' Pac was a sprite. As were the ghosts and the dots. Even the maze walls were sprites. Each sprite can be animated to move about a game board or "world," or it can stay in one place, acting as border or barrier. Usually, the character or machine you controlled in a game (ol' Pac!) was a sprite. It could be decoration. It could collide and react to other sprites, just as we learned to do in TGF.

By the time the first round of home computer systems debuted, the ability to draw sprites on the screen was available in just about every computer language. Some processors were even created with them in mind. As such, sprites ruled games for more than a decade.

But sprites had one inherent flaw: They were 2D – flat, without depth. You could paint it anyway you want; it was still flat 2D. 3D would make games so much better. Developers wondered: "There had to be something that could be used to build 3D objects – or objects that looked 3D enough. Yeah, something simple... ."

Wherefore Art Thou, Polygon?

In 1984, a game made its way to the arcade. It never progressed much beyond it either – a mere few hundred machines were produced – but it paved the way for Quake, Kingpin, and all those death matches you've fragged around in.

The game was I, Robot, from Atari. Hardly based on the Isaac Asimov story of the same name, in I, Robot, you guide a robot around a "world," looking for and walking onto red squares. Once in contact with the red, the robot lasers a foreboding red eye at the other end of the world. Touch all the red, the eye dies. After a small fly-through-space-shoot-objects game, you reach another world with more red, and another eye.

Yeah, it's simple, but fun. What is more important here is that I, Robot was the first game to use polygons.

You've probably heard of polygons. They're the latest buzzword in game advertising. "Each world consists of 40 bazillion polygons, all rendered on-the-fly!" Polygons are the key to 3D games and those more "realistic" worlds that developers want to create and gamers want to play in.

The year 1984 and I, Robot was the impetus to develop 3D worlds. For a long time, such amazing stuff would stay in the arcade in games like Hard Drivin' and Virtua Fighter. The processors in home computers couldn't handle all the necessary computations to draw polygons and what they represented – three-dimensional graphics. But, you know, it was only a matter of time... .

rol $62 = "Make a COOL game!"

In the meantime, many programmers tried like the dickens to get away from the opaque complexity of Assembly. Some programmers used other languages, but by-and-large, Assembly was the most powerful choice. But for all its power, it was a pain. You couldn't port a game to a different processor easily. Plus, it was a bit of a memory hog. Or, at least, assembly handled precious memory resources inefficiently.

In answer to these and other problems, Dennis Ritchie and Brian Kernighan at Bell Labs introduced a "flexible" programming language, C, in the late 1970s. They called it a "high-level" programming language and it quickly became very popular. It took up less memory, was much easier to learn, and was more "human-readable."

Human-readable is not a difficult concept to grasp. Remember our assembly example? Well, some programmers wanted to get beyond those cryptic codes to something humans could "read." Here's another example. If any of you remember WordPerfect for DOS, then you remember that after you typed a line of text and wanted it to be bold or italicized, you had to type a bracketed command before and after the word to tell the printer what you wanted the letters to look like.

Example:

I want the last words in this sentence to be bold and italicized.

Add the commands in the word processor:

I want the last words in this sentence to be <ITAL> <BOLD>bold and italicized<ITAL> <BOLD>.

The printed version:

I want the last words in this sentence to be ***bold and italicized***.

This is also very similar to HTML, or Hyper Text Markup Language, which is what Web browsers use to display a site's pages.

<FONT COLOR="#000000" FACE="Times New Roman,Times,Times NewRoman">

I want the last word in this sentence to be <B><I>bold and italicized</I></B></FONT>

I stripped a lot of HTML code out, too! These commands tell the Web browser what font (style of letter) to use, as well as the color of the font. And you can see the <B> and <I> commands for bold and italic.

Now, we simply highlight the text we want to change and click a button or menu command for bolding or italicizing.

The point was to make programming languages easier to read and, ultimately, easier to use to make games.

In a lot of respects, the push toward "human-readable" languages parallels the push toward WYSIWYG (What You See Is What You Get) interfaces. From codes in word processors came buttons that quickly and easily formatted the words in the document and showed you on screen, what you'd seen on paper.

Home computers were not as plentiful or prevalent when C first debuted. It found success! But only with tinkerers, hobbyist programmers, and business folk. It never gained the popularity of its second-generation – C++. Bell Labs debuted it in the late 1980s.

C++ revolutionized programming and game development in two distinct ways. First, it took advantage of a newly created programming structure called "Object-Oriented Programming," (OOP). OOP, in a nutshell, takes functions, and the data those functions operate on, and places them in separate, independent structures that float inside a larger house program. This structure is the "object." The main program can, at any time, call upon the object to perform its function. The data created would then be served up to the main program, or even to other objects, which would have their own specific functions. Objects are portable, movable to, and usable in, any other C++ code.

By the time C++ came about, computers — especially IBM clones — had become affordable. So, hobbyist and even professional programmers spread C++ objects and code throughout Bulletin Boards and, ultimately, the Internet. Any programmer who had a handle on C++ didn't have to recreate the wheel every time he wrote a new program.

Need a routine that created sounds as the game played? An object existed. Download, modify a bit, and presto.

C++'s portability exploded beyond anything developers imagined and became that second revolution. Developers created whole 3D engines for games like Doom, Quake, and Unreal; then they'd sell them to other developers to use in other projects. Can't afford one? That's cool, because free 3D engines started to appear on the Internet – along with code for sound cards, objects for polygon calculation, and so much more, all of it nearly plug-and-play.

Hardware! Assist Me!

The ease of use and the portability of C++ revolutionized game development, and hardware support took it to the next level.

Sound, calculations, sprite and polygon rendering, player control, collision detection – these are just a few of the things that, just a few years ago, one processor would have to handle. Nintendo changed that.

Back in the 1970s when Atari and the like debuted their consoles, processors were expensive. So, the 2600, Intellivision, et al., had to rely on less processor power to do all the tasks necessary. In 1984, Nintendo was creating its new video game console, The Family Computer (or Famicom), which later became the Nintendo Entertainment System (NES) in the United States. Chip prices were more affordable and easier to come by. So, instead of doing what other console makers had to do because of the higher costs (and, to Nintendo, bad engineering decisions) when they made their consoles back in the late 1970s, Nintendo inserted several "processors" in the Famicom, each with specific tasks. The breakdown went like this: The main CPU, the 6502, controlled the larger functions – math calculations, floating point instructions, system management, etc. Another chip controlled the creation and administration of graphics – how they appeared on the screen and what sprites would do when they collided into one another. And yet another would manage, create, and "play" sounds. This whole system created a looser, more efficient structure, allowing programs to harness the power of each processor individually. The first Famicom games appeared in Japan in 1985, a year when Atari's 2600 was still king in America. But if you've ever seen a 2600 and Nintendo game side-by-side, you know that NES games blow 2600 games to smithereens.

A few computers of that day employed this type of structure already; the Commodore 64 had separate video, audio, and CPU chips. But Nintendo showed to what advantage such a system could be. The word was out: This was the way to better games. Commodore's Amiga and Atari's ST computer series took the model to an extreme, creating amazing graphics and audio processors, even if it had to huddle around mediocre CPUs.

PC manufacturers would, however, approach this system with more caution. For a long time, IBM and their clone-makers thought their customers didn't want graphics. Computers inside businesses don't need high-powered graphics or polygons or full-on surround-sound stereo. And business was all a "real" computer like a PC should do, right?

Some third-party manufacturers thought otherwise. Graphics card manufacturers, like Creative, created cards with better video processors, all with their own RAM. As the cards became more powerful, the main CPU became free to do other things. CGA, the first PC graphics standard, turned to EGA and then to VGA and SuperVGA. Soon, "Graphics Accelerator Cards" like the 3Dfx and ATI series appeared — cards that assisted the video card and enhanced graphics-intensive applications (i.e., games!), rendered polygons into the tens of thousands, and applied textures for a "real-life" look.

The same push for "better," happened in the sound world, too, though the battle ended pretty early. Two cards, the Ad-Lib and the SoundBlaster, appeared in the early 1990s. By the middle of the decade, the SoundBlaster was an unofficial standard. Today it comes in nearly every new PC and creates and plays sound unimagined a decade ago – full stereo music and effects, sounds that even rival real life. The screeches in Grand Theft Auto sound as if they're outside your door.

For game developers, cards made programming even easier. Each card came with drivers and libraries that could be inserted into new games. A new game could look and sound fantastic right out of the box, with no need to rewrite basic sound and graphics routines. Flat, 2D games with tinny sound, gave way to fully rendered 3D worlds filled with music and sounds around every darkened corner. In Unreal, the growls fall from the platforms above. In Quake 3: Arena, you can actually hear the sound of someone getting fragged two rooms away. Quick! Run! Frag the fragger!

The Future of Game Development

We've come to the end of game development's road of progress. But this is by no means a dead end. There will always be room for advancement and improvement.

Some developers believe easier programming and game development tools make for worse games. This is not true. Sure, we have a lot more games out there because they are so easy to crank out, that ease of creation being the cause of some poorly done games. But we are also seeing better games because of the fact we can actually have a real artists work on the title and use what they create, not a degraded version of it. We can also focus more on the production values of the game and not the technical details.

The typewriter didn't create bad writing, just more of it, both good and bad. In any artistic endeavor, it's the output that is to be judged, not the tools that made it.

Whereas before you'd have to learn the specific language of a processor before you even went near the definition of "game," now programs like TGF or The Pie GCS can help you create games in a matter of hours. Easier programming tools give professionals a broader range of talent to pull from. And it gives amateur developers stronger tools to hone their skills.

Games and game development are becoming more and more popular due to the increasing ease of entry into the game development field (you no longer have to be a programmer). There is a demand for artists, animators, and designers. As a result, we have larger teams and more diverse teams working on games. In the development office and the marketplace, we have had to develop a common vocabulary to communicate about the growing field of computer games.

In order to design and develop computer games, you will find that, as in most professions, you will need a common vocabulary to communicate with all the individuals involved in the life of a game title. Among the most important of those terms is "genre." Genres in computer games, like in the movies and books, help the designers form a unified vision, help the businessmen sell the title, and help the audience know what they are getting in the box.

NOTE

GameDictionary.com (www.gamedictionary.com) is an online resource you can visit to brush up on the terminology of the game development industry.

As you will see, the concept of the genre in computer games starts simple and gets rather complex. We have more forces and influences at work on our product in the computer field than in any other medium. In printed fiction, the genre started simple, like the thriller, then branched off into subgenres, such as the "legal thriller" or "psychological thriller." Having subgenres branch off main genres is simple to understand for everyone involved, from the writer to the reader. But in computer games, we have many factors that create many genre hybrids and combinations. Things are also moving so fast that there is barely time for a consensus on how genres should be divided and labeled.

Game Genres

Following we will look at the many genres, subgenres, and hybrids of computer games. You will need to know the genre of your game before you design it, but chances are, if you have an idea for a game, it already fits into one of the following categories. Genre is important at this point, since it will help determine the amount of art, technology, time, and money you will need for your game. And if you plan on getting your game published, you will need to be able to quickly and clearly position your title in the publisher's mind by comparing it to other games and discussing your game in terms of its genre.

MAZE GAME

Maze games have been around almost longer than any other genre. These are the very familiar games like Pac Man and Ms. Pac Man. Maze games are simply that — you run around a maze, usually eating or gathering something while being chased by something. Maze games started in 2D with an overhead view of the maze and can be easily made by The Game Factory.

Many don't realize that from a design point of view, the modern high tech full-blown 3D games are simply the player being brought into the maze. We still chase, are chased, gather power, and die in a maze. We tried our hands at a maze game once, as seen in Figure 4.8.

FIGURE   *Crak Man was not well-received by any audience.*
4.8

BOARD GAME

When a traditional board game like Monopoly, Clue, or Sorry is recreated on the computer, they retain their original genre classification of "board game." This is usually done with a very close adherence to the original game, with no innovation in game play, no original use of computer technology other than to make the game function as it did in real life, and usually no artistic improvements on the original game board and pieces. Initially, the challenge of getting the Artificial Intelligence to play the game was enough to keep the developers busy, so new innovations in art and game play had to wait.

Board games have been moving more recently in the computer world from straight copies of their 2D ancestors to newer 3D versions. These newer games sport a 3D look, as the pieces move and have animated cut scenes at highlights or low points (victory and defeat points) of the game, but still they are usually not innovative. They are simply more lavish productions. Some players and designers argue that this takes away from the game itself, as the animation and videos in many cases slow the game down.

CARD GAMES

Card games like Solitaire, Poker, Hearts, and Strip Poker are on the computer and are a huge genre. And, like board games, these titles have so far seen little innovation in most ways. Hardwood Hearts by Silver Creek Entertainment is a well produced card game (See Figure 4.9) that is showing some really cool innovations, such as multiplayer modes and custom decks.

FIGURE
4.9 *A screen shot of the innovative Hardwood Hearts. A demo can be downloaded at www.silvercrk.com.*

BATTLE CARD GAMES

Battle card games came about with the Magic The Gathering craze, which spawned such card games as Spellfire, Legends of the Five Rings, and Poké-mon. Battle card games play very much like traditional card games, only with pretty pictures and an emphasis on being collectible. Naturally, the decks are open-ended, and if you buy more cards you will be more powerful. Their move to the computer has been much like the traditional card game's move to the computer.

QUIZ GAME

Quiz games are big, especially online, and TGF makes them easy. Games like You Don't Know Jack, Jeopardy, and Trivia Wars are some of the biggest in this genre. While the logic behind these so-called "multiple-choice games" is rather easy, since all you do is display a question and three or four answers, the hard part is in the researching and organizing of all the content — the questions and answers. Figure 4.10 shows the typical quiz game interface.

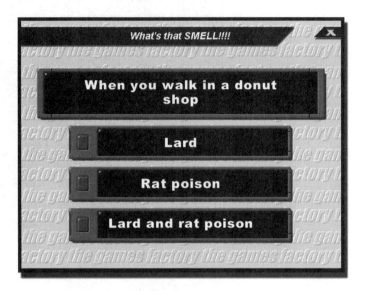

FIGURE   *Trivia game in TGF, What's That Smell?*
4.10

PUZZLE GAME

Puzzle games include Tetris, Dr. Mario, and others. Usually, there are pieces falling from above that you have to line up before they hit bottom, and you have to fit them all together in the most efficient manner — your goal being to have no open spaces between the pieces. The pieces become more complex and fall faster as the game progresses.

SHOOT 'EM UP

Space Invaders, Asteroids, Sinistar, Space Battle, and the original Spacewar are examples of this genre. (In Part 2 of this book, we make a shoot'em up game.) These are the 2D games where you are in a ship in space and you shoot things before they hit you — aliens, missiles, etc. Space Defiler is a typical shoot 'em up and can be seen in Figure 4.11.

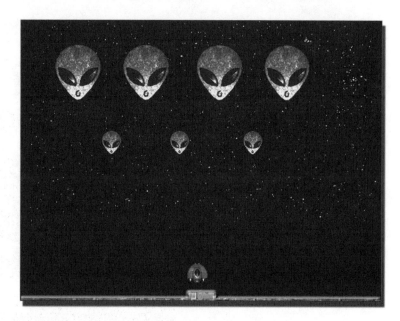

FIGURE *Space Defiler, a shoot em' up you can make with The Games Factory.*
4.11

SIDE SCROLLERS

Side scrollers are what made id big. Remember Commander Keen in the "Invasion of the Vorticons?" The original Duke Nukem', Prince of Persia 1, and Zeb are also examples. Zeb, coincidentally, was made with The Games Factory. Side scrollers usually have the hero running along platforms and jumping from one to the next, while trying not to fall into lava or get hit by projectiles. A typical side scroller interface can be seen in Figure 4.12.

FIGHTING GAME

There are many fighting games: Street Fighter 2, Samurai Showdown, Martial Champion, Virtual Fighter, Killer Instinct, Battle Arena Toshinden, Smash Brothers, and Kung Fu (See Figure 4.13). Fighting games started as flat 2d interfaces and now feature full 3D arenas and animated characters. The focus in a fighting game is the almost endless fighting moves and special moves you can use against your opponent.

FIGURE *Zeb is a side scroller made with The Games Factory.*
4.12

FIGURE *The Kung Fu game is a fighting game made with The Games Factory.*
4.13

RACING GAME

Racing games center around the concept of driving really fast around different tracks. Wipeout, Destruction Derby, Mario Kart, and South Park Derby, to name a few, are all racing games. There were 2D racing games made with a scrolling road and the sprite of the car moving over the surface. With the explosion of the color Gameboy on the scene, these games are making a comeback.

FLIGHT SIM

A flight simulator (sim) attempts to simulate real flying conditions by giving you control over such things as fuel, wind speed, and other instruments, and even control over the flaps and wings of your craft. A sim will respond with the same limits as a real vehicle, as opposed to a more simple flying game where you just go and don't have as much to think about. Wing Commander, X-Wing, and The Microsoft Flight Simulator are all flight sims. A screen shot from a flight sim can be seen in Figure 4.14.

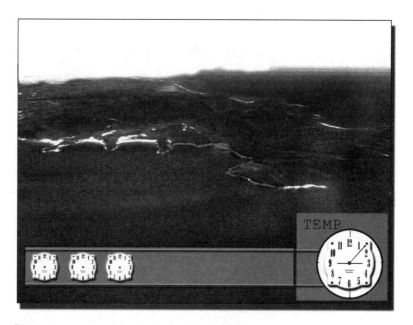

FIGURE   *A flight sim mock-up for a game company.*
4.14

TURN-BASED STRATEGY GAME

In games such as Breach, Paladin, Empire, Civilization, Stellar Conflict, and Master of Orion, players each make their decisions and the game progresses after each person has taken their turn. A lot more strategic thought and planning go into your game, much like chess.

REAL-TIME STRATEGY GAME

Populous, Command and Conquer, Warcraft, and Syndicate are a few popular real-time strategy games. In these games, you don't have forever to take your turn before the next person makes theirs. The faster player can make many moves in a short period of time. These games are also a bit like sims, since you are usually overseeing a large battle or war and the building of towns and outposts. Resource management is important — like determining the amount of gold you can get in Warcraft before you run out and can build no more.

SIMS

Sim City, Sim Earth, Sim Ant — Sim Everything. You run a simulation of a town, world, or ant colony making decisions and managing resources. Sounds too much like real life to me. Often called God Games because you are playing the part of God in the game world.

NOTE

First and third person refers to the point of view of the player. Just as in literature we write in first person ("I shot the rocket.") or third person ("She shot the rocket."), in gaming we have points of view as well.

FIRST-PERSON SHOOTER 3D (FPS)

Castle Wolfenstein 3D, Doom, Duke Nukem', Quake, Dark Forces, Sorcerer: The focus in these games is on technology and atmosphere. These games attempt to put you into the action as you are literally looking out of the eyes of the character, seeing and hearing what they see or hear. As you can see in Figure 4.15, the point of view is from a person on the street.

FIRST-PERSON 3D VEHICLE BASED

These game are much like the above first-person shooter, except the first-person vehicle-based shooter has you in a vehicle that may be a tank, ship, or giant robot. This genre is more similar to an FPS shooter than a racing game because you are not simply driving as fast as you can to cross a finish line. Your goals are more similar to the FPS — kill or be killed. Examples of vehicle-based shooters are Descent, Dead Reckoning, and Cylindrix. You can see a screen shot of a vehicle-based shooter in Figure 4.16.

FIGURE   *Screen shot from Sorcerer, a First Person 3D game.*
4.15

FIGURE   *Screen shot from Dead Reckoning, a first-person 3D vehicle-based game.*
4.16

THIRD-PERSON 3D

Tomb Raider, Dark Vengeance, Deathtrap Dungeon, and Fighting Force are all third-person. Although there are games where you can switch from first- to third-person perspective, most games are designed primarily to be one or the other. Tomb Raider in first person is not as much fun, since it is designed around seeing Lara Croft jump, roll, and tumble. In first person, you would not see these acrobatics. In Figure 4.17, you can see a third-person game. Notice how you can see the spell effects you cast (the protection circle) when in third-person mode. Likewise, when playing a first-person shooter, like Quake 3 Arena, you depend on speed and accuracy in battle to win — that is the point of the game. If you were able to play Quake 3 in third-person mode, you would die an awful lot since you would not be able to run, aim, shoot, and run some more as quickly.

RPG (ROLE-PLAYING GAME)

Wizardry, Ultima, NetHack, Dungeon Hack, Might and Magic, and Daggerfall are all RPGs. These games are focused on the emulation of the traditional pen-and-paper games where you play characters who have a lot of data

FIGURE   *Screen shot from Sorcerer in third-person mode.*
4.17

attached, like health, intelligence, strength, and areas of knowledge and skill. RPGs are like a simulation of an adventure.

ADVENTURE GAME

Zork, Hitchhiker's Guide to the Galaxy, and King's Quest are all adventure games. In an adventure game, you walk around a lot and try to fulfill a quest or unravel a mystery. You typically collect information and items. Battle is light and not the focus of this game type.

INTERACTIVE MOVIE

FMV, or Full-Motion Video, like MYST, RIVEN, and . . . well, no other FMV game is worth mentioning. Full-motion games require a lot of art and animation or video production, and precious little of anything else. There is simply no room for it, since FMV is a limiting genre at present. In FMV, you mostly watch a movie and then select what portion of the movie you watch next, kind of like a computerized version of the "choose your own adventure" books.

Other Genres

EDUCATIONAL AND EDUTAINMENT

Some games or interactive products fall under this genre head, which seems to be more determined by the intention of the product than the content or technology. A first-person game would be an edutainment title if its intention was to educate and entertain, as would a quiz game. These genres are instructional and informative. The edutainment variety attempts to make learning fun while the educational variety is straightforward learning.

SPORTS

Sports is a huge-selling genre all by itself, but also another genre label that doesn't convey the technology, game play, interface, or other aspects of the game. "It's just 'bout sports." In fiction, a thriller that takes place at a football game may be called a "sports thriller." An inspirational nonfiction book with a sports theme may be called "self-help/sports." But in games, they don't bother to put "quiz game/sports" or "quiz game/football" or "third-person football simulation" — it's all lumped under "sports."

SCREEN SAVERS/DESKTOP TOYS

While not games, and not even very interactive for that matter, these products are generally entertaining and lumped in with games and interactive products.

FIGURE   *Swarming Roaches is a screen saver Goldtree made for a local Web site as a*
4.18   *novelty give away.*

These are fairly lucrative products that you can make with The Games Factory, like the screen saver we made in Figure 4.18 for a local company's Web site.

GENRE MADNESS

Even with all these genre breakouts, we still have a lot of games that cross over and combine the above genres. Generally, a good game will have elements of the other genres; puzzle-solving in a 3D game, etc. We also see genre breakouts where technology permits; for example, many fighting games started out as side scrollers for the 2D platform and evolved into 3D shooters or 3D games. Duke Nukem' is a good example. Duke's progress can be seen in Figures 4.19, 4.20, and 4.21.

When designing your title, keep genre in mind. It is the first step in communicating your vision clearly to all involved. Once you have a clear idea of your game ("it is a first-person adventure game with shades of military simulation"), you can proceed to describe it in visual terms on paper, eventually breaking it down into the elements that will comprise the design document. Once you are at that point, we can move on to the next chapter where we look at the elements of design.

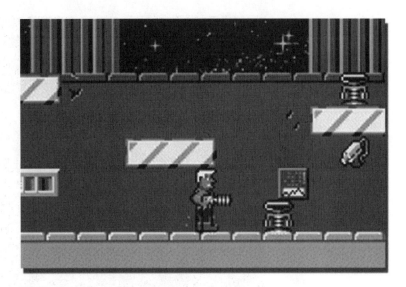

FIGURE   *The original 2D side scroller Duke Nukem.'*
4.19

FIGURE   *The first 3D Duke Nukem.'*
4.20

FIGURE *The latest Duke Nukem', using the Unreal Engine.*
4.21

5 THE ELEMENTS OF DESIGNING A GAME

So far we have looked at the most fundamental parts of game design and development; your equipment, the building blocks of a game (sights and sounds), the truth about game design and development (facts and fallacies), and finally the genres, or classifications, of games. Now we are at last ready to look at the stage of game design where we actually start designing the game; where you start to marshal your resources, explore your limits, form your ideas, and put it all down on paper. We start to head toward being able to actually generate a design document in the early stages of predevelopment.

All too often, many individuals start generating their design documents and jumping right into development all at once. While recording your ideas and other information, and prototyping and testing as you go, can be invaluable, an unbridled jump into development can be a waste of time and will usually physically and mentally lock you into a tight spot. It is far harder to change the course of something that has momentum than to set it rolling on the right path to begin with.

This is not exclusively a beginner's mistake. Often a newbie to game development will do a better job at this phase precisely because they are a newbie and have to plan out everything they are going to do. Planning is important and can not be stressed enough.

Not planning can be disastrous if you are putting a lot of time, talent, and money on the line — dashed hopes can throw a small team or business asunder. This stage of breaking out the specific elements of your game cannot be jumped into, or you will develop yourself into a corner. Building the proper groundwork is essential or you may very well design and develop a game which no one wants, which you can't legally use, or which otherwise represents wasted time and money.

The actual elements of a computer game are no secret. They are just mysterious to most because most people think of the design document as something you just dash off, and the number of pages should suffice to impress any reader. They have trouble filling these pages as they struggle through each item trying to fill in the blank. The truth is, it is only after you have decided upon your game idea, genre, and the overall feasibility of the game idea, that you are ready to tackle this phase. The elements of your game should flow on paper once you know what your game is.

NOTE

Design documents are not fill-in-the-blank forms. If you approach it this way, you will be frustrated and your game will not be half as good as it could have been had it been planned up front. Design documents are the end result of your game idea. Design documents are not game ideas waiting to happen; they are guidelines for the areas you should develop in your game, but they are not the end all.

In the three phases of game design — Predevelopment, development, and post-development — we are most concerned with predevelopment at this point. During predevelopment, you should be defining your limits and strengths, researching the feasibility of your game idea, and, of course, defining and refining your game idea.

Before you develop a game, you will have to determine if your audience will like the game you developed. As mentioned previously, you have to design for an audience, whether it is for one person or a million. And you have to know who these people are: which computer systems they like or dislike, etc. We looked at this aspect of design in the previous chapter.

You audience will also determine what type of computer system you design for, how complex your game will be, how long it will take to play, and even the content.

You have to not only design for the market's technology, but obviously you have to design using the technology you are familiar with and have access to. We will look at this in the latter part of the book.

You have to include all the *needed* elements in your game. We make the distinction *needed* because many designers throw in all the elements of a game they can think of and in some predetermined order.

What the proper parts of a game are is not at issue here; what will make a game successful is.

Remember, those bold and conclusive statements stating what a game has to be are wrong. The truth is, a game has to be fun for the intended audience. What a game should be and/or contain continues to evolve and is never set in stone.

Game Elements

Now we are down to the elements of a game. I could have just listed them up front, but where's the fun in that?

Anyone can mindlessly list game elements and attempt to fill in the blanks, but it takes more than that to design a game worth developing.

Important: anyone can make a game, but few can make a game worth playing.

ELEMENT ONE: GAME TYPE

We looked at game genres previously in detail. Now is the time to fill in the blanks. Write down your game type from the following list. You need to at least know this tidbit of information.

In the book *Game Architecture and Design,* genres are defined in their truest sense and can be broken down into the following seven types:

1. Action — Lots of frantic button-pushing
2. Adventure — The story matters
3. Strategy — Nontrivial choices
4. Simulation — Optimization exercises
5. Puzzle — Hard analytical thinking
6. Toys — Software you just have fun with
7. Educational — Learning by doing

This is a good start for our design decisions and will greatly simplify the other decisions. The basic genre you develop will determine the focus on technology, art, content, and research. It will even determine the approximate size of your team, budget, and other resources.

You can also, at this point, make notes about the other genres or game types you hope to incorporate into your game. Keep in mind that adding, or layering, genres, on your game increases everything — time, money and resources needed, and the complexity of the project.

After you have a good idea of the type of game you want to do — depending on your strengths and weaknesses — you are ready to move on to the next step.

ELEMENT TWO: GAME TREATMENT AND GAME IDEA

You are now ready to write your game idea down, but not the treatment. The idea and the treatment are two very different things and people often confuse the two.

Game Idea

A game idea is just that, an idea. It is written first to convey your game idea to others.

Game Treatment

A game treatment is written after substantial research, design, and even development has been done, and serves primarily as a "selling document" to "pique" the interest of publishers, investors, and department heads in larger companies. This is a concise document of an already well-formed game project.

In other words, the game idea represents the sum total of what is known about the game, whereas the game treatment is a distillation of a much larger body of work and is only hitting the highlights of the project.

Initially, you should write a rough draft of your game idea that presents as much information as possible about the game in as clear and concise a fashion as possible, while spelling out the general resources (time, talent, and cash flow) that the game will take and why you think it is such a great idea. This document then is used to discuss and research the feasibility of the game.

As the game project gears up, you will line up resources and team members, determine needs, develop budgets and schedules, and define the game to a great degree. The original idea will change, evolve, and grow more solid. A mountain of information will have been generated.

At the end of all this is the task of writing the game treatment, which will explain the exciting game development effort you have underway.

NOTE

Most of the advice floating around the Internet tells you to write the treatment first, then this document, then that document. This is not the best advice. This comes from people looking at a game proposal and attempting to reverse engineer it.

The treatment *generally* contains the following items: the (proposed) title, genre, feel of the game play as well as the overall look of the game, and even planned features and any marketing information that will back up the feasibility of the title. Money, budgets, and dollar amounts should wait until *after* the publisher is interested in your game.

As a selling document, the treatment should open with the most marketable feature of you or your game development effort. If you are a top-selling developer, or if you developed a technological wonder or an artistic masterpiece, those facts should be presented first.

NOTE

Be careful. This document is deceptive to many because of its brevity, but writing this short and concise document effectively requires a great deal of industry knowledge and writing skill. What you are attempting, in as few words as possible, is to get a publisher or investor to invest in your idea. This document is the equivalent of the query letters writers send out to get book and article publishing deals and the cover letters that accompany business proposals. These are all selling documents and contain the same basic elements.

Even if you are making a game on a small scale, you should still get in the habit of writing down your ideas and documenting the development of your title. This will give you a focus that will benefit your title, and the practice will clarify your thoughts and clear the way for new thoughts to bubble up.

Element Three: Technology

This element consists of the game platform and the technology needed to play the game.

You should know what the system requirements are for your final game. Will it require a CD-ROM, special video card or peripheral, certain amount of RAM, or other special resources? What operating systems, drivers, or special software may the user need? These are all considerations the publisher will want to hear about.

Element Four: Audience

Who did you develop the game for and why?

Did you get audience input? What were their suggestions?

Remember the previous sections dealing with "game design and the audience"?

Element Five: Team

You need a team, even if you are the only one working on your game.

What team members will you need; what jobs need to be done?

Who are your team members and where will you get them from?

What are their strengths and weaknesses?

How will you manage them; do you have any experience managing people?

Element Six: The Design Elements

So what should a design document contain? The design document is the after-effect of a good game idea and the breakdown of the elements needed to develop that idea into a game.

Upcoming developers always want to see a design document, and with good reason, as it represents a complete game and the elements it takes to make a complete game. It is what the developer aspires to create. While a design document can be very useful as a guide, it is someone else's title and most likely will not be a perfect fit for your game. Like the game treatment, a design document is a product of your game and should not be the genesis of it.

If you are doing a 3D Shooter that is action-oriented, you don't need a huge back story. In fact, that may be a detriment to the document from a development and selling point of view.

To best illustrate the design document, I used the sample design document from G.O.D. Games. This is probably the "fill-in-the-blank" form most of you were hoping to find, but hopefully it will serve as a guide for you in defining your game, and not simply be a "fill-in-the-blank" exercise.

Take note of the elements of this design document, but realize that your own game may have none, more, or all of the listed elements.

Sample Design Document Outline from G.O.D. Games

I. Treatment/Intro This section's purpose is to introduce the overall game concept to the Gathering's Development Board. The suggested guidelines for completing this section are as follows:

    A. 1-2 pages of **overall** game idea
    B. Use broad strokes; specifics will be addressed at a later time
    C. Stay concise and focused
    D. Include these elements:

        1. Game title
        2. Game genre
        3. Brief story description
        4. If applicable, main character or units description (including general actions)
        5. Brief description of settings and scenarios
        6. Overall look of the game
        7. General computer AI description
        8. Minimum/recommended hardware specs
        9. List of necessary development tools
       10. List of team members and skills required to produce game
       11. Estimated completion/release date
       12. Similarities to other genre games
       13. Standout features—"competition killers"

II. Design Document The completion of this section will be required as an early milestone subsequent to the Development Boards approval of the submitted title. It will also be used by the Gathering Review Team as a measure of progress throughout the titles development cycle.

    A. **OVERVIEW/STORY**
        1. Define the games key ambience/attitude
        2. Describe the games overall style
        3. Describe the general world(s), and the state of that world in which the game takes place

4. Team members who will be working in this area, and their specific duties

5. Production art

B. **CHARACTERS/UNITS**

1. Thoroughly describe player characters/units
   a) Current status/situation/ambition
   b) Personality traits, history, relevant relationships
   c) Abilities, special abilities (powers and/or techniques), and their accompanying animation (and effects)
   d) Weapons or utility items

2. Describe persistent non-player characters/units (See previous list:B/1/a-d)

3. Describe persistent arch-enemies (See previous list:B/1/a-d)

4. Team members who will be working in this area and their specific duties (include necessary technological implementation)

5. Production art

C. **LEVEL DESCRIPTION**

1. Break the game into manageable sections according to its genre
   a) Levels (action/platform)
   b) Chapters (RPG/adventure)
   c) Geographical areas (RPG/adventure/action/strategy/sim)
   d) Mission (sim/strategy/action)
   e) Races/tournaments (driving/sports)
   f) ...ad infinitum

2. Description of each level
   a) Level name
      (1) Describe the level in referential terms that everyone can understand: Blade Runner Metropolis,
          Spider King's Lair, Atlantis, Third Stage (Waterfall)
   b) Environment
      (1) Appearance
      (2) Geographical features (main and subareas)
      (3) Inactive (background)
      (4) Active (foreground)
      (5) Puzzles/traps/environmental challenges
      (6) Key area for artwork
      (7) Maps may be helpful

      (8) Team members who will be working in this area, and their specific duties (include necessary technological implementation)

      (9) Production art

  c) Main goal of level

      (1) Explains the purpose of the level

           E.g., Pascal needs to navigate through the Hellhole to rescue Auntie Garfungiloop, so she can give him the Jeweled Monkey's Head.

  d) Level's relevance to story

      (1) How the results of the player's success or choices in this level affect the overall story (particularly in a game with a branching storyline)

      (2) How the level, and the events portrayed within, fit into or advance the overall story (contextual placement)

      (3) How these story elements are related to the player (through dialogue, in-game events, or framing cinematics)

      (4) Keep track of subplots

  e) Characters/enemies encountered

      (1) Conversation/dialogue

      (2) Non-player character actions

      (3) Attack moves

      (4) Physical appearance

      (5) Brief character sketch

      (6) Relevance to story

      (7) Technical description

      (8) Key area for artwork

      (9) Team members who will be working in this area, and their specific duties (include necessary technological implementation)

      (10) Production art

  f) Actions/animations specific to level

      (1) Explicit actions performed by main character to accomplish level goal(s): defeating a boss, discovering or recovering an artifact, special abilities granted by power-ups, etc.

      (2) Explicit actions performed by other characters in the level

   (3)   Terms like run and jump are insufficient. It is important here to describe how a character jumps, and what he looks like while doing so.

   (4)   Team members who will be working in this area, and their specific duties (include necessary technological implementation)

   (5)   Production art

g)   Music for level

   (1)   Technical aspects (event-triggered, Redbook Audio, etc.)

   (2)   Desired effect on players

   (3)   Purpose of music (e.g., background ambiance, tension-building, or clue-supplying)

   (4)   Team members who will be working in this area, and their specific duties (include necessary technological implementation)

   (5)   Production art

h)   Sound effects for level

   (1)   Level of realism

   (2)   3D aspects of sound

   (3)   Hints provided by cues (e.g. T-Rex shockwave thuds getting louder as something approaches) or sounds that result from certain actions (e.g., hollow sound resulting from shooting a false wall)

   (4)   Scripted dialogue

   (5)   Background ambiance

   (6)   Team members who will be working in this area, and their specific duties (include necessary technological implementation)

i)   Items per level

   (1)   Powerups

   (2)   Weapons

   (3)   Any other items that the player can interact with—pushed, climbed, thrown, switched, clung to, hung from, triggered, blown up, ridden on, eaten, examined, etc.

   (4)   Key area for artwork

   (5)   Team members who will be working in this area, and their specific duties (include necessary technological implementation)

   (6)   Production artwork

D. **SCHEDULE**

Since every development cycle varies greatly, the following are to be viewed more as guidelines than as hard requirements:

1. Technological development milestones

    a) First year: Engine/tools development should be broken into quarterly milestones.

    b) Following 12 months of engine/tool work: Technological additions should be scheduled with 8-10 monthly milestones.

    c) For titles using licensed engines and tools, adjust the previous schedules accordingly. Budget three months for mid-production engine upgrade.

2. Art and non-technological content development milestones

    a) Pre-production art—character sketches and model sheets, architectural rendering, color studies, etc., should coincide with the engine/tools schedule (see above). Should be complete at the end of the first 12 months.

    b) Crucial story elements, plot devices, level and character concepts, etc., should coincide with the engine/tools schedule (see above). Should be complete at the end of the first 12 months.

On completion of concept stage, art production should begin concurrent with monthly milestones of technological progress.

IN CONCLUSION

There are no set rules for game design and development, but there are plenty of guidelines and areas where the practices are age-old — like the proper way to budget or plan a project. One of the most awesome things about game development is the fact that our genres are so flexible and our technology is so powerful. There are no barriers to entry. In fact, it is incredibly easy to get started in game development. It is all about knowing what tools and resources you have at your disposal and where you want to go with your ideas. Then you have to work very hard at it.

Speaking of work, are you ready to start working on a game? Now that you know the basics of game design and development, let's make some games. We will start with the 2D game types and move up to 3D later in the book.

PART

2

AWESOME 2D GAME CREATION

6

INTRODUCTION TO THE GAMES FACTORY

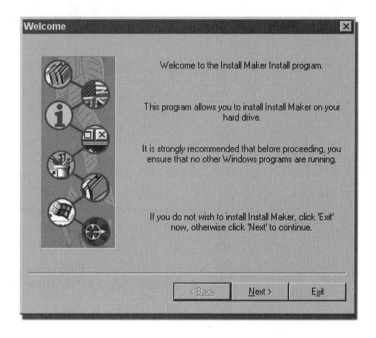

I n the following chapters, we will actually make a game step by step. It will be exciting to see your creations come to life on the computer screen as we work through the tutorials.

Once you have been led through the process of making a 2D game, you have the basis you need to go further into game development. Much of what you learn here will apply to more complex applications and tools later on. You will find it easier to pick up new software and tools and learn them after having learned one application.

We will be using The Games Factory (TGF) thanks to the wonderful people at Clickteam (See Figure 6.1).

FIGURE *Clickteam makes The Games Factory, Install Maker, and other fine products.*
6.1   *Please visit them at www.clickteam.com.*

NOTE

IMPORTANT TUTORIAL SETUP Instruction: Please copy the three files on the ROM in the back of this book in the 'samplegames\tgflibs' folder to the TGF Library Folder on your hard drive. If you did a default installation the folder will be 'C:\GFactory\Libs' Do not copy the folder itself, but the three files in the folder.

Once you are comfortable with TGF, you will be able to use it to produce games and interactive applications with ease. TGF is a very powerful 2D game creation package. It contains state-of-the-art animation tools, sound tools, multimedia functions, and fabulous game structuring routines that make it very easy to produce your own games — with no programming.

NOTE

You can also make slide shows, interactive tests, presentations, and screen savers with TGF.

We will start by installing and getting familiar with the major areas of TGF. Make sure the CD-ROM from the back of this book is in the drive of your computer. On it is a copy of TGF.

What You Are Getting on the CD-ROM

On the CD-ROM in the back of the book, you will find both 32- and 16-bit versions of TGF. If you are running Windows 3.1 or Windows NT, you need the 16-bit version; all other operating systems should use the 32-bit version.

Operating Systems

Windows 95 and 98 users can install the 32-bit version of The Games Factory on their machines. To do this, simply double click the My Computer icon on your Windows desktop. Click the button next to the My Computer text box and select the CD-ROM icon from the drop-down list. Look down the list for the folder that contains the 16 bit or 32 bit version you are installing.

Double click this file to start the installation.

Windows 3.x users can use the 16-bit version of The Game Factory, GFCR16.exe.

Installation Note

The installation procedure is very similar for both the 16- and 32-bit versions.

During the installation you will be given the choice to install the unregistered, home, or pro version figure (See Figures 6.2 and 6.3). You should install the unregistered version. This is a normal unregistered version of TGF, but as a special contribution to this book, Clickteam has removed the time limit. You can use TGF as long as you like, but you will see a start-up screen each time you start TGF and you cannot save stand-alone games, screen savers, or Internet applications.

This unregistered version allows you to save your creations as GAM files (.gam files). Anyone wishing to play your game needs to have TGF installed on their computer to load and run the GAM files.

WHAT IF I WANT TO "SAVE STAND-ALONE GAMES, SCREEN SAVERS, AND INTERNET APPLICATIONS?"

You will have to surf on over to the Clickteam site (www.clickteam.com) and register TGF. You will buy a registration code that will allow you to run either the registered home version or the pro version. We included these files on the disk to save you the download. All you have to do is reinstall TGF, select the proper registered version from the menu during installation and enter the registration code, as seen in Figure 6.4.

FIGURE *The welcome screen.*
6.2

FIGURE *Unless you are a registered owner of TGF, you should select the Unregistered*
6.3 *option.*

FIGURE   *The registration code window during installation.*
6.4

NOTE

Note: The registered versions of TGF are home and pro. Both can save stand-alone games, screen savers and Internet applications, but:

The home version *saves stand-alone applications that have an end screen, and games produced with the Home Version cannot be sold for profit.*
The pro version *saves stand-alone applications that have no end screen and games made with the Pro Version can be sold for profit.*

I am assuming that you have selected the unregistered version of the disk from the back of this book.

After this choice is made, TGF will install itself onto your system and ask if you want to read the README file. It would be a good idea to do so. Click Finish at the bottom of the screen when you are ready to move on.

The next screen asks if you want to install either Video for Windows or a QuickTime video driver for showing AVI and QuickTime-compatible video clips. Unless you want to install one of the drivers, click Next. The next screen asks you to type in your full name. When you have done so, click Next.

At the top of the next screen are two tick boxes, one for the 16-bit version and one for the 32-bit version. If you are running Windows 95/98 on your machine, you can install the 32-bit version. The tick box will be filled already. If you are running Windows 3.x, then the 16-bit tick box will be filled (See Figure 6.5).

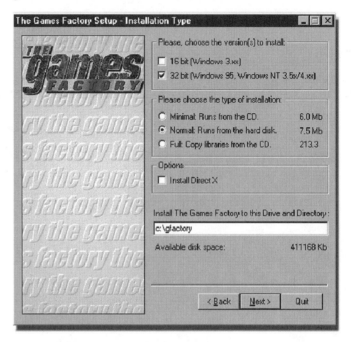

FIGURE *Installation Type screen.*
6.5

For 32-bit (Windows 95 and 98) users, there is a tick box for Direct X, which is Microsoft's own graphics driver. Unless you specifically don't want to install Direct X, check the box. If you experience problems using Direct X, you should change the graphics driver.

For 16-bit (Windows 3.x) users, there is a tick box for Win G, which is Microsoft's own graphics driver.

At the bottom of this screen is the file name that The Games Factory will use. Unless you specifically want to enter a different name, click the Next button. You will then be told that the directory does not already exist, and you will be asked if you want to create it. Click the OK button to proceed. Now wait while The Games Factory installs. When installation is complete, click the Return to Windows button to return to Windows. Now you can double click The Games Factory icon to run the program.

Tutorial Setup Note

You MUST copy the three tutorial files from the CD ROM that are located in the *samplegames\tgflibs folder onto the TGF LIBRARY FOLDER*, now installed on your hard drive. (If you did a default installation, the folder will be called **C:\GFactory\Libs.**) DO NOT copy the folder itself, but each of the three files in the folder.

A Quick Intoduction to TGF

TGF is centered around three main editing screens that allow you to control the three main parts of your game.

The Storyboard Editor is the screen that allows you to decide the order of the levels in the game.

The Level Editor allows you to decide which characters, backgrounds, and objects to put in your level and how to animate them.

The Event Editor allows you to assign the actions and responses that will make your game come alive.

Some of the functions overlap, so look out for the Handy Hints along the way.

NOTE

You can easily move from one editor screen to the next by clicking the Editor icons from the toolbar at the top of each editor screen. Don't worry if you cannot remember what each one looks like. As you move the mouse pointer over the icons, a text balloon will appear underneath the mouse pointer telling you what each one is. Following is a brief description of the functions of each of the editor screens. These functions are described in more detail in the chapters of the user's manual relating to them.

STORYBOARD EDITOR

Most games are composed of several different levels, and this screen allows you to add levels to your game, copy levels, and change the order of the levels by moving them around. This is also where you decide on the size of your playing area, add and edit professional-looking fades to each level, and assign passwords to enter each level (See figure 6.6)

NOTE

Until you have created a level, the only way to move out of this screen is by clicking in the 'Thumbnail' with the right mouse button, and select the 'Edit this level' option.

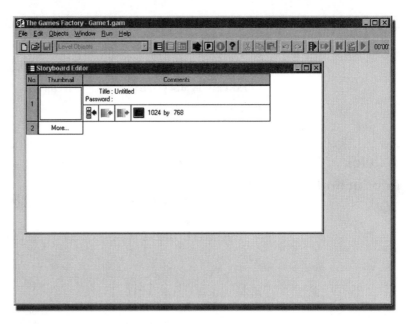

FIGURE   *The Storyboard Editor.*
6.6

LEVEL EDITOR

The Level Editor (See Figure 6.7) is the initial "blank page" for each of your levels. It displays your play area and is where you put background objects and the main characters of your game. You generally access this screen from the Storyboard Editor screen.

It is from this screen that you have access to the libraries of all the different objects that you can use in your game. This is also where you can create your own animated objects, text, and other object types. Basically, all the objects that you want to play with have to be placed on this screen first before you can start manipulating them. It is also here that you change the animation and movement of objects, and change the basic setup of all your objects.

You will frequently find that before you can manipulate an object from the Event Editor, you must make sure that it is set up correctly on this screen.

EVENT EDITOR

This is where your game will really come to life. The actions you assign here are called interactivity. Once you become experienced with The Games Factory, you will find that this editor is where you will spend most of your time. It is here that you decide all the events in your game.

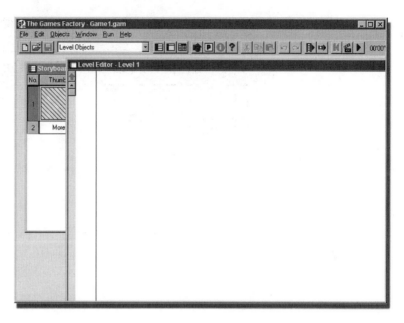

FIGURE   *The Level Editor.*
6.7

The Event Editor (See Figure 6.8) is set up like a spreadsheet, where you can assign relationships to each object in your game. This setup makes game-building, since as you can visually see what happens in your game. Examples of the game play you can build are aliens colliding with a spaceship; the main character collecting a power-up or getting hit by a missile; setting a time limit; or assigning a sound event. You can create an explosion, destroy an object, add to the score, subtract a life, or even add complicated events like changing the direction of a character or randomly moving object.

That was the quick tour of TGF. We saw that a game is built in TGF in three stages: First you lay out the flow of your game in the Storyboard Editor, then you lay out your level and its objects in the Level Editor, and finally you use the Event Editor to assign relationships and behaviors to your objects.

For the next chapter, you will want to have TGF installed and running, if possible since we will be digging deeper into The Games Factory.

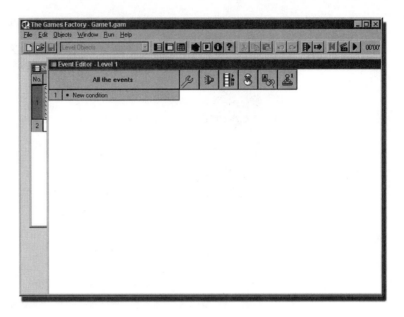

FIGURE   *The Event Editor.*
6.8

CAUTION

As mentioned on page 102 You MUST copy the three tutorial files from the CD ROM that are located in the *samplegames\tgflibs folder onto the TGF LIBRARY FOLDER*, now installed on your hard drive. (If you did a default installation, the folder will be called **C:\GFactory\Libs.**) DO NOT copy the folder itself, but each of the three files in the folder.

If you do not copy the three files into the proper folder, you will not be able to use the sample game tutorials with TGF software.

CHAPTER

7

BEHIND THE SCENES OF THE GAMES FACTORY

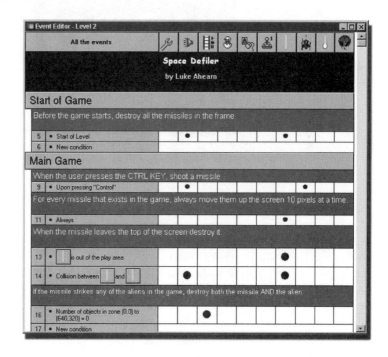

N ow we will take you through the step-by-step process used to construct a very basic shoot-'em-up game for this book. I named my retro-creation Space Defiler (See Figure 7.1), my own version of Space Invaders. You will see that, with TGF, we can do a lot more than what the original Space Invaders could.

FIGURE *Space Defiler, a retro-creation using TGF, inspired by Space Invaders.*
7.1

NOTE

Retro gaming is still rather popular. People still love to play Pac Man, Asteroids, Space Invaders, and other older games. Many can be found online in the form of Java applets that can play in your Web browser window. A great site for this is http://spaceinvaders.retrogames.com.

Loading Space Defiler

Select the Open option from the File menu at the top of the main screen in TGF, and look for the the sample game folder on the CD-ROM.

Open the the sample game folder and look for the spacedel2.gam file, as shown in Figure 7.2. Open this file.

Notice as you are searching for the file that TGF has a thumbnail preview of the GAM file (See figure 7.3).

FIGURE   *Opening the spacedel2.gam file.*
7.2

FIGURE   *Opening the spacedel2.gam file. Notice the thumbnail of your game in the lower*
7.3   *right-hand corner.*

Space Defiler will show you the very basics of creating games with TGF. But those basics will go a long way in game development since a lot of the procedures that you will be using for this game are basic to all games. With this tutorial, you will learn the different functions of the Editor screens and how they relate to each other. Once you understand those basics, you are home free.

We will be dealing a great deal with the actual interactivity of a game, the aspect not touched on in Part 1. You will see how integrated the interactivity aspect of a game is to the specific application you are using.

NOTE

Although Space Defiler is a very basic game, you will be introduced to a set of interactive behaviors that you will be able to add to and expand on. You can make any game as complex as you like by adding levels, monsters, behaviors, and additional complexity by changing the movement, sounds, power-ups, scoring, etc.

Space Defiler – The Storyboard Editor

Once you have loaded the Space Defiler game, you will be presented with a Storyboard Editor screen, as seen in Figure 7.4.

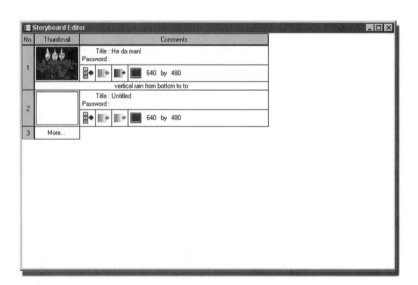

FIGURE *The Space Defiler Storyboard Editor.*
7.4

Starting from the top of the screen, we shall describe the various features of the Storyboard Editor screen.

Note that a lot of the features are the same for all of the Editor screens, but what they actually perform on each Editor screen can be quite different. So you may want to get used to looking at what screen you are in before clicking buttons.

At the top right of the main TGF window are the Standard Window Manipulation icons: Minimize (Maximize), Restore, and Exit. By clicking these you can control the window size or close the application. This is mentioned here since the different editors also have their own set of Window Manipulation icons and you could accidentally close the entire TGF, when all really want to do is close a specific editor.

On the very top of the screen is the The Games Factory header bar. This displays the current game name — in this case, spacedel2.gam. Next to this is the name of the current Editor screen, Storyboard Editor. Below this is the pull-down menu bar. From here you can save your games, change the size of the screen, change preferences, access the Help pages, and customize your display.

Below the menu bar is The Games Factory toolbar. From here you can very quickly and easily move around the Editor screens by clicking their icons, save games, cut and paste objects or events, and conduct test runs of your games See Figure 7.5).

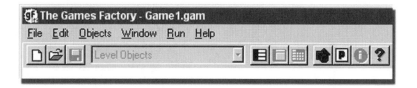

FIGURE   *Tool bar icons.*
7.5

Each level is displayed as a thumbnail, or very small screen shot on the main window area of the Storyboard Editor. By default, the thumbnail is displayed immediately next to the number of the corresponding level, as shown in Figure 7.6.

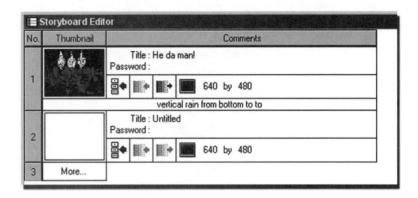

FIGURE *Closeup of the Storyboard Editor's level window.*
7.6

Next to the thumbnail are the comments for that level, the title of the level, and the password. To change these, simply click the text that you want to change with the left mouse button. You can then edit or add a title or password.

Underneath the comments are several buttons, as shown in Figures 7.7 - 7.10.

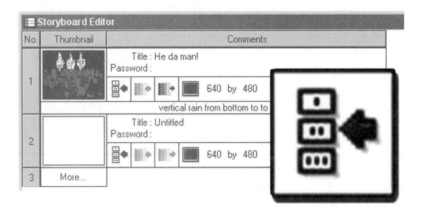

FIGURE *The multimedia level button.*
7.7

This denotes a multimedia level, which is what all your levels will be by default. If you were to make your level an animation frame, this icon would change.

You can add a fade-in transition to your level by using the icon in Figure 7.8.

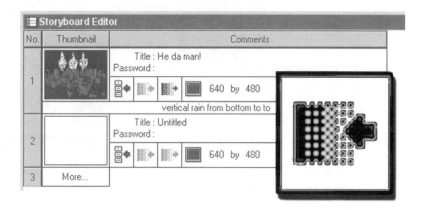

FIGURE   *Fade-in transition button.*
7.8

You can add a fade-out transition to your level using the icon seen in Figure 7.9.

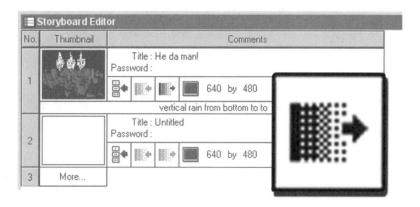

FIGURE   *Fade-out transition button.*
7.9

You can select the size of your play area by using the button in Figure 7.10. The play area can be much larger than the screen size, if you want. Then you can scroll around it using a scroll function.

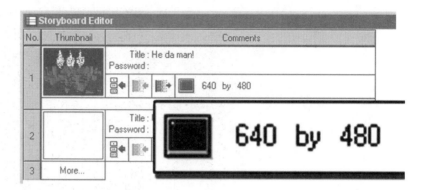

FIGURE *Play area size button.*
7.10

By clicking the numbers, you can enter your own screen sizes via the keyboard, or by clicking the monitor icon, you can pick one of the default (common or standard) monitor sizes. Space Defiler is set at 640 x 480, which is a standard monitor size, and will allow the game to play faster than a larger screen size.

Now that you've got a general idea of what all the different features are on the Storyboard Editor, let's look at how I put all the objects on the screen. Any questions you may have about the Storyboard Editor will be answered soon and in more detail.

Space Defiler – The Level Editor

If you are just opening the Space Defiler file, right click inside the thumbnail to get the pop-up menu. Select Edit the level\Level Editor. This will take you to the Level Editor.

NOTE

If you open a new file at this point and then open the Level Editor, you will be presented with a white, empty screen. When you open the spacedel2.gam file, you see the screen as it looks in the game (See Figure 7.11) and several items to the left in a vertical row. In the next chapter, we will look at getting those items into the editor.

Once you have been in the Level Editor or the Event Editor using the thumbnail from the Storyboard Editor, all you have to do is click the icons on the toolbar to move through the different Editor screens in the future.

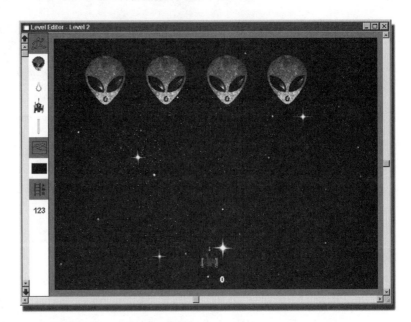

FIGURE   *The Space Defiler Level Editor, with objects and a background.*
7.11

Now that you are in the Level Editor, you will notice that the toolbar at the top of the main window is exactly the same as on the Storyboard Editor screen, only now you can access the object libraries via the Level Objects window in the toolbar, as shown in Figure 7.12. Notice also that you can see all of the objects that have been used to create Space Defiler in their own Object Window on the left-hand side of the screen.

When there are a lot of objects in a level, not all of the objects will fit inside that window, so there is a scroll bar to look through them. Scroll the object libraries now. You will find many premade items that you can use. Notice that as you select a library, it appears in the left-hand vertical window of the Level Editor. When you change libraries, all the items go away, unless you have used one. If so, that item is retained.

You can also make the window a "moveable window" using the Objects-Display objects in a movable window option from the menu bar at the top of the screen.

NOTE

If you move your mouse pointer over the objects in the object window, a "Handy hint" will show you the name of each object, as shown in Figure 7.13. You could now select one of the objects with the left mouse button and then place it anywhere on the screen. Try it now — just don't save the file!

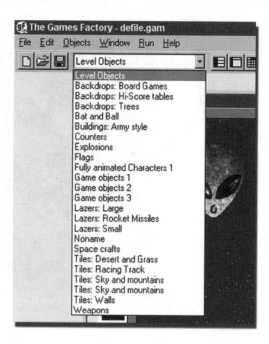

FIGURE   *The Level Objects pull-down list.*
7.12

If you had fun placing objects all over the level screen, then select them with the left mouse button and use the Delete key to erase them. You must do this before you continue or you will change the contents of the other Editor screens. If that happens, what you see will no longer correlate with the contents of this book.

Also try moving the mouse pointer over the objects that have already been placed on the screen. You can move them around by clicking them with the left mouse button and dragging them around by holding the left mouse button down. Now go to the scroll bars at the side of the screen, and try moving around the play area using them. You will notice that there is a gray area, which is the edge of the play area. Any objects placed here will not be shown on the screen when you play your game. But it can be a useful "holding area" for placing objects in a level, which you can move onto the play area later on by using the Event Editor.

Now let's look at the menu options for each object. Different types of objects have different menus. Press the right mouse button when you have the mouse pointer over the backdrop object, as shown in Figure 7.14. Look through all the different options, but don't change anything. Now try it over any of the other objects on the screen. We shall be using these menus in a later

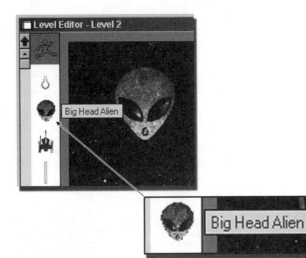

FIGURE *Handy hint balloon over objects in the Level Editor.*
7.13

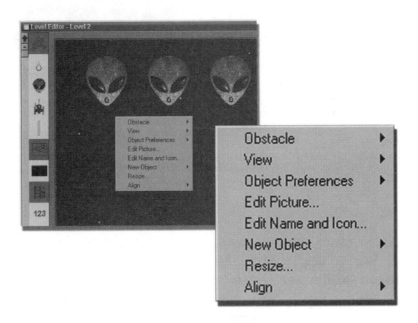

FIGURE *Right mouse menu over space backdrop.*
7.14

tutorial. Now that we've had a quick tour around The Games Factory's more basic features, let's look at how the game plays!

To be sure that you have made no changes to the game at all, simply reload the game. To do this, click the File menu at the top of the screen, then select the Open option. Now reload Space Defiler, right click in the thumbnail, and select and open the Level Editor.

Look at the top right of the toolbar. There are several control buttons there which control the testing of your game. For now we are just going to use the Play/Pause button and the Restart button, as shown in Figure 7.15.

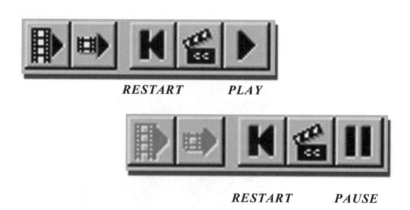

RESTART   PLAY

RESTART   PAUSE

FIGURE *The Play/Pause buttons and the Restart Button.*
7.15

The controls for the game are Left/Right (cursor keys) and fire is the Ctrl key.

Now click the Play button. To stop the action, click it again. When you want to finish playing, be sure to use the Restart button to reset everything.

**Space Defiler –
The Event Editor**

To get into the Event Editor, simply click the icon on the toolbar at the top of the screen. You should now see a screen that looks like Figure 7.16.

You decide upon the action and strategy of your game in the Event Editor. This is where you add sound and explosions, move onto the next level, and display Hi Score tables; the list is almost endless.

We will look more specifically at how to change and edit the events and actions in the Event Editor in the next chapter. Right now we will be familiarizing you with the logic of the Event Editor.

FIGURE *The Space Defiler Event Editor.*
7.16

In addition to the menu bar and toolbar, the Event Editor basically consists of one horizontal line. At first this line is like the first line of a spreadsheet before you enter any information. In Space Defiler, you will see many events already entered.

Look at the Event Editor and you will see a row of icons across the top that represent possible actions. Beyond those, to the right, are all the objects we placed in our game from the Level Editor.

You will also notice that there is a vertical column of gray "event lines." Look below the heading "Start of Game Actions," and you will notice that next to each event line, there is a grid of boxes. Each box lines up with an object icon above it. For example, the first event states that 'start of level' 'destroy' the 'missile object'. We shall discuss how to insert and edit events and actions in the next chapter.

You can see the horizontal line at the top of the Event Grid in Figure 7.17. It looks like this in Space Defiler.

"All the events" is the heading for the vertical column, which is where you insert all the events for the game. We shall describe this after talking you through the icons in the horizontal bar at the top.

FIGURE   *The Event Grid in Space Defiler.*
7.17

The icons at the right of the bar refer to all the level's objects. Shown here are all of the objects (except backdrop) that have been placed on the play area. You can see the enemy objects here, as well as the player's ship and the missile. It will also show any object that you use for bullets or that you create from within the Event Editor, even if they are not already on the play area.

NOTE

How to shoot an object is described in the next chapter.

The first six icons denote Game Objects, and are always on the event grid by default. They are in order, and can be seen in Figure 7.18.

Special Conditions. Performs special functions when an event occurs.

Sound. Plays or stops sound or music, even a CD track.

Storyboard. Allows you to start, stop, and change levels, as well as control the flow of the different levels of your game.

Create New Object. Allows you to place or create a new object on the screen at certain times or due to certain events.

Mouse and Keyboard. Lets you control how the player interacts with the mouse and keyboard — interactivity!

Player One. Allows you to change lives and scores.

Before we go any further, use the vertical scroll buttons on the right side of the screen to move down through the events until you can see events 18 and 19 just appearing on the bottom of the screen. You should now have a screen that looks like Figure 7.19.

You can now see three event lines within the group "Missile Destroys Aliens." You can see, starting from left to right, that there are two events that involve the two alien head entities and the missile object.

The logic in line 17 is stated clearly with text and pictures:

Collision between missile and enemy

Now move your cursor over the dots in the grid to the right and you will complete the logic.

Play sound sample.

Add 10 to the score.

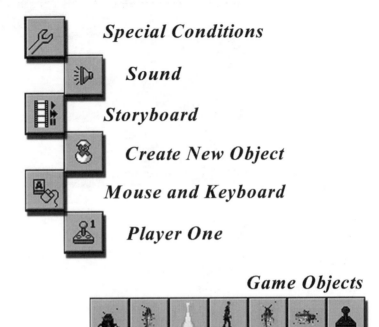

Icons of the Event Grid

Special Conditions

Sound

Storyboard

Create New Object

Mouse and Keyboard

Player One

Game Objects

FIGURE   *The six icons on the Event Grid.*
7.18

Destroy the ship object.
Destroy the missile object.

Notice how the pattern for these two events is identical, except for the alien that is destroyed. Since the two events each refer to the two different ships when they are struck by a missile, logically each different ship is destroyed in each event.

Now look through the rest of the events and move your cursor over the check marks so that you can see which actions are associated with which objects. As you see this relationship unfold, you will see the simplicity of game creation with TGF.

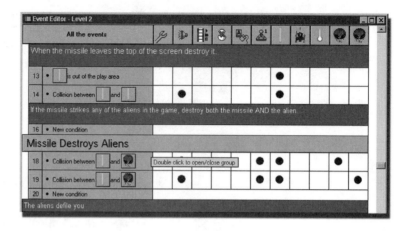

FIGURE   *The Space Defiler Event Editor, events 18 and 19.*
7.19

Creating Event Lines

Let's quickly create an event line. Creating event lines and adding actions is very much like working with a standard spreadsheet and is very easy. All the options are pulled down from menus and all the information is.

1. To create a new event line, move the cursor directly over the text *New condition* on an empty event line. *New condition* means that this line is completely empty. Notice that it has no grid next to it.
2. Now click the text with the right mouse button. You will now have a dialog box that looks like the one in Figure 7.20.
3. If you move your mouse pointer over each icon in the New Condition window, you will be shown what each one is via the handy hint text balloon.
4. Now right click the Storyboard controls icon. You will pull down a menu.
5. Click the Start of level option with the left mouse button in this menu.

You will now be taken back to the Event Grid, and the new event will read *Start of level.* You've created your first event and now all you need to do is put in an action associated with that event. Notice the line is devoid of actions.

Go across the empty check boxes on line number 10 until you get to the box underneath the icon of the missile. Click the empty box with the right mouse button. You will then see a menu of all the things you can do to the missile object; movement, animation, direction, position, etc. We will look at all these option in the next chapter.

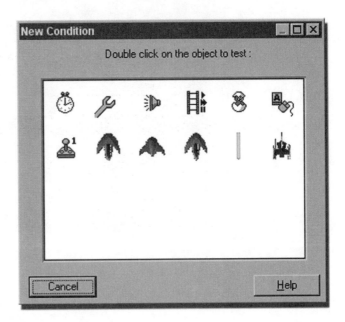

FIGURE *New Condition window that pops up when a new condition is added.*
7.20

Now move down the pop-up menu and, using the left mouse button, click the Destroy option. You will then be taken back to the Event Grid and the new event line with the logic that states:

At the start of the level destroy the missile object.

Well, that's the bare bones look at TGF. If you are comfortable with the concepts presented in this chapter, we can move on to the next chapter where you create a game from the ground up.

CHAPTER 8

MAKING A GAME YOURSELF WITH THE GAMES FACTORY

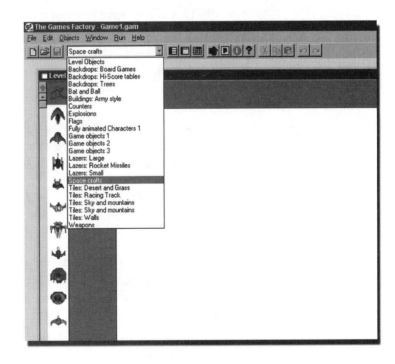

G et the caffeine pumping in your system and prepare your mind —
you are ready for the serious stuff. In this chapter, we will go deep into
TGF and really get our game tweaked out. We will attempt . . . drum
roll, please . . . to make Space Defiler from the ground up.

By the end of this chapter, you will be able to lay out multiple levels, or-
chestrate game effects, play music off a CD from within your game, and more.

Creating Space Defiler Yourself

Okay, now that you've had me hold your hand on a guided tour around TGF,
let's look at how Space Defiler was assembled. I will move faster when it comes
to areas we covered in the last chapter. For instance, I will tell you to create a
new event line without telling you exactly how to do it each time as in the last
chapter.

CREATE A NEW FILE

Go to the File heading on the menu bar at the top of the screen. Select the New
option. The Games Factory will ask you if you want to save the changes that
you have made to Space Defiler if it is open. Select No.

You will be asked to select a playfield size. Click the 640 by 480 size, then
click OK. This screen size will run faster because it is small, but it is still big
enough to be playable.

You will now be taken to the Storyboard Editor, with an empty level 1 display. To enter a name for the level, click the "Untitled" text within the level 1
display, enter the name you would like, then press Return.

NOTE

*Although the point of this chapter is to have you build Space Defiler from the
ground up, you can go to the CD-ROM and open the file spacedel2.gam to look
around the finished version of Space Defiler.*

Click inside the empty Thumbnail with the right mouse button. From the
menu produced, click the Edit this level option, then the Level Editor option.
You will then be taken to an empty Level Editor screen, ready for you to place
your objects on.

To place new objects on the screen, go to the Level objects text box on the
toolbar at the top of the screen, and click the pull-down button at the side of
the text (See figure 8.1).

Now look through all the different object libraries until you get to one
called (Tutorial) SPACE DEFILER. Click this library.

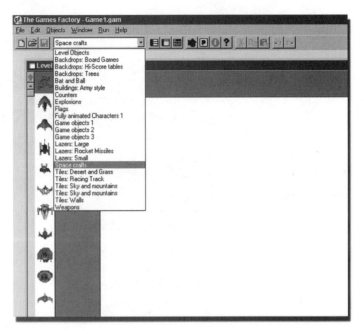

FIGURE   *The pull-down Level Objects button.*

8.1

You will now have all the objects from this library displayed in the Object window down the left-hand side of the screen. You will notice that there are large icons within this window. These denote the type of object below it, as shown in Figure 8.2, 8.3, and 8.4.

Try moving your mouse pointer over the different objects in the window. A handy hint text box will tell you what each one is called.

Before we place the active objects of our game on the play area, we are going to put a backdrop into place, align it perfectly with the edges of the screen, then 'lock' it into place so it cannot be selected or moved while we are putting all the other objects on the play area.

PLACING THE BACKDROP AND LOCKING IT IN PLACE

To place the backdrop on the screen, go to the Object window and click the Backdrop icon, called Space Defiler Backdrop, using the left mouse button.

Now move the mouse pointer over the play area — anywhere will do— then press the left mouse button again. This places the backdrop object on the play area. Your screen should look like Figure 8.5.

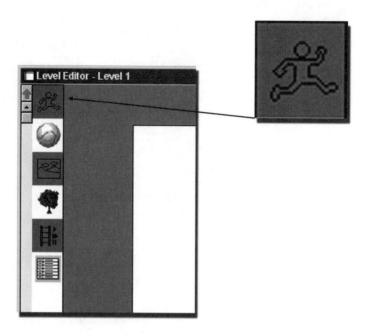

FIGURE **8.2** *The Active Objects icon denotes active objects.*

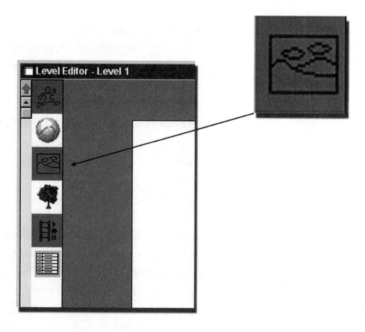

FIGURE **8.3** *The Backdrop icon denotes backdrop objects.*

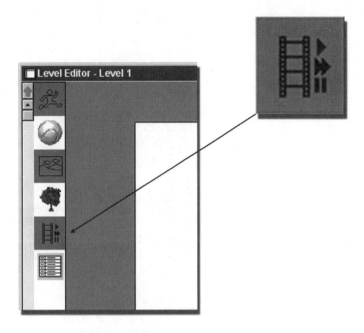

FIGURE
8.4
The Storyboard icon denotes storyboard objects.

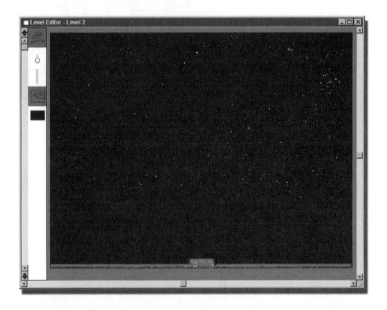

FIGURE
8.5
The Space Defiler background on the playfield.

NOTE

When the backdrop object and the size of the play area are identical, The Games Factory will automatically align the backdrop object to fit.

We are now going to stop the backdrop object from being selected every time you click it with the mouse. This will make it far easier when you start putting other objects on the play area.

Go to the toolbar at the top of the screen and click the Preferences icon with the left mouse button. You will see the Level Editor Preference window, as shown in Figure 8.6.

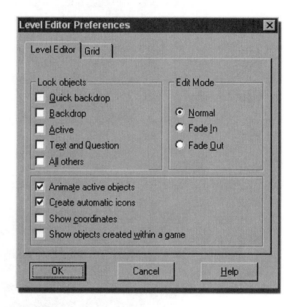

FIGURE *The Level Editor Preferences window.*
8.6

In this dialog box, look in the Lock objects heading for the Backdrop option. There will be an empty check box. Click in the check box with the left mouse button. It will now be filled with a small *X*, which means that you have locked the backdrop into place. Now click the OK button.

NOTE

If you lock the background or any other object in place, don't forget that you did it! There is no indication that the background is locked in place, other than the fact that you cannot move it — it simply doesn't respond to your cursor. This may be confusing if you forget you locked it.

Now try clicking the backdrop object. You cannot! As you saw from the different options in the Preferences dialog box, you can also lock many different types of objects into place. To unlock the backdrop object, click the Preferences icon and then click the Backdrop object radio button again.

PLACING OBJECTS ON THE SCREEN

Now that we have a nice backdrop for our game, we are going to place the active objects on the play area: the enemies, the missile, some obstacles, and the player's spaceship. The trick to getting all the objects lined up so neatly on the screen is to use the grid tool.

Go to the Preferences icon again, at the top of the screen. Click the icon using the left mouse button. Now in the Preferences dialog box, select the second tab called Grid. You can see the Grid preferences in Figure 8.7.

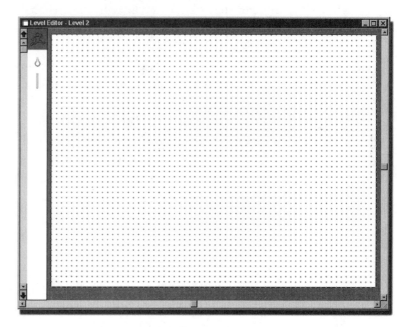

FIGURE   *The grid is used to precisely align objects in the game.*
8.7

On the Grid tab, you will see several options:

Origin. This dictates where the grid starts. Leave it at zero.

Square size. This dictates how far apart the "line up points" of the grid are. The larger the number, the farther apart the points, and the less fine control you have over where an object is placed.

Click the numbers in the Width and Height boxes and change them to 10.

At the bottom of the dialog box, there are two radio buttons: **Snap-to** and **Show grid**.

Check the Snap-to radio button. This means that any object you place on the screen will snap to the grid points. If you would like to see the grid, check the Show grid button. You do not have to have it visible to use it, and I prefer not to see it.

Now click the OK button at the bottom of the dialog box to take you back to the Level Editor screen.

We are ready to actually start placing the objects on the screen. Now that we enabled the grid, you will see the objects jump a little as you drag the object across the background. This is the grid in effect. If you were to go back into the Preferences dialog box and make the grid squares larger, you would see the objects jumping more.

Now go to the Object window and select an object — use the left mouse button. Move the object to where you want it on the screen. Next click the **left** mouse button and you will place a single copy of the object down. If you were to click the **right** mouse button, you could place multiple copies of the object down without having to return to the object shelf every time you want to place an object. This is handy for placing an army of drones or building a maze dungeon with many obstacles.

Let's use the right mouse button to lay out a wave of Space Defiling aliens!

Go to the Object window and click the big alien head with the left mouse button. Now move the mouse pointer over the play area. Let's go to the top left of the screen and start placing our aliens there. Select the place where you want to place the first alien, but don't press any buttons yet. Don't place it too close to the edge of the screen or it will disappear off the screen when you play the game since the aliens move. I placed the alien heads in a row in the center of the play area, as shown in Figure 8.8.

You can still scroll around the display area using the scroll bars even when you are "carrying" an object.

NOTE

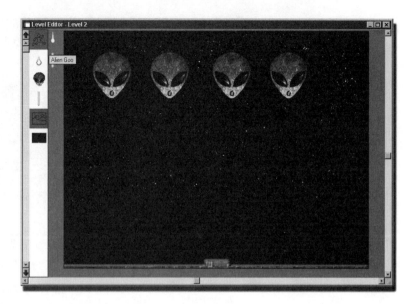

FIGURE   *The big alien heads on the playfield.*
8.8

You can use the right mouse button to place aliens quickly. You should end up with a line of alien heads evenly spaced across the top of the screen. When you are placing your last alien head on the screen using the left mouse button, this will stop you from placing any more clones and free up the cursor.

Next go to the objects, select the Player's Ship, and place that on the bottom of the play area. Place it just slightly above the bottom of the screen.

Next go to the Object window, click a Space Defiler Obstacle, and place a row of about four of these immediately above the Player's Ship using the same method as above. Try not to have them too close to the ship — give it some room.

Now place the bullet, Missile, anywhere on the screen. When we use the Event Editor, we are going to remove any missiles from the display when the level first starts. We are only placing it on the screen so that it will appear in the Event Editor and we can assign behaviors to it.

Scroll through the Object window until you find the Score object. Place that on the bottom of the screen, out of the way of everything else, as shown in Figure 8.9.

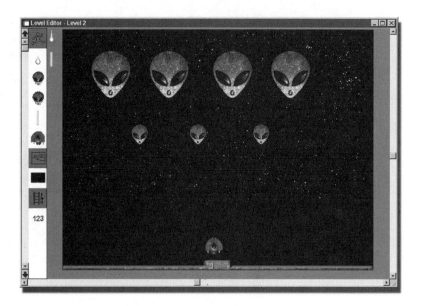

FIGURE *The objects all laid out in the Layout Editor for the Space Defiler game.*
8.9

ASSIGNING MOVEMENTS TO OBJECTS

Assigning movement and animation to objects is done here, in the Level Editor. This is rather easy to do. Right click an object in the layout area and you will see the pop-up menu shown in Figure 8.10.

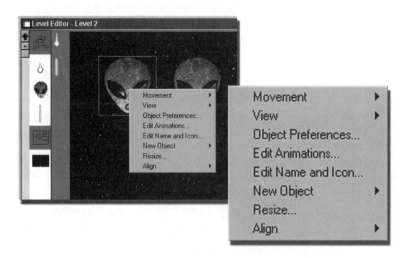

FIGURE *The pop-up menu associated to an object in the Level Editor.*
8.10

Of all the options in this menu, there are two we will look at now: Movement and Edit Animation.

Movement has an arrow indicating more choices are available — Change or Edit, in this case.

Edit Animation will open up the Animation Editor if selected.

NOTE

The distinction between movement and animation in TGF is important and should be understood. **Animation** *is the ability to have an active object function like a short movie, playing frames over and over like an animated cursor in Windows. This makes the active object appear to be walking or running in place, or moving in some way.* **Movement** *dictates where the active object goes in the game and how it is controlled.*

An active object can have more than one animation assigned to it. We will look at that next.

Examples of animation are:

Walking; legs are moving back and forth, arms swinging

Running; like walking, only faster

Dying; body falls to the ground

An example of Movement is: The active object following a path or being controlled by the player. The active object can play the walking animation while being moved by the player and will, therefore, look like it is using its legs to move.

To best see this illustrated, go to the Level Editor and right click the big alien head. The same menu as in Figure 8.10 appears. Select Change Movement and you will see the Change Movement menu appear as shown in Figure 8.11.

As you can see, you can make the object computer-or player-controlled. We have our alien heads computer-controlled. Since we have a Space Invaders-type game, the best way to emulate that back-and-forth track-type movement is to use the Path option.

The Path option allows you to select a track the object moves on, whether it loops or plays once, the speed of the movement, and, most importantly, it allows you to test your movement.

Cancel this after playing with it, right click the Spaceship, and select Edit Animation from the pop-up menu. This opens the Animation Editor, as shown in figure 8.12.

In the Animation Editor, you will see three main areas: the Animation window, the Direction window, and the Animation Frames window. The Animation window has a pull-down text box that stores animation tracks for many events for each active object. This is used later in the Event Editor where you

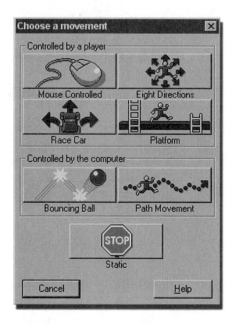

FIGURE   *The Change Movement menu.*
8.11

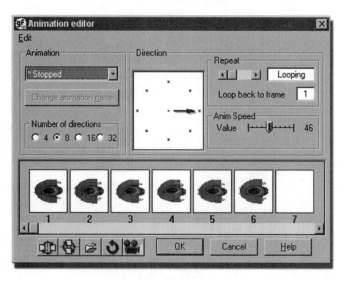

FIGURE   *The Animation Editor.*
8.12

can make a character using the default walking animation play the dying animation track when he gets hit.

You can pull this list down and select another animation. There will be an asterisk next to the selections that contain an animation. In this case, there are two: **Stopped** and **Getting Hit**. Stopped is the Player Ship swaying and Getting Hit distorts and changes color.

NOTE

When you add your own active objects, you will be brought here. Even if the object is not animated, you will still have to import the images here. This is done by clicking the Create New Object icon on the toolbar and selecting the active object. Next you double click in the first frame and then click the Open Folder icon in the Picture Editor.

After all of that layout is done, you can check your work.

CHECKING YOUR WORK

To have a look at what you've done so far, click the Play button on the toolbar at the top of the screen (See Figure 8.13). Remember to click it again to pause the game, then use the Rewind button to reset the game.

RESTART   PLAY

RESTART   PAUSE

FIGURE *The Play button from the toolbar.*
8.13

You should have a field of alien heads moving around the screen and hocking big wads of alien goo down at you. You should also be able to move the spaceship from left to right by using the cursor keys.

Now that we have the basic objects on the screen, we need to add some actions, sound, etc. To do all this, you need to go to the Event Editor. But, before we do this, save the work that we have done.

The Proper Way to Save a File in TGF

If you have created anything unique that you want to keep in the previous exercises stop and save your work now!

Go to the File option in the menu bar at the top of the screen. Click it using the left mouse button, then click the Save as... option.

You will now see a file selector. Select the disk drive that you want to save to. Next type in the name that you want to save the file as. If you are using Windows 3.1, this can be up to eight letters long, and must always have *.gam* after it, denoting this as a game file. Windows 95/98 allows you file names with up to 256 characters.

Once you have safely saved your work, close your file.

MAKING SPACE DEFILER EVENTS AND ACTIONS

For this section, please open the file spacedel2.gam and right click the thumbnail of level 2 in the Storyboard Editor. Click the Event Editor option (See Figure 8.14). This will take you to the Event Editor.

The Event Editor is where your gaming really comes to life. You have seen how easy it is to place your objects on the screen, but now you want to fire missiles, destroy aliens, add sound, and change the score.

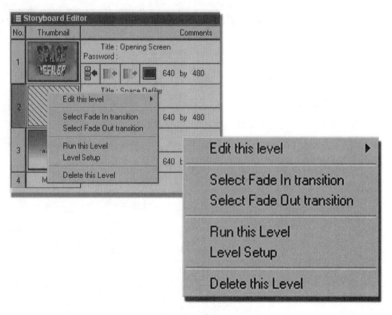

FIGURE *The pop-up menu to get to the Event Editor.*
8.14

Step by step, we are going to take you through creating a complete set of events that brings Space Defiler to life. A lot of what you will learn in this chapter is basic to all game creation using The Games Factory and other applications.

To start with, before we even create events, we are going to show you how to create comment lines, which do nothing other than provide you with notes to refer to in the Event Editor. Although Space Defiler is a very simple game and presents no problem for the experienced user to find their way around, writing comments in the Event Editor is a very good habit to get into. When you start writing longer, complicated games and applications, you will need to refer to these comments.

We are also going to show you how to define groups of events, which again make your event editing far easier to follow, and allow you to simplify your game-writing.

CREATING A GROUP OF EVENTS

The first thing we are going to do is to create a group of events called "Start of Game Actions."

To do this, right click the number 1 on the New condition line. Next, select the Insert option from the menu, then the A group of events option from that menu.

You will now have a dialog box asking you to enter the name of the group. Type in the text "Start of Game Actions." When you have done this, make sure that the Active when frame starts radio button is selected. It will be selected by default, but check it anyway.

When you have the name entered, either press Return or click the OK button.

You should now have a group called Start of Game Actions. Event line number 2 will be indented slightly, denoting it as being within that group.

Next we are going to make event line number 2 a comment.

CREATING A COMMENT LINE

Now right click the number 2 of event line number 2. Select the Insert option, then the A comment option.

You now have a dialog box where you can select the font, color, and background color of your text. We are going to use the standard font, but write in white, so…

1. Click the Set font color option, then click the white square. Next click the OK button.

2. Click the Set back color option, select dark green, then click the OK button.

Click in the top left of the empty text box. Now you can type in the words that you want to appear in the comment.

Enter the text "Before the game starts, destroy the missile in the frame to make sure only the missiles fired from the ship are used in the game." Then click OK.

You will now have a comment with a green background and white letters. If you have made a mistake, you can edit your comment line by right clicking the text of the comment, then selecting the Edit Comment option.

CREATING AN EVENT LINE

Time to get down to the nitty-gritty of your games creation! We are going to insert an actual event, Start of level, which means that when it is the start of the level, all the actions associated with this event line will be performed.

This event is going to be within the group Start of Game Actions. So click on the text "New condition" of event line number 3 with the right mouse button.

You will see a with a dialog box titled New Condition, with the subheading Double click the object to test. Move your mouse pointer over the Storyboard controls icon, (The handy hint text will tell you which one it is as you move your mouse pointer over the objects), and either double left click or single right click it. This will produce a menu from the object (See Figure 8.15).

Select the Start of level option with the left mouse button. You will have an event line number 3 that reads "Start of level". You can now insert an action.

SAVE YOUR GAME!

If you are working on your own game from the ground up, before you go any farther, save your game.

ADDING ACTIONS TO EVENT LINES

Next we are going to insert an action into event line number 3, to destroy the missile.

Destroying Objects

Right click in the empty box below the missile icon, on line number 3. This will produce a large menu of all the possible actions that you could do to the missile.

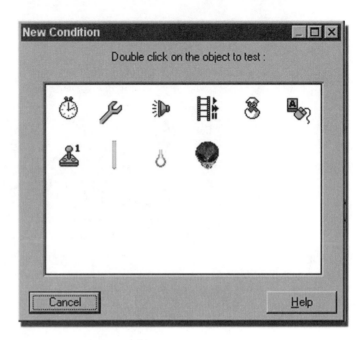

FIGURE *The New Condition dialog box.*
8.15

Select the Destroy option with the left mouse button. You will have a complete event line that will destroy the missiles at the very start of the level, within the group Start of Game Actions.

Now it's time to start adding the rest of the events. Create a Group called Main Game. Next insert a comment. The text of the comment line should be:

"When the user presses the Ctrl key, shoot a missile."

Testing the Keyboard for a Specific Key Depression

During the game, you will want certain keystrokes to do certain things; in this case, the Ctrl key will fire a missile - *Interactivity, baby!*

Right click the "New condition" text. Now use the right mouse button to select the Mouse pointer and keyboard icon. Select the Keyboard option from this menu, then select the Upon Pressing a key option.

You will now be asked to press the key that you want to associate your actions with. So press the Ctrl key (next to the arrow keys on most keyboards, like in Figure 8.16).

You will now be taken back to the Event Editor screen, with an event line that reads 'Upon pressing "Ctrl"' — you are half way there.

Shooting an Object

Now that you've made your event line to test when the Ctrl key has been pressed, you need to actually shoot something when it is pressed.

FIGURE *The Control, or Ctrl key.*
8.16

Go to the empty box that lies directly underneath "Player's ship" and on the same line as the event line we just created. Click it with the right mouse button and select the Shoot an Object... option from the pop-up menu (See Figure 8.17).

You will see a dialogue box displaying all the active objects from the current level. We want to use the Missile object as our bullet, so select that, then click OK.

You will now be asked to select a speed and direction for the bullet. By default, the speed is 100, which is very fast. Use the mouse to move the pointer to 50.

FIGURE *The relationship between the event created and the object it affects.*
8.17

Next you want to select the direction to fire in, which, in this case, should be up. To do this, click the Shoot in selected directions button.

You can now select the direction that you want to fire the bullet in from the "direction clock face." You can select/deselect directions by clicking the black buttons around the clock face. See Figure 8.18.

Make sure you have just one arrow pointing straight up. Note that if you have more than one direction showing, The Games Factory will select of those directions at random. We will use this feature later on the aliens.

Now click all the OK buttons to take you back to the Event Editor screen. You should have a complete event line, so that when you press the Ctrl key, a missile is fired up the screen. Save Your Game before you go any farther.

The Aliens Shoot Back

What fun would it be if the aliens just sat there? They need to shoot back, and this is where the real *defiling* comes in. To make the aliens shoot back, go to the Level Editor and follow the same steps we used earlier to place a missile into the scene; only this time, choose the alien goo object. Place this under the missile object in the Level Editor simply to keep things neat.

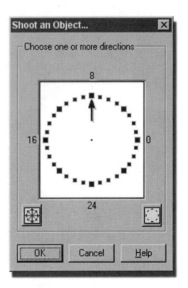

FIGURE   *The direction clock face.*
8.18

Back in the Event Editor, you need to follow the same steps to destroy the goo object at the start of the game. And also destroy the goo if any goes off the screen, just like the missile.

Next, go to the Event Editor where we make the aliens fight back. Create a new event by right clicking the "New condition" line, and then right clicking the clock face. Select the Every option from the pop-up menu. In the window that pops up, set the time to 1 second. This means that the event will take place every one second .

CAUTION

Warning! The default active window is minutes. If you fail to move over to the seconds (middle) window, and accidentally set the event at "every 1 minute" instead of "every 1 second," it will look like your event is not happening at all in the game, since it will take a minute instead of a second to happen.

Now go over to the empty box that lies directly underneath the big alien head and on the same line as the event line we just created. Click it with the right mouse button and select the Shoot an Object... option from the pop-up menu.

You will see a dialog box displaying all the active objects from the current level. We want to use the Alien goo object as our bullet, so select that, then click OK.

Next you will be asked to select a speed and direction for the bullet. You should make it a bit slower than we made the player's missile, for game play reasons as well as aesthetics.

By default the speed is 100, which is very fast. Use the mouse to move the pointer to 50 or below.

Now click the Shoot in selected directions button and deselect the arrow pointing up by clicking the little black square it is pointing at and clicking the down, or 6 o'clock, arrow. If you remember, selecting more than one direction makes TGF select a direction at random. This can be annoying if the missile is coming from the player's ship, but coming from the aliens selecting a square immediately on either side of the 6 o'clock direction gives it a nice random feel that adds to the game.

Press all the OK buttons to take you back to the Event Editor screen. Press the Play button to check your work.

Adding Sound Effects

If you remember the discussion we had on sound in the previous section, you will be anxious to add some sounds to your game. Try running the level with no sound event (or turn your speakers down), and then running the level with sound. You will see firsthand how important sound is in a game.

Right click the empty box beneath the Sound icon on the active event line. Select the Play sample option from the menu produced. You will then be taken to a file selector.

First, you have to select the correct drive to look in. You can click the button under the Drives heading to pull down a list of the drives available.

Look down the list of directories (use the scroll bars) until you find one called *samples*. Double click this directory with the left mouse button.

Next look down this list until you find *weapons*. Double click it. You will now have a list of all the noises contained within the weapons directory.

Scroll through the list of all the noises until you get to one called *phaser03.wav*. Click it once with the left mouse button.

Now click the Play button on the right side of the dialog box. You can preview the noises using this button. You can always select another sample and preview that using the Play button, or even move to another sound directory. Simply double click the samples directory, then choose another sound directory.

When you are happy with the sound that you want to play every time a missile is fired, click the OK button.

Adding CD music to your level will be looked at later in this chapter.

NOTE

Create a comment on the next line, containing the following text:

"For every missile that exists in the game, always move them up 10 pixels at a time."

Create an Always event on the line after that. To do this, right click the New Condition text, then right click the special object. From the Always/Never option, select the Always option.

Moving an Object by Changing its Coordinates

Now insert an action on the Always event line, beneath the missile icon. Click the empty box with the right mouse button. From the menu produced, select the Position option (See Figure 8.19).

FIGURE *The relationship of the Always action to the missile object.*
8.19

1. From this menu, select the Set Y coordinate option.
2. Click the Edit button. This will take you to another Expression Editor.
3. Click the Retrieve data from an object button.
4. Next right-click the missile from the objects displayed.
5. When you select the missile, it will produce a menu. Select the Position option.
6. From the menu that this produces, select the Y coordinate option.
7. You will now have the text Y("MISSILE") in the text box of the Expression Editor. Without changing this text, add -10 to the end of the text, so that you have an expression that reads Y("MISSILE")-10.

This means that every time The Games Factory cycles through the Event Editor, it will always subtract 10 from the Y coordinate of the missile. Click the OK buttons to take you back to the Event Editor.

Lean back and rub your eyes.

This method of movement is actually somewhat redundant in this game, since we are already firing the missile at the speed of 50. But this exercise does show you that you can move objects around quite easily by changing their co-ordinates. This will help you in the future with more complex games.

Testing the Position of an Object

Keeping track of objects in the game can be important for the efficiency of the game. For now we will start with a simple exercise in object tracking. Insert a new comment on the next event line that reads:

"When the missile leaves the top of the screen, it is not needed any more, so destroy it."

Now insert an event on the line below it to test the position of the missile.

1. Right click the New condition line and select the missile from the dialog box.
2. Select the Position-Test position of "Missile" option.
3. You will have a dialog box that allows you to test the position of the missile in several different ways. Move the mouse pointer over the different buttons and look at all the options available.
4. Click the Is the object outside? button. Note that from here, you could select more than one button. You can deselect a button by clicking it again.
5. When only the Is the object outside? button is depressed, click the OK button to take you back to the Event Editor.

You will now have an event line that reads (Missile) is out of the play area.

Next insert an action to destroy the missile, on the same event line (See Figure 8.20).

When the missile leaves the top of the screen destroy it.

13	•	is out of the play area							●		
14	•	Collision between	and		●				Destroy		

FIGURE *The relationship between the missile object and the action to destroy it if it goes*
8.20 *outside of the play area.*

Insert the following new comment:

"If a missile strikes another missile, destroy it."

Now insert the following Event:

Collision between (missile) and (missile)

1. Right click the New condition text, right click the missile object, and select the Collisions-Another object option from the menu.
2. Select the missile from the dialog box with the left mouse button, then click OK. You will have an event line as described above.

We are doing this in case the player is very fast on the keyboard and fires out too many missiles that end up running into each other. If they do, the missiles will destroy each other. This can also be useful if you apply the same action set to any other two objects in a game.

Next insert another action in this group to destroy the missile.

NOTE

You can copy the action from one of the other event lines by clicking and holding on one of the Destroy tick-marks, then dragging it into the empty box beneath the Missile icon, on the Collision between (Missile) and (Missile) event line .

Save your game if you need to!

Destroying an Alien

In order for your missiles to have any effect when they hit an alien, we have to assign that behavior as well. We will create the necessary events for this next.

On the next line, insert the following comment:

"If the missile strikes a big alien head, destroy the missile AND the alien."

Next insert the following event:

Collision between (missile) and (big alien head)

Do this by right clicking the New condition text, then right clicking the Missile icon, and selecting the Collisions-Another object option. Now select the big alien head object.

Insert the following event next:

Collision between (missile) and (alien head)

Next insert the following event:

Collision between (missile) and (baby alien)

You should now have three event lines.

Insert a sound action on the first event line, **Collision between (missile) and (big alien head)**.

Pick something appropriate for an explosion. (Right click the empty box under the sound icon, select the Play sample option, and look in Samples-Impacts.)

Copy the sound action into the lines for the alien head and baby alien. You will now have that sound being played every time a missile collides with any of the aliens.

Destroying the Missile Upon Impact

We want the missile to be destroyed when it hits the alien, or it will just keep going. If the missile is destroyed upon impact, it adds realism.

Insert another Destroy action into the empty box under the missile on each line. (Right click the box and select the Destroy option.)

To save a lot of time, drag the Destroy action, using the left mouse button, into all the empty boxes beneath the missile, for when the missile collides with an alien.

Check your logic. Make sure that it is the big alien head that is destroyed when a missile collides with a big alien head, and not one of the others! If you make a mistake, you can select a check mark, and then press the Delete key.

Do the same for the other alien entities. The events should look like the screen shot in Figure 8.21.

Save your game!

Keeping score

Now we want to add to the score every time one of the missiles destroys one of the aliens. We are still working with the same three event lines from the previous section.

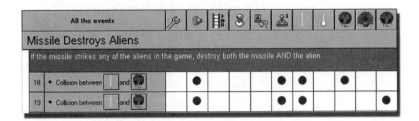

FIGURE *The two alien collision events.*
8.21

Right click the empty box underneath the Player 1 object and select the Score option. Then select the Add to score option (See Figure 8.22 for the Add to Score menu).

You can choose how much you are going to add to the score when a big alien head is destroyed. Since he is big and nasty, you may want him to be worth a hundred points. Click OK. Do the same for the other alien entities.

You can also make items deduct points when destroyed. You can make an item worth negative points by typing in a minus sign before the number, thus creating an item the player does not want to hit. To make levels harder later on, you can introduce friendly, or civilian, crafts you are not supposed to hit.

*You will notice that as you develop a game, you will make decisions such as the harder a target is to kill, the more points it will be worth. This type of decision in your game design is called **game balance**.*

NOTE

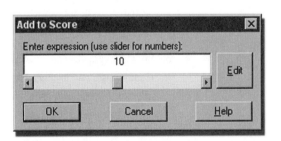

FIGURE *The Add to Score menu.*
8.22

It Ain't Over Till It's Over

And you need to tell the TGF when it is over — the game, that is.

The way we will do that here is to have the computer look at the playing area, and if all the aliens are dead and gone, it will be ended.

Insert a comment line, if you wish, that says the following:

"Check the area above the player's ship where the aliens are. If there are no more aliens, the game is complete."

Now we are going to insert an event to end the game when all the aliens have been destroyed. To do this, we are going to test if there are any objects in a zone on the play area.

1. Right click on the New condition text line.
2. Right click the New Objects icon.
3. Select the Compare to number of objects in a zone option. You will be taken to a Zone setup screen.
4. Click in the first box, Horizontal. Type a 0 in the box. Go to the next box on that line, to, click it and type 640.
5. Next click the first box on the next line down, Vertical. Enter a 0 in the box.
6. Now enter 320 in the last box, to. You should have the four boxes filled as follows: 0 to 640, then underneath, 0 to 320. If you have done this successfully, click OK.
7. Next you will be taken to a dialog box where you can enter a number which you are comparing to the number of objects in the zone that you just defined.

In the top of the dialog box are several radio buttons, which is where you decide how you are going to compare the number. By default, it is set at Equal. This is the comparison that we want to use, because when the number of objects is equal to zero, we want to end the game. Make sure the Equal radio button is selected.

8. Now you can enter the number you want to compare. In this case, it is 0, so make sure the text box at the bottom of the dialog box has a 0 in it. You can change it by using the slider, or by clicking the text box and entering the numbers directly.

When you have the comparison set to Equals 0, click the OK button.

Your event line will read: **Number of objects in zone (0,0) to (640,320) = 0.**

Next we are going to insert an action to finish the game. Go to the empty box underneath the Storyboard controls icon.

1. Right click the box.
2. From the menu produced, select the End the game option.

That's it! Space Defiler is ready to play!

Oh yeah — SAVE YOUR GAME!

In the next chapter, we will take our development with TGF up a notch or two by introducing a new game type.

MAKING ANOTHER GAME WITH THE GAMES FACTORY

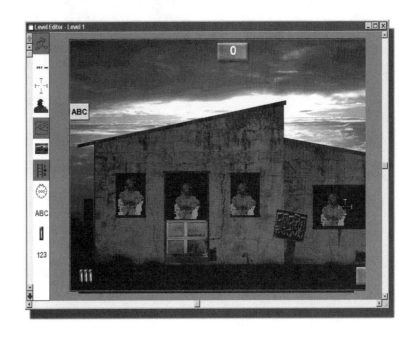

Okay, are you ready to make a game that will sell a million units and blow right off the sales charts? Well hold on tight because we are going to make Ghost Hunter (See Figure 9.1) — a surefire hit! Think about it — *Deer Hunter,* only with ghosts....

FIGURE *Ghost Hunter — a surefire hit.*
9.1

Well, the design needs work, but we will develop Ghost Hunter for fun. And behind all this fun, you will be learning the next step of working with TGF. We will be using several more features of TGF and doing a lot more actual development, as far as the tweaking of the assets and game flow. As you will see, Ghost Hunter is from a different viewpoint than Space Defiler. Instead of shooting up, we will be shooting at the targets. This will introduce a few new techniques to your growing TGF knowledge base.

In this chapter, we will not only learn new functions of TGF, but we will also learn a few new techniques to keep productions made with TGF organized and running smoothly.

Let's look at Ghost Hunter.

Loading Ghost Hunter

You will find the completed version of Ghost Hunter if you go to the File menu, select Open, and then look for the gametuts directory where you installed TGF. You are looking for the file ghosthunt. Once you open it, we can begin.

Ghost Hunter — The Storyboard Editor

You The first thing you will see is the familiar Storyboard Editor. When you have loaded Ghost Hunter, you will have a Storyboard Editor screen that looks very similar to the one for Space Defiler, and all the same options are available (See Figure 9.2).

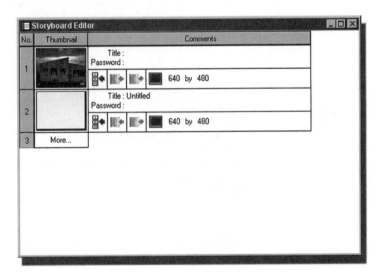

FIGURE   *The familiar Storyboard Editor, as used by Ghost Hunter.*
9.2

While we are here, let's look at a few more things you can do from the Storyboard Editor screen that we didn't look at last time. Click the Preferences icon and look at the dialog box, as shown in Figure 9.3.

In the box, you see one slider bar and two check boxes. The boxes allow you to remove the comments and the header bar, as shown in Figure 9.4.

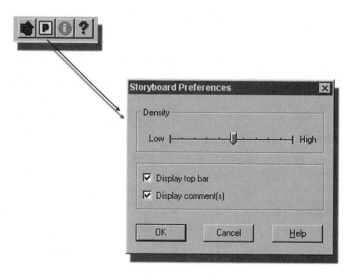

FIGURE
9.3 *The Preferences icon and the Properties dialogue box that pops up from the Storyboard Editor.*

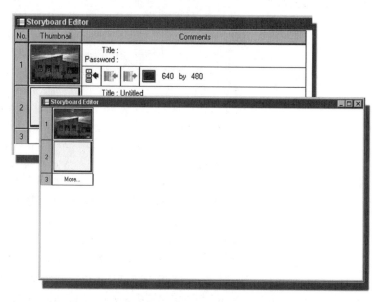

FIGURE
9.4 *The Storyboard Editor with the various options enacted from the Properties dialog box.*

The slider bar allows you to change the density of the display, which means that the thumbnail picture can be larger or smaller, as shown in Figure 9.4 .

You have to click OK and exit the dialog box to see the difference it has made to the display.

NOTE

Setting the density lower can be useful as you get more proficient with TGF and don't need all the visual help. Making the thumbnails smaller makes them harder to see, but if you have been working a lot on a game, you will be intimately familiar with the level names, layout, and general appearance. As your games become more complex and contain more levels, the smaller thumbnails will be preferred.

You will notice while we are here in the Storyboard Editor that I set the screen at 800 x 600. Since the average computer today is displaying at larger resolutions, I have decided to make the game a bit bigger.

Now let's go to the Level Editor. Right click the thumbnail of the level, bring up the Edit this level option, and select the Level Editor.

Ghost Hunter – The Level Editor

Remember that you can look at all the objects in the editor by simply placing your cursor over them and reading the handy hint balloons. If you do this, you will see how Ghost Hunter was created and what objects are contained in the game (See Figure 9.5).

Notice that in the Level Editor, you can see all the ghosts, but later when you run the level, you will see that they drop down and hide (for good reason) a little while after the game is started. When the game is running, all the ghosts are going to be hidden from view, then at random they are going to emerge from hiding to scare you and then hide again. The only shot you have is going to be when they are out of hiding. You will use the mouse to put the crosshair of your Ghost Vaporizer over them and then, pressing the left mouse button, you will fire at them.

To make the ghosts look like they are actually hiding behind something and then emerging from behind it, we have to use a chopped up copy of the backdrop. As you have seen before, active objects are placed on top of backdrop objects and appear in front of the backdrop objects. In order to hide the ghosts properly, we are going to make an active object out of part of the backdrop and use it as a Mask object in front of the ghosts.

FIGURE   *The Ghost Hunter Level Editor.*
9.5

NOTE

You will remember the term mask from Part 1.

This not only hides them from view and makes them look like they are hiding and popping up, but it also prevents them from being shot while they are hiding, thus increasing the challenge of the game. The mask fits exactly over the background, and it is not obvious when the game runs that there is another object on the screen because of the way the two pieces fit together (that is, unless we do a sloppy job and place the ghosts or the mask improperly).

Ghost Hunter – The Event Editor

To enter the Event Editor, click the Event Editor icon on the toolbar at the top of the screen or right click the thumbnail if you have gone back to the Storyboard Editor. You will now be able to look through all of the events used to make the game actions for Ghost Hunter and read the comments. You will see that now we have more events and a few new icons we will be working with. Figure 9.6 shows the Ghost Hunter Event Editor.

You will also notice that groups are used to a much greater degree in this game. One reason is because the game is larger and you will need to use groups more to help with the organization of the game. But groups are also used because you can deactivate and activate them during the game, and this makes the game easier to control.

FIGURE *The Ghost Hunter Event Editor.*
9.6

If you scroll through the events and move your mouse pointer over the check marks in the boxes to see the actions that are associated with the events, you will get a feel for the logic, or flow, of the game. Some of the first events you will see are the group deactivation events I mentioned. We will look at these more closely later, but what these deactivation events are for is to literally help speed up the game during play by preventing unneeded events from running. This will be useful in boosting performance when you start making larger and more complex games.

For example, you will notice a group of Level Won events, as shown in Figure 9.7. This group is inactive until it is needed, when the player wins the game. Then it is activated and other groups are deactivated.

You can also collapse a group of events by double clicking the header. Do this to all the groups and you will be able to see how this can make it far easier to move around the Event Grid. This will also make it easier for you to see the major steps of the game. You will notice that we have five major groups of events in our game (See Figure 9.8).

As you double click each group and open it, you will be able to see the events that make up that portion of the game. Now that we have had a look around in the Event Editor, let's play the game a little before we start to recreate it, so you have a frame of reference for the events we are setting up.

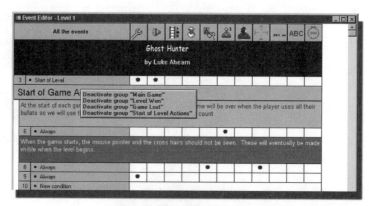

FIGURE *The events for activating and deactivating groups.*
9.7

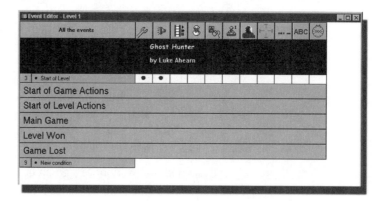

FIGURE *The Event Editor, with all events collapsed into group headings.*
9.8

Use the Run Game button on the toolbar at the top of the screen to run Ghost Hunter.

When you are ready to exit the game, you must press Alt and F4 together.

NOTE

Assembling Ghost Hunter Yourself

We will now walk through the steps of assembling Ghost Hunter. When you are finished playing Ghost Hunter, load a new file. You should by default be in the Storyboard Editor. Set the play area to 640 by 480 and then click OK.

IN THE GHOST HUNTER LEVEL EDITOR

To get into the Level Editor from the Storyboard Editor, click the empty thumbnail with the right mouse button, and select the Edit this level and the Level Editor options.

First we need to go and get all the assets and objects we will be using for this project, so go to the Level Objects pull-down menu on the toolbar. Click the button at the side of this menu to pull down a list of all the object libraries, and select the library called *(Tutorial) GHOST HUNTER* (See Figure 9.9).

FIGURE *The library of items used in Ghost Hunter*
9.9

You can see all the objects used to create Ghost Hunter in the Object window down the left-hand side of the screen.

Placing the Backdrop Object

First we will place the backdrop object onto the screen. Select it, then place it anywhere in the play area. You will remember from the previous chapters that because it is exactly the same size as the play area, it will align itself automatically.

Placing the Ghosts

Next click the active object for the ghost, named Ghost, and, using the right mouse button, place copies of it in the window part of the house, on the door, and over the fence. Line up the bottom of the ghost so it fits nicely into the areas. You will also remember that using the right mouse button will allow you to lay down more than one copy of the ghost, and using the left mouse button will lay down a single copy.

The Mask Object

Now you can place the mask object in front of the ghosts. Be careful to line it up with the backdrop perfectly. It should cover up the bottom part of the ghosts a little. The mask is to stop you from being able to shoot the ghosts when they are hiding. Since they are behind an active object, the mask, they will be protected (See Figure 9.10).

FIGURE *The mask (notice the blocks of color that will be used for transparency.*
9.10

NOTE

You will notice that the mask is nothing more than the backdrop image copied, with the large areas being filled in with a color that is very different from the rest of the image, to be used as the transparency color. If you are creating your own mask object, be careful to use no anti-aliasing (see previous chapters), since this will cause a colored line to be around your masked portions of the image. The reason for this is also explained in the previous chapters on image manipulation.

Placing the Crosshair Object

Now we are going to place the object that we will be using as the crosshair of our gun onto the play area. Later, this crosshair will replace the mouse cursor in the game.

Go to the Object window and select the Crosshair object. Place it anywhere on the screen. It does not matter where you place it, since we are going to hide it at the very beginning of the level. We will deal with making it replace the mouse cursor later on in the Event Editor.

Placing the Countdown Object

Select the countdown object and put this on the play area in a place where you will be able to see it readily, but not so as to interfere with the ghosts, such as one of the corners.

Placing the Text Object

Now place the IT'S A SHAME! text object on the far left of the ghost play area, at about the same height as the top of the ghosts.

Placing the Ammo Object

Place the live ammo on the bottom left of the play area. This is the display for the number of bullets that you have left.

Placing the Score Object

Place the score object on the play area near the countdown object. This will display your score during the game. You should now have a screen that looks like Figure 9.11.

CHANGING THE VIEW ORDER OF OBJECTS

While we are in the Level Editor, let's look at a small but useful feature of TGF — changing the view order of objects.

Let's say that you accidentally placed the mask object on the screen before the ghosts, then placed the ghosts over the top of the mask. You then noticed that the mask does not cover the ghosts and the ghosts are on top of the mask object. If you had done this, you would not need to delete everything and start over. You could simply right click the mask and change the order of the layers, just like you can in Photoshop, Paint Shop Pro, and other paint programs. What this means is simply that you can make the mask move forward and be on top of the ghosts.

The Ghost Hunter Level Editor, with objects laid out.
9.11

To change the order of the layer of either the ghosts or the mask:

1. Right click the mask object. This will produce a menu with several options, as shown in Figure 9.12.
2. Select the View option from this menu.
3. Now select the To front option. This will place the mask object "in front" of all the other objects on the screen.

This is a simple and very useful tool to be aware of. You may have noticed that your other options were to bring forward one or go back one. You can see how this will save you time if you have many items on the screen, or if you decide to stick another active object in and have to get it behind the mask. You can lay it in and then change its order.

CHANGING THE GAME SETUP

We are going to look at the the Game Setup menu before we go any farther. We are going to change the game setup because some of the objects we are using need to have their initial values changed. We also want to hide the mouse pointer and the menu bar that is normally displayed when you do a full run of your game using the Run Game button (See Figure 9.13).

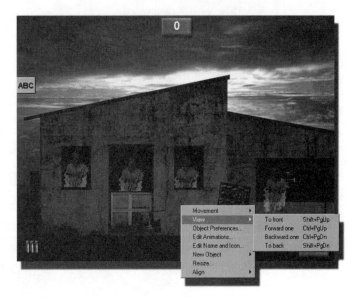

FIGURE *The pop-up menu from the mask object.*
9.12

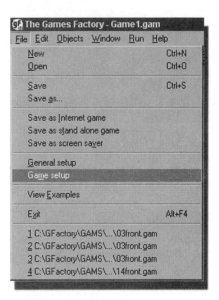

FIGURE *The Game Setup menu.*
9.13

1. Select the File menu heading at the top of the screen.
2. Select the Game setup option from this menu. Be careful not to select the General Setup by accident.
3. On the first "layer" of the dialog box, you can enter a name for your game in the Title text box, then your name underneath in the Author text box, as shown in Figure 9.14.

FIGURE *The About tab of the Game Setup dialog box.*
9.14

4. Now go to the Window layer by clicking its tab at the top of the dialog box, as shown in Figure 9.15.
5. Next make sure that all of the tick boxes are unselected; i.e., that they are all empty. This will stop the menu bar and heading from being displayed when you run your game.
6. When you have done that, select the Players tab. In the Lives box at the bottom right, change the Initial setting to 15. You can enter the numbers directly by clicking the text box, using the Delete key to clear the box, and then entering 15 (See Figure 9.16).
7. Change the Maximum value to 15 also.
8. Click the OK button.

We didn't look at several options in the Game Setup dialog box, but we will get back to these later.

NOTE

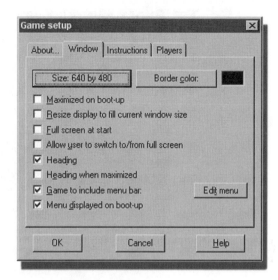

FIGURE *The Window tab of the Game Setup dialog box.*
9.15

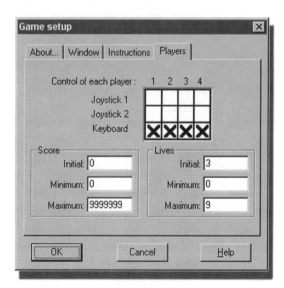

FIGURE *The Players tab of the Game Setup dialog box.*
9.16

THE GHOST HUNTER EVENT EDITOR

Once you have those changes made to the Game Setup dialog box, and you have all the game objects placed the way you want them on the play area in the Level Editor, go to the Event Editor. Select its icon from the toolbar at the top of the screen to do this (See Figure 9.17).

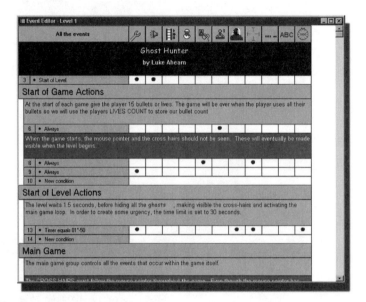

FIGURE *The Ghost Hunter Event Editor.*
9.17

We are now going to start inserting events. We will start with a Start of level event, then put in some actions.

Right click the "New condition" text of event line number 1.

Right click the Storyboard icon, then select the Start of level option from its menu.

Playing Music

The first thing we are going to do at the start of the level is play some music, so we will insert an action to play some music on this event line. We are also going to add four actions to deactivate other groups of actions like we talked about earlier. Since we have not yet created these groups, TGF will not let us deactivate them yet.

1. Right click the empty box directly beneath the Sound icon. Select the Play and loop music option. You will then be able to select a file. If you have done a normal installation of The Games Factory, the sound files will be on your hard drive in the default installation folder.

Go to the directory called *Midi*, and then look for the file named *Melanitr.mid*. When you have selected this file, click the OK button.

You will now be asked to enter the number of times you want the music to loop. Enter 99 times.

When you have entered the number 99, click the OK button.

You will have a check mark under the sound icon. If you move your mouse pointer over it, the event will read **Play music Melanitr.mid 99 times** (See Figure 9.18).

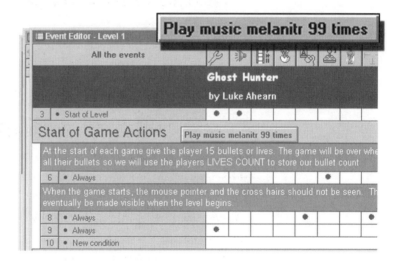

FIGURE   *The pop-up handy hint balloon for the Start of Level event,* **Play music**
9.18   *Melanitr.mid 99 times.*

Inserting The Start of Game Actions Group

Now we are going to create a group called Start of Game Actions.

Right click event line number 2.

Select Insert from the pop-up menu, and then select A Group of events.

Type in "Start of Game Actions" in the text box, then click OK.

Inserting a Comment

We are now ready to place events within this group. Make sure that each event line that you insert a new condition on is indented slightly from the left. This denotes that specific event line as being within the group directly above it.

Insert a comment on line number 3 that reads:

"At the start of each game, give the player 15 bullets, or lives. The game will be over when the player uses all their bullets, so we will use the player's LIVES COUNT to store our bullet count."

To insert a comment, right click the number of the event line. Select the Insert option, then select the A Comment option.

Of course, to make the comments stand out, you can change the text and background color. This also is useful for grouping the events visually. As your games get increasingly longer and more complex, color-coding the comments will help you keep track of your game.

Inserting an Always Event

Insert an always event on line number 4.

Right click the "New condition" text line.

Right click the Special Object icon in the window.

Then, from the Always/Never option that pops up, select the Always option.

Setting Lives

Now we will insert the Set number of lives to 15 action.

Right click the box under the Player 1 object, on line 4.

Select the Number of lives option, then select the Set number of lives option.

You can enter the number in the text box, or use the slider.

When it is set to 15, click OK.

Inserting a Comment

Insert the following comment on line 5:

"When the game starts, the mouse pointer and crosshair will not be seen, but the crosshair will be made visible when the game starts."

Inserting an Always Event

Insert an always event on line 6. (Right click New condition, right click the special object, and select the Always option.)

Hiding the Mouse Pointer

Now we are going to always hide the Windows mouse pointer, so we can replace it with the custom crosshair object. On the same line as the always event we just created, insert the Hide Windows mouse pointer action .

To do this, right click the empty box beneath the Mouse pointer and Keyboard icon, and then select the Hide Windows mouse pointer option.

Making the Crosshair Object Invisible

Insert another action on line 6 to make the crosshair invisible. To do this, right click the box under the crosshair object, select the Visibility option, and then select the Make object invisible option.

We are hiding the crosshair at the start of the game to add to the game play. Maybe you noticed that when you run the game, the ghosts taunt you for a second before hiding — you can't shoot them at this time. This adds a bit of production value as a sort of introduction to the action of the game.

Inserting an Always Event

Insert an always event on line 7. We are going to activate and deactivate some of the groups here, but as explained earlier, you cannot do this until you have created those groups.

Save your game.

NOTE

Inserting Start of Level Actions Group of Events

Insert a group of events called Start of Level Actions on line 9. You must create this group on a line that is not indented, so it will function properly in the game.

When you have done this, line 8 should be empty, and still be within the Start of Game Actions group as shown in Figure 9.19.

Inserting a Comment

Insert the following comment on line 10:

"The level waits 1.5 seconds before hiding all the ghosts, making the crosshair visible, and activating the main game loop."

To increase the game play, we will create a sense of urgency and set the time limit to 30 seconds. Right click the number in the border and select the Insert-A Comment option.

Enter the above comment line and click OK.

Not Indented

Indented

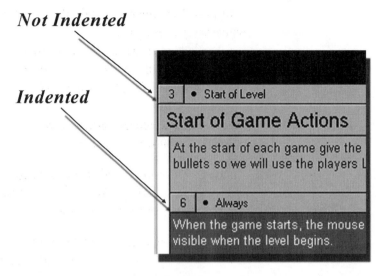

FIGURE *The Start of Level Actions group on line 9, not indented.*
9.19

Reading the Timer

Now insert an event on line 11 **Timer is greater than 1"-50**.

To do this, right click the "New condition" text and right click the timer object.

Select the Is the timer greater than a certain value? option.

Now you can enter the time. By default, the value is 1 second, so you only need to change the 1/100 box. Click in it and enter the number 50, then click OK.

Changing an Animation Sequence

Insert a Change animation to hiding action under the Ghosts icon on line 11.

Right click the box, select the Animation option, select the Change option, then select the Animation sequence option.

From the dialog box that this produces, select the Hiding option. Click OK.

Making the Crosshair Reappear

Insert reappear action on line 11, under the Crosshair icon.

Right click the box and, from the menu, select the Visibility option, then select the Make object reappear option.

Next insert an action to set the counter to 30.

Right click the empty box under the countdown object on line 11, then select the Set counter option.

You will see a dialog box where you can either enter the numbers directly in the text box, or use the buttons on the slider to change the number. Make sure that the value entered is 30, then click OK.

Inserting the Main Game Group

Insert a group called Main Game.

NOTE

You must do this on line 13, which is outside of the Start of Level Actions group . If you used line 12, which is indented, then you would put a group within a group, which The Games Factory will not allow.

To insert a group, right click the number of the line (13), select the Insert-A group of events option, type in the text, and click OK.

Inserting a Comment

Insert the following comment on line 14:

"The Main Game group controls all the events that occur within the game itself."

Right click the number, select the Insert-A comment option, type in the text, and then click OK.

Inserting Another Comment

Insert another comment, preferably in a different color;

"The crosshair will follow the hidden mouse pointer throughout the game."

NOTE

Even though the Windows mouse pointer has been hidden, it is still there, moving about and functioning as though it were visible. If your game window is smaller than your screen size, then you will see the cursor reappear if you move it off the game and onto the Windows Desktop.

By taking the mouse pointer's X and Y coordinates, we can make the crosshair follow the movement of the mouse pointer.

Inserting an Always Event

Insert an always event on the next event line (line16).

Making an Object Follow the Mouse Pointer

Now we will make the crosshair follow the invisible cursor. Insert an action on line 16 to set the coordinates of the crosshair to be the same as the mouse.

1. Right click the empty box under the crosshair object on line 16.
2. Select the Position option.
3. Select the Set X coordinate... option.
4. Click the Edit button.
5. Click the Retrieve data from an object button.
6. Now right click the mouse pointer and keyboard object.
7. Select the Current X position of the mouse option.

You should have an action under the crosshair object that reads "Set position to X mouse." To set the Y coordinate to be the same as the mouse, do the following;

1. Right click the filled box under the crosshair object on line 16.
2. Select the Position option.
3. Select the Set Y coordinate... option.
4. Click the Edit button.
5. Click the Retrieve data from an object button.
6. Now right click the mouse pointer and keyboard object.
7. Select the Current Y position of the mouse option, then click OK. This will set the crosshair object to follow the movement of the mouse pointer exactly.

Save Your Game

Inserting a Comment

Insert the following comment on line 17:
"Every second, deduct 1 from the counter that holds the time limit."

Testing the Timer

Now insert an every 1"-00 event .

Right click the "New condition" text of line number 18, then right click the timer object.

Select the Every option.

Make sure the time entered is 1 second, then click the OK button.

Changing the Value of the Counter

Insert the subtract 1 from counter action.

Right click the box under the countdown object.

Select the subtract from counter option.

Now enter the number 1 in the text box of the Expression Editor produced, then click OK.

Inserting a Comment

Insert the following comment on line 19:

"Every 2 seconds, select one of the many ghost objects from the game, and if that ghost is currently hiding, run its appear from hiding animation."

Right click on the number and select the Insert-A Comment option.

Testing the Timer Every 2 seconds

Insert an event, every 2"-00.

Right click the "New condition" text of line number 20.

Right click the timer object, then select the Every option. Make sure the time entered is 2 seconds, then click the OK button.

Adding a Condition to a Timer Event

Now add a condition to the above event. To do this, right click the text "Every 2"-00," and select the Insert option.

Now right click the ghost object, select the Pick or Count option, then select the Pick "ghost" at random option.

Adding a Further Condition

Next add a further condition to line number 20, "Ghost" animation Hiding is playing.

To do this, right click on any of the texts of line 20, and select the Insert option.

Right click the ghost, then select the Animation option.

Select the Which animation of "Ghost" is playing? option.

Select the hiding animation from the list in the dialog box. Then click the OK box.

You will have three conditions all on one event line.

NOTE

You should move the every 2"-00 event to the top of this event line, so that The Games Factory will only go through the rest of the conditions once every 2 seconds. This will help to speed up your game play slightly, especially if you have many event lines like this, for example: if you placed the Pick one of "Ghost" condition at the top, then The Games Factory would go through the actions of picking a ghost before looking at the other conditions.

Changing an Animation Sequence

Insert a Change animation sequence to Appear from Hiding action into line number 20.

To do this, right click the box under the ghost object on line 20.

Select the Animation option, select the Change option, then select the Animation sequence... option.

From the dialog box, select the Appear from hiding animation, then click OK.

Inserting a Comment

Insert the following comment on line 21:

"Four times a second, select one of the ghost objects from the game, and if that ghost is currently hiding, run its appear from hiding animation."

Testing the Timer

Insert an every 00"-25 event on line 22.

Right click the "New condition" text, right click the timer object, and select the Every option from its menu. Make sure that the time entered is 25 hundredths of a second, then click OK.

Picking a Ghost at Random

Insert a condition to line 22, Pick one of (Ghost).

Right click the text "Every 00"25" of line 22, and select the Insert option.

Right click the ghost object, select the Pick or count option from its menu, and then select the Pick "ghost" at random option.

Testing Which Animation is Playing

Now insert another condition to line 22, "ghost" animation Stopped is playing.

Right click either of the condition texts on line 22, select the Insert option, right click the ghost object from its menu, and select the Animation option.

Next select the Which animation of "ghost" is playing? option. From the dialog box produced, select the Stopped animation, then click OK.

Changing the Animation Sequence

You can insert an action into line 22 to hide the "ghost" that has been picked.

Right click the empty box on line 22, underneath the "ghost" object. From its menu, select the Animation option, select the Change option, and then select the Animation sequence option.

From the dialog box, select the hiding animation, then click OK.

Inserting a Comment

Insert the following comment on line 23:

"If the player manages to click the mouse pointer (appearing as a crosshair) on a ghost, destroy the ghost and add 10 points to the score."

Testing the Mouse to See if it has Clicked a Ghost

Insert a user clicks with left mouse button on "ghost" event on line 24.

Right click the "New condition" text of line 24, then right click the mouse pointer and keyboard object.

Select the The mouse option, then select the User clicks on an object option.

You will be taken to a dialog box. Make sure that there are tick marks in the Left button and Single click radio buttons, then click OK.

Select the ghost object, then click OK.

Inserting Sound

Now we will insert two sound actions on line 24.

Right click the empty box under the sound object, and select the Play sample option.

You will see a file selector. If you have done a normal installation, the sound files are on your computer in the default directory. Look for the directory *samples*.

Within the samples directory, look for the sub-directory *weapons*. It is from here that we are going to select the noise for the gun being fired. Try the gun3.wav file. You can preview the sound by clicking the Play button. Then click the Open button.

Now insert a second noise, the yelp of the ghost, from the Ghost Hunter tutorial folder.

To insert a further Action in the same check-box, left click in the box you want to add an action to.

NOTE

Click under the sound object again, then right click the New action option. Select the Play sample option.

Now look again in the samples directory, but this time look in the Ghost Hunter sub-directory. Look for the file *Ricchet2.wav* Try playing it a few times. If you are happy with your selection, click the OK boxes until you are returned to the Event Editor.

Changing the Score

You are now going to change the score at the same time as you destroy a ghost, so that every time the user clicks a ghost, not only are you going to play a gun sample and a Ricchet2.wav sample, but you will also add to the score and destroy the ghost.

Right click the empty check box underneath the Player 1 object. From the menu produced, select the Score option, then select the Add to score option.

Here you can enter the score via the keyboard, by clicking within the text box, or you can click the slider. You can add any score you like, but we are going to add 10 to the score. Click the OK button.

Destroying a Ghost

Now right click in the empty check box underneath the ghost object. From the menu produced, select the Destroy option.

Deducting a Life (ammo)

Next add an action to deduct a life from Player 1. In the context of this game, it means that Player 1 has used a bullet each time he fires the gun. When there are no more bullets, the game is over, since there is nothing else to do. This is an example of using set tools in a different way than they are labeled to make a better or more interesting game. Just because the word *life* is used, doesn't mean you have to literally make the action apply to a life.

Cick the box underneath the Player 1 object, where you just inserted the action to add to their score.

Right click the New action option, select the Number of lives option, then select the Subtract from Number of Lives option. Now enter the number 1 into the text box, or use the slider bar to change the value.

Click the OK buttons to return to the Event Editor.

Inserting a Comment

Insert the following Comment on line 25:

"'When the player presses the left button and misses, deduct 1 life and play the sample gun04.wav. The sound condition makes sure that these actions are not repeated very rapidly."

Testing the Mouse to See if the Left Button has Been Clicked

Insert an event on line 26 to check whether the user has clicked the left mouse button. We are then going to add a condition to this, so the actions associated with this line will only take place if a sound is not playing; i.e., if the player has not hit a ghost.

Right click the "New condition" text of line 26, select the mouse pointer and keyboard object, select the The mouse option, then select the User clicks option.

Make sure that the Left button and Single click radio buttons are selected then click OK.

Testing to See if no Samples are Already Being Played.

That is, make sure that the user has not already just killed a ghost.

Insert a condition to line 26 to check that no samples are being played. Right click the text of line 26 and select the Insert option. Then click the sound object. Choose the Samples option, then select the Is a sample not playing? option.

Playing a Sample and Deducting a Life

Now you can insert actions into line 26 to play a sample and to deduct 1 from Player 1's lives; i.e., one bullet.

First, right click the empty box under the sound object and select the play sample option.

Look in the samples directory, then in the weapons sub-directory. From here, select the sample gun04.wav.

Next, right click the empty box under the Player 1 object, select the Lives option, then select the Subtract from number of lives option. Set the Expression Editor value to 1, then click OK.

Inserting a Comment

Insert a Comment on line 27;

"If all the ghosts in the game have been destroyed, the player has completed the level. Reveal the 'It's a shame!' message and activate the Level Won group."

Testing to See if all the Ghosts have Been Shot

Insert the last "ghost" has been destroyed event on line 28.

Right click the "New condition" text, then right click the ghosts object.

Select the Pick or count option, then select the Have all "ghosts" been destroyed? option.

Playing Victory Music and Displaying the Victory Text

As previously stated, we cannot activate or deactivate a group until it has been created, so we will insert the action to activate the Level Won group after it has been created. For now, you can insert several Actions on line 28. First, insert an action to play some music.

Right click under the sound object, select the Play Music option, then look in the midi directory and select the soldier2.mid file. Now insert an action to display the text "It's A Shame."

Right click under the good shooting object, then select the Display text... option. You will now see a position selector. Enter 0 into the X coordinate box and 64 into the Y coordinate box, then click OK.

Inserting a Comment

Insert the following comment on line 29:

"There are two ways in which the player can lose the game. The bullets can run out or the time limit can expire. In each case, the Game Lost group will be activated."

Insert an event on line 30, right click the "New condition" text, select the Player 1 object, then select the Compare to player's number of lives option. Now make sure that the value is 0, and that the Equals radio button is selected. Click the OK button.

Inserting Sound

Insert a sound action on line 29. Play a piece of music that you feel is appropriate to losing the game.

Comparing the Value of the Countdown Object to a Number

Insert an Event on line 31. Click the line's text, then select the countdown object. Next select the Compare the counter to a value option. Make sure the value it is being compared to is 0, then make sure that the Equals radio button is selected.

Copying an Action

Click and drag the music action from line 30 down into line 31. This copies that sound action onto line 31.

Inserting a Group

On line 33, insert a Level Won group. Note that this must go on this line so that it falls outside of the Main Game group. If you were to place it on line 32, The Games Factory would be unable to run your game.

Inserting a Comment

On line 34, insert the following comment:

"When the congratulations music has finished, restart the level, which keeps the score and allows the player to play again with all the ghosts back as they were at the start of the level."

Testing to See if no Music is Playing

Insert an event on line 35. Right click the line, select the sound object, select the Music option, then select the Is music not playing? option.

Restarting the Current Level

Insert an action on line 35. Right click under the storyboard object, then select the Restart the current level option.

Inserting a Group

Now insert a Game Lost group on line 37.

Inserting a Comment

Insert the following comment on line 38:

"When the game lost sound has ended, restart the game to clear the score and begin the entire game from the very start."

Copying an Event

Copy an event onto line 39. Click and hold on the "No sample is playing" text of line 35 and drag it into line 39. This will copy that event.

Restarting the Game

Insert an action on line 39 to restart the game. Right click the box under the storyboard object, then select the Restart game option.

INSERTING ALL THE ACTIONS TO ACTIVATE/DEACTIVATE THE GROUPS

That's almost it. All we need to do is go back and insert all the actions to activate/deactivate the groups, now that we have created them all.

Go to line 1, right click the box under the special object, select the Group of events option, then select the Deactivate option. You will then be taken to a dialog box where you can select the groups that you want to deactivate (See Figure 9.20). First of all, pick the Start of Level Actions group, then click OK.

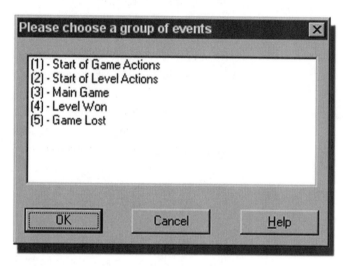

FIGURE *The dialog box where you activate and deactivate groups.*
9.20

Now you need to insert the rest of the actions into the same check mark. To do this, click the check mark. This will produce a dialog box which lists all the actions from within that check mark. You also have a New action option. Right click this option. You will see the same menu produced as when you first right clicked under the special object. Select the Group of events option, then the Deactivate option. Now select the Main Game group.

You will be able to deactivate the Level Won and Game Lost groups using the method above.

Go to line 7 and insert the following actions: deactivate group — Start of game actions, and activate group — Start of level actions.

Right click under the Special object, select Group of events, select Deactivate, Start of game actions, then click OK.

Click the check mark, right click New actions, select Group of events, select Activate, select Start of level actions, then click OK.

Go to line 11 and insert the following actions: deactivate group — Start of level actions, and activate group — Main Game.

Go to line 28 and insert the following actions: deactivate group — Main Game, and activate group — Level Won.

Go to line 30 and insert the following actions: deactivate group — Main Game, and activate group — Game Lost.

Now copy these actions into line 31 by clicking and holding on the check mark, then dragging it into line 31.

CONGRATULATIONS

And that's it. Ghost Hunter is ready to take the market by storm. You have just completed a more advanced game in TGF and learned some functions and techniques to help you with your organization while making a game with TGF, and also to help TGF run more efficiently.

Next we will take yet another big step in game development and create a game that adds to our growing bag of tools. Once again, we will change the perspective you have of the game world and attempt a different type of game to further explore the abilities of TGF.

CHAPTER

10

MAKING A MORE ADVANCED GAME WITH THE GAMES FACTORY

185

Okay. Ready to make another game? This time we will do a game that is a bit more advanced. We will explore a few more functions of The Game Factory. We will look at side scrolling on a screen larger than the play area and use groups to speed up game development and make the Event Editor easier to look at.

We will be developing Dragon Flight.

FIGURE *A screen shot of Dragon Flight.*
10.1

Dragon Flight

By now you should really have a good feel for the different Editor screens and their purposes. As you can already see, most of your game action is created in the Event Editor, and the levels themselves are assembled in the Level Editor. The Storyboard Editor allows you to control the flow of your game as a production — level order, transitions, and the progress of your game. Now we will look deeper into some fairly complex game-creation techniques, but don't be intimidated. We will go through these step by step.

Dragon Flight is a simple game where you are racing against the clock. The dragon is trying to take off out of its cave and has to dodge the walls and its own firetraps. Although fairly simple in terms of game play, Dragon Flight uses some fairly advanced techniques to achieve the end result. Before we go any farther, let's load up the game and have a look around.

Go to the File menu heading at the top of the screen, and select the Open option.

Now look for the directory *sample games*, and then look in the sub-directory *dragon* for the file *dragon.gam*.

STORYBOARD EDITOR – DRAGON FLIGHT PART 1

Let's have a look around the Dragon Flight Storyboard Editor and see the changes that have been made here, as well as look into the various preferences that have been changed (See Figure 10.2).

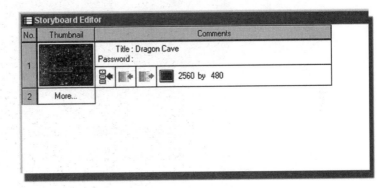

FIGURE *The Dragon Flight Storyboard Editor.*
10.2

First, go to the File menu in the toolbar and select the Game setup option. You can see on the first layer of this dialog box the author and title of the game. You can see that the panic key has been enabled (See Figure 10.3).

The panic key is in case you panic during the game (like when your boss walks in when you are playing). If you hit the key (F5), during the game The Games Factory will take you back to the Windows screen, leaving the game to run in the background. The panic key turns off the sound and minimizes the display. When you click the button in the Windows Bar to restore the game, the sound effects will work, but the looped music will not play again until the level is restarted.

Click the Windows tab and look on the next layer. There are some significant changes here from the default settings. These have a dramatic effect on the final look of the game when it is run, and it is important to understand these changes (See Figure 10.4).

The first line is Maximized on boot up, which maximizes the window used to display the game when it is first loaded, not the game itself. That is, as in any Windows application, The Games Factory uses a window to display your

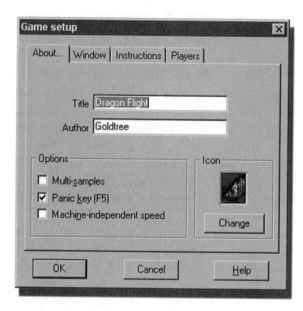

FIGURE *The Game Setup menu for Dragon Flight, with the panic button activated.*
10.3

FIGURE *The changes made on the Windows tab of the Game Setup menu.*
10.4

game. Having this option turned on will stretch the window out to fill the screen to the very edge (See Figure 10.5).

NOTE

You will not be able to change the dimensions of the window using the mouse pointer when this option is enabled.

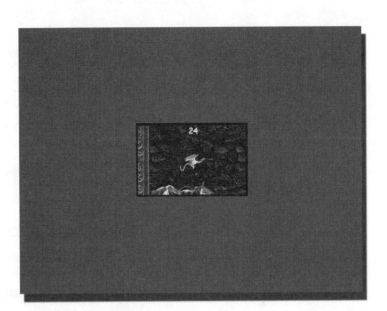

FIGURE   *The maximized game window (note the game is not maximized).*
10.5

The Resize display to fill current window size option will fill whatever window size you are using with the game display.

NOTE

If you disable the Maximized on boot up option, then you will be able to shrink or stretch the window used to display your game, using the mouse pointer to "grab" the edges of the window. When the window is large, this option can dramatically slow down the game action due to the complicated nature of the calculations necessary to resize the display.

The Full screen at start option is for use on the 16-bit version only. It was designed specifically for use with the 320 by 200 graphics mode that is supported by the 16-bit version.

NOTE

Changing this option will have no effect when used with any other window sizes, only on the 320 by 200. It allows very fast game play of a low resolution that still fills the screen. Notice at the top of this layer, the size of the window has been changed to 320 by 200, which means that only an area 320 by 200 will be shown on the screen. By enabling the Full screen at start option, you "expand" this small chunk of the play area to fill the screen.

When you go back to the Storyboard Editor, look at the size of the play area and note that it is, in fact, larger than the size of the screen (See Figure 10.6). The Window preference being set to 320 by 200 means that only a window 320 by 200 will be shown from this play area, and Full screen at start means this is expanded to fill the screen. This is a very important feature of The Games Factory and can be used to change the way your games are displayed.

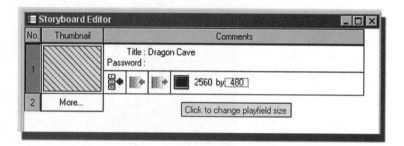

FIGURE　*The playfield size is set larger than the screen size.*
10.6

For 32-bit users to achieve the same effect as the Full screen at start option has on the 16-bit version, they should enable the Maximized on boot up and Resize display to fill current window size options. This will make the window being used to display the game fill the screen to the edge. Then the display is resized to fit this larger window.

NOTE

If you maximized the window without resizing the display, then the screen will show a chunk of the play area 320 by 200, surrounded by a huge black border.

While having a look around the Windows tab, notice that the Heading and Game to include menu bar options have been disabled as well. This means that when your game is run, there will be no menu heading at the top of the screen, and no heading telling what the game is (See Figure 10.7).

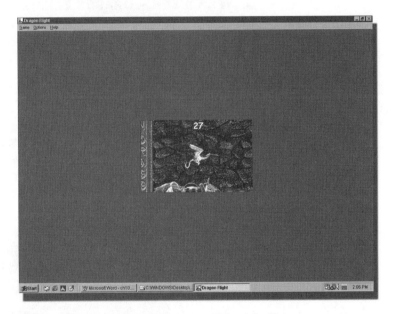

FIGURE   *The different Header Bar options, enabled and disabled.*
10.7

NOTE

Only the actual play area window will be displayed and nothing else, so the only way to escape from a game when these options are turned off is to use the Alt + F4 keys. The mouse pointer is hidden via the Event Editor and is inaccessible. There are no menus to click even if it was there.

No other changes have been made to the default settings in the Game Setup menu so you can "OK" your way out of this dialog box or cancel if you are not sure if you made any changes.

Now we will look around the levels of Dragon Flight. The main thing you may want to take note of first is the play area size. It is 2560 by 480, a long horizontal strip.

We made the game world much longer than it is wide because one of the things we are going to do in Dragon Flight is to scroll the screen through the main character of the dragon's lair. We need a long screen so the whole level isn't visible all at once.

Now let's look in the Level Editor. I am sure you remember how to open the Level Editor by now.

LEVEL EDITOR – DRAGON FLIGHT, PART 1

As you have done in previous tutorial games, run your mouse pointer over the different objects on the screen to see what they are and how they relate to each other. Not all of the objects that we are going to use are on this screen yet — they are being saved for later tutorials.

Move your mouse pointer over the Cave wall backdrop object and right click it. Select the Obstacle menu option and note that the No option is selected. This means that active objects cannot collide with it. This is the "wall" of the cave in the background. Our dragon is going to move through the cave with this wall in the background. See Figure 10.8 for the backdrop pop-up menu.

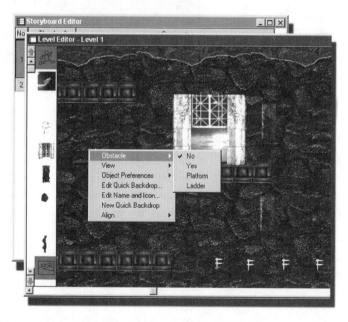

FIGURE **10.8** *The pop-up menu for the cave wall, indicating that it is not an obstacle.*

Look at the other pop-up menus of the other objects and notice that the Obstacle menus all have the Yes option checked. This means that active objects can collide with them, as you can see when you run the game.

Now go and find the dragon object. It is on the far left of the play area, which is where the game starts.

Right click the dragon object to show the menu options.

Look at the Movement option and the Edit movement option. Note that the Eight direction movement is being used. The maximum speed is set quite low, making the object slow, and the deceleration is set quite high, making the object slow down quickly. To make the dragon reasonably responsive, the acceleration is set quite high. (See Figure 10.9).

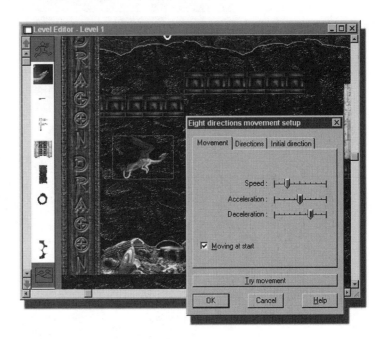

FIGURE *The Movement options for the dragon.*
10.9

While you are here, you can look around at the other objects. Make sure you don't change anything, or make a backup copy if you want to experiment. If you look at all the different menu options of all the different objects on this screen, you will recognize many functions from the previous chapters.

Now look at all the objects in the Object window. There are many different active objects in this game level, mostly the cave walls.

NOTE

There are two different walls, but they look exactly the same. One is going to be indestructible; the other you will be able to shoot out of the way during the game.

You can make two different objects look exactly the same by placing the first object on the play area, and then from its menu, selecting the New object option (See Figure 10.10), making the second object an active object, then selecting its Edit name and icon option to change its name. Apart from that, they are identical. The other differences in the way they behave are all done in the Event Editor.

FIGURE *The pop-up menu in the Level Editor to make a new object from an existing* **10.10** *one.*

As you scroll through all the other objects in the Object window, you will see that the background has been made out of many different objects, placed individually onto the screen. Using The Games Factory's many different libraries, you will be able to do the same thing to create similar backgrounds or platforms.

At the very bottom of the object library is the counter object, which is used to display the time left, and also a lives object, which in this case, is used to keep count of the number of fireballs the player (dragon) has left.

When you are finished looking around the Level Editor, move onto the Event Editor by clicking its icon from the toolbar.

EVENT EDITOR – DRAGON FLIGHT, PART 1

One of the first things that you will notice is that there are lots of objects displayed across the top of the Event Grid; so many, in fact, that you may have to scroll through them using the scroll bar at the base of the screen. You will also notice two funny face icons — Group.Bad and Group.Neutral. Ignore these for now. We will talk about them at the end of the chapter.

NOTE

If you have a small monitor or are displaying at a low resolution, you can make all the events fit onto the screen. You can do this by clicking the Preferences icon on the toolbar, selecting the display layer of the dialog box, then moving the number of events on the screen slider to High.

Try experimenting with this slider until you are happy with the result. This is similar to the Storyboard Display properties that we looked at earlier.

Read through all the comments in the Event Grid. These will clearly explain what has been done at each stage of the game. Remember that you can collapse groups, sort events, and manipulate the display for your convenience to see all the events.

An interesting side note: As we spoke about way back at the beginning of this book, the drag-and-drop tools available to us now, like TGF, have made our lives a lot easier. So much so that we may take things like this first actual event line for granted. In this event, we click one button and make a few menu selections to tell TGF to allow the screen to scroll. This used to take hours of extensive programming. This is done in just one line with TGF. This event line makes the rest of the screen scroll about, using the dragon object as the center when it is moved. The dragon will always be in the center of the screen and the play area moves instead.

Making the Dragon always in the Center

To make this event, create an always event.

Right click the square under the Storyboard Actions icon and do the following:

Click the Center horizontal position in the playfield button.

Click the Center vertical position in the playfield button.

Click the Retrieve data from an object button from these menus, and then select the dragon object to use the X and Y coordinates of the dragon object for the scrolling actions. See Figure 10.11 for the menu progression of this function.

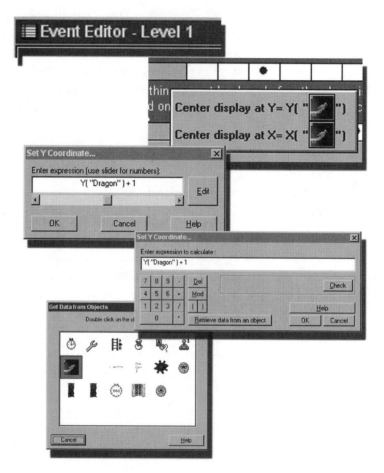

FIGURE   *The menu progression for making the screen scroll with the dragon object.*
10.11

Decreasing the Counter

In the game, we make the counter decrease in value by 1 for every second that passes. This is the clock you are racing against. This event was created by adding the event line Every 1"00, then selecting the Subtract from Counter option, and setting the value to 1.

Moving Firetraps

To move the firetrap objects, you start by making their Y values the same as the Y value of the dragon. This means that the firetraps are always "in the way" or in the same location as the dragon going up and down, but not side to side. The player has to shoot the firetraps in order to get past them.

This was done in a similar manner to the scrolling function above. If you right click the square below the firetrap, and then select the Position option from the pop-up menu, you can then select the Set Y coordinate option. Then all you have to do is click the Retrieve data from an object button and select the dragon object from the pop-up window.

During the game, the firetrap objects will get, or *retrieve,* their Y coordinate values from the "position" of the Dragon.

Use the Play button on the top right of the toolbar to see how all of these events and actions fit together, and save your game file if you are creating this from the ground up.

LEVEL EDITOR – DRAGON FLIGHT, PART 2

Let's look at another significant feature of Dragon Flight — an easy one to pull off, but a very useful one. Look in the Object window for an object called the real collider. This is the object that is actually going to be tested for collisions instead of the dragon object. The reason for this is that the dragon object itself is fairly big — or the square image it is contained on is — but the body of the dragon is actually rather slender.

It is the flapping wings and flames that make the image so big, and the players will never get through the cave if the entire area of the dragon image is tested for collisions, so we will make things a bit more fair for them by testing another object.

To explain further, TGF by default detects for a collision using the entire image borders. Thus a collision would be detected if any part of the dragon collided with anything else, including the flames and wings. Since we want the actual portion of the dragon's body to be what causes a collision, we will use an active object created for this purpose that has an outline shape matching that of the dragon object. This is helpful to artists, since some of us may want to have an impressive object that shoots lightening bolts off in every direction, but that also has a small body for passing through the caves or tunnels of our own game. The problem would obviously be that if the entire image was tested, even the tips of a lightening bolt with supposedly no mass would cause a collision. See Figure 10.12 for a visual representation of these concepts.

The real collider object is then made invisible, and given the same X and Y coordinates as the dragon, via the Event Editor.

Let's see how that looks in the Event Editor.

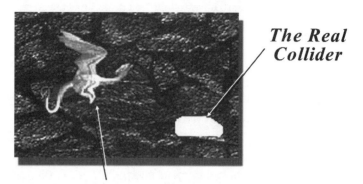

The Real Collider

The Dragon Object

FIGURE *The large dragon bitmap and the real collider objects, and how they function in*
10.12 *the game.*

EVENT EDITOR – DRAGON FLIGHT, PART 2

Let's look at the groups, Lost Race and Won Race (See Figure 10.13). These groups perform groups of actions when the race is either won or lost. They are deactivated here to stop their actions from being performed during the game. Then when the game is won or lost, one of the two groups is activated and the Main Game group will be deactivated.

You can see that this very much simplifies your game creation. Rather than having a condition on all the lines for the Lost Race group that tests to see if the game has been lost, the group is simply deactivated, then activated when needed. Also on this line is the action to make the real collider object invisible. The next significant new line is line 23. This is where the real collider object is given exactly the same position as the dragon.

Lost Race

When the race has been lost, wait 4 seconds then RESTART THE GAME loosing all the score points accumulated thus far.

46	• No sample is playing																		
47	• Every 04"-00			•															
48	• New condition																		

Won Race

When the race has been won, increment the score which will be deducted from the seconds given in the following race.

51	• No music is playing			•		•													
52	• New condition																		
53	• New condition																		

FIGURE *The Lost Race and Won Race groups of events in the Event Editor.*
10.13

To give the real Collider object the exact same position as the dragon object do the following:

Set up an always event and right click the square under the special object, and select the Position option from the pop-up menu.

Select the real collider object.

Select the Select position option.

The position should be set at 0,0, relative to the dragon object.

Loosing the Game by Collision

The game can be lost if the dragon hits the walls of the cave. Line 25 is where you make this happen.

Insert an event that detects if a collision has occurred between the real collider object and the background. Remember, do not use the dragon object for this collision test.

To set this line up correctly, select on the New condition text.

Right click the real collider object.

From the pop-up menu, select the Collisions menu option.

Next select the Backdrop option.

Then the Main Game group is deactivated, to stop the game from continuing to run, and the Lost Race group is activated.

An explosion sample is also played on this line. The player's control is taken away from them here, and the dragon object is destroyed.

Because the Main Game group is deactivated here, all the lines hereafter will be ignored when the game is lost, and only the lines in the Lost Race group will be active.

The Racing Flavor

The next line is the one that controls when the game is won. To give the game a true racing flavor, only the X coordinate of the finishing portal object has to be passed in order to win, making it a true "finish line."

To create the finish line, we must do the following:

Select the Position option of the dragon object.

Select the **Compare X position to a value** option.

The X position of the finishing portal is retrieved via the Retrieve data from an object button.

This was compared using the **Greater than** comparison.

Then, on this line, the Main Game group is deactivated and the Game Won group is activated. Notice that in order to stop the player from moving any farther, the player's control is ignored.

The Lost Race group, at this stage, merely waits 4 seconds and then restarts the game, which resets the score.

The Game Won group waits 1 second then restarts the level, which does not reset the score. It also adds 2 to the value of the score. The score is not going to be used to display the score, but will be used to subtract from the time at the beginning of the game. So each time you win, yo, have less and less time to reach the end.

Now run this version of Dragon Flight and see how the dragon collides with obstacles and how the won/lost game sections work.

Right now, let's look at the last part of this chapter, which gives you a finished, running race game!

LEVEL EDITOR – DRAGON FLIGHT, PART 3

Now we are adding yet another important function. If you look in the Object window and on the play area, you will see our fireball object. This will be used to replenish your stock of Fire Breath, without which you would be unable to get past the various traps and obstacles.

Something that you may have noticed is that there are bad and neutral groups in the game. The groups are Group.Bad and Group.Neutral. Find out which objects belong to which groups by right clicking them on the play area, then selecting their Object preferences menu. This will show you which groups they belong to.

EVENT EDITOR – DRAGON FLIGHT, PART 3

This time we look at the event that will destroy all the fireball objects that might be left on the play area before the game begins. Also we will add a neat little start to the game for effect. While the music is being played, the dragon moves down and along a path as if it has just launched off of its perch and is ready to fly out of the cave.

As soon as the music that was played from line 11 has finished, this line plays another sound sample and then deactivates the Start of Race Actions group, which stops the dragon from being moved any farther. It also launches you into the main game by activating the Main Game group.

Launching a Fireball

The next major event is blasting something with a fireball. First we must check that we have fireballs in our possession. To do that we check to see if the number of lives (fireballs) is greater than 0. If they are, when the key is pressed, then all the actions on this line will be performed.

To create this line, first create the Upon pressing the key event.

Then insert the Number of lives >0 condition.

Right click the Upon pressing the key text.

Then select the Insert option. The player 1 object is tested by selecting its Compare to the player's number of lives option.

Now associate the following action to this event line, using the Event Editor as a guide (See Figure 10.14):

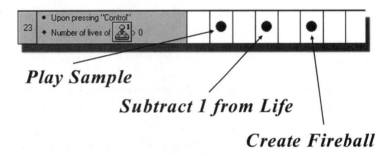

Play Sample

Subtract 1 from Life

Create Fireball

FIGURE   *The events associated with breathing a fireball.*
10.14

1. Play a sample.
2. Create a fireball just in front of the dragon. Note that the fireball is not fired out, and is in fact stationary when it is first created. It needs an event line to accelerate it placed elsewhere in the Main Game group. The reason that the fireball's movement is controlled in this way is to create a realistic effect of the fireball slowly accelerating through the air.
3. Subtract one fireball, since one was just fired. In addition to the above actions, 1 is subtracted from the player's number of lives (fireballs) to signify that a fireball has been used up.

Accelerating a Fireball

Farther down is where the fireballs are accelerated up to a maximum speed of 50. This is done by doing the following:

Select the fireball object's Movement menu.

Select its Compare speed of "fireball" to a value option.

Using the Less than comparison, compared this with the value 50.

Place the action to set its direction in the check box first.

Insert the action to increase it's speed afterwards by left clicking the box, right clicking the "New action" text, selecting the Movement option, and then selecting the Set speed option. Retrieve its own speed by using the Retrieve data from an object button, then adding +5 onto the end of the expression. See Figure 10.15 for a visual aid of these steps.

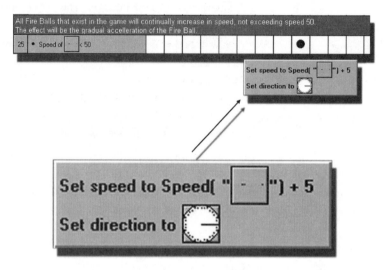

FIGURE *The steps for accelerating a fireball from a dead stop to 50, but no faster.*
10.15

The logic of these steps is: The speed of the object is set to the speed of itself, +5.

You can then set an action to destroy the fireballs if they collide with the background. This is associated with a sound sample as well.

To speed up game development and simplify it, you can use the Bad and Neutral groups. You can set an event to say, "Anything belonging to the Group.Neutral is destroyed when hit by the fireball," as opposed to going through the motions for every object you want destroyed by the fireball.

Game Balance and Indestructible Walls

In this game, we have also placed some walls that react when hit with a fireball, but which are in fact indestructible. While the steps to do this are easy (we will look at them next), I wanted to make some observations about this easy action's impact on the game while we are here.

Placing these walls, at first, seems cruel to the player since they will no doubt waste precious time and fireballs trying to get through them and they will loose the game a few times. But these initial defeats make the player want to play the game again and again, since they know what to do differently the next time around to win — or they think they do, until they hit your next trick.

This is ultimately a gift to the player, since they will have a more enjoyable experience in the long run. They will gain a feeling of accomplishment after having played your game a few times and eventually winning. I bring this up here to illustrate game balance since, we just illustrated a simple aspect of a rather simple game that increases game play enormously. With game balance you literally are balancing the game play — too hard and you loose the player to frustration, too easy and they are done in a flash and are bored with the simplicity of the game play.

Also, these walls also add to the atmosphere a great deal. Remember from our discussions on game design that interactivity is a very important aspect of game development. Game worlds that feel flat and dead reduce the playability of the game. Adding little things like this make a big difference in the quality of your game. This is called production values, professional polish, tweaking, or some state it as "God is in the details." Walls and objects that can be poked or prodded and tested for a result make the players feel that they are, in fact, exploring a real world and not just driving through tunnels.

Back to the Game Steps and Destructible Walls

Now we will also create walls that are destructible. Theses are actually animated active objects that allow a hole to be blasted through a weak wall. The object is not completely destroyed, but the animation is changed to create hole, the fireball is destroyed, and a sound sample is played. And the dragon can pass through the hole.

Collecting Fireball Energy

The action that controls the collection of fireballs is done simply by adding 2 to the number of lives and destroying the fireball power rune object when the real collider object collides with the ammo object.

Countdown

The countdown object actions. If the value of the counter is zero, then the game has been lost. The associated actions deactivate the Main Game group and the player's controls, as well as playing a sample and activating the Lost Race group .

Real Collider Hits Backdrop

This is where the game is lost if the real collider object hits any of the backdrop objects. The same actions are performed as above, with the addition of destroying the dragon object.

Real Collider and the Group.Neutral

This tests to see if the real collider object hits any of the other active objects that belong to the Group.Neutral, which includes the walls, both weak and indestructible, and any of the firetrap objects or boulder objects.

And guess what? You just made another game with TGF. By now you should understand how this game was constructed, as well as why it was constructed in this way, using groups.

If there are any points you are finding difficult to understand, it can be very helpful to try and recreate an event line on a spare "New condition" line. You can always delete it afterwards. You can also "have a look around" most of the actions and events by right clicking them and selecting the Edit option. Note that you cannot edit some of the very simple actions, such as Destroy.

Now that you may be itching to get on with game developments of your own and to move on in TGF, the next few chapters will look in depth at some of the most commonly used tools in game development with TGF.

11

ADVANCED CONTROL OF ACTIVE OBJECTS

Now that you have a firm background in TGF, you will want to experiment on your own more. You will start digging deeper into the menus. Detailed here are a few of the most important things you will do with active objects in TGF.

You may have noticed that in the previous chapters, you were never called upon to create assets or animate objects. Over the next few chapters, we will look at ways to create and manage assets. We will start by looking at all the active objects and their movement menus, the text objects, and the backdrop objects — the mainstays of TGF games.

Active Objects

Active objects are mostly used as the main characters of your games. These are the characters and objects we have been using to assign behavior and controls to. We did this by either allowing the player to use the mouse or keyboard, or we had the computer control the objects for us. You can also make your active objects animated, making them run, jump, or whatever you decide.

Active objects are denoted by the icon on the object shelf on the Level Editor screen (See Figure 11.1). Open one of the past tutorials that had a moving character, like the dragon in Dragon Flight, from the last chapter. Try grabbing the dragon active object and dragging it onto the screen of the Level Editor.

You can also create your own active object by clicking the New Object icon on the toolbar at the top of the Level Editor screen, as shown in Figure 11.2. Once you have done this, you can change the options by clicking the object with the right mouse button. Don't worry about the images and object animation just yet. We will talk about that in the next chapter.

Movement

To change an object's movement from the Level Editor, select the object using the right mouse button, select the Movement option from its pulldown menu, and then select the Select Movement option. The menu seen in Figure 11.3 will pop up.

The first area on this menu is the Player-Controlled Movement area. Obviously, this allows the player to control the object in several ways.

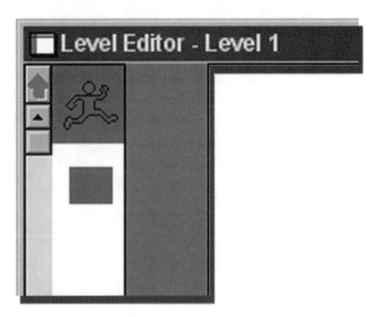

FIGURE   *The Active Object icon in the Level Editor screen.*
11.1

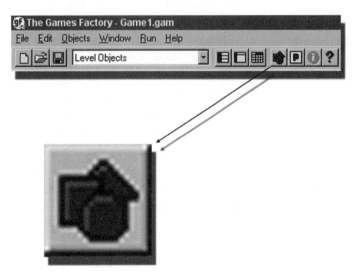

FIGURE   *The New Object icon from the toolbar.*
11.2

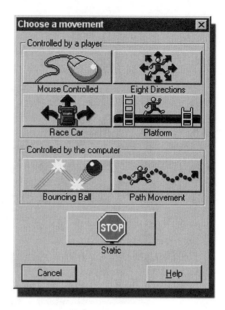

FIGURE *The Movement pop-up menu.*
11.3

Player Controlled Movement

MOUSE CONTROLLED

This assigns your object to exactly follow the movement of the mouse. Notice that when you call this option, (See Figure 11.4), your object will be surrounded by a box, which represents the limits of movement of your object, as shown in Figure 11.5.

You can stretch or shrink the area by grabbing the pick points with your mouse and dragging them around. Note that this box takes its position from the object, not the screen. So if you move your object to a new position on the Level Editor screen, you may well need to edit this box again.

The following movement parameters are used for several of the movements, so they have been summarized here.

Speed

Speed sets the maximum speed at which your object will be able to move.

Acceleration

Acceleration sets the rate at which your object will reach its maximum speed. If your object was a car, for example, you may want the acceleration

FIGURE *Mouse controlled icon.*
11.4

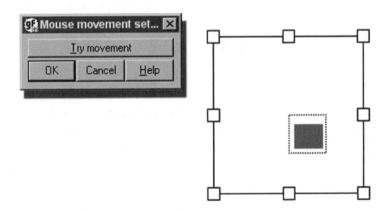

FIGURE *The mouse movement area control box.*
11.5

quite high. If it were a "heavier" object, like an elephant, you would want it set quite low.

Deceleration

Deceleration affects the rate at which your object slows down. Having a high value will stop your object quickly when you release the key to move it. Having it set low will result in a very gradual slowing down, as though the object were really heavy, like an oil tanker.

Initial Direction

Initial Direction allows you to decide what the first direction of the object will be. If you select more than one direction, the computer will select one direction at random.

Moving at Start

Moving at Start toggles whether or not you want your object to be moving at the start of a game.

Try Movement

Try Movement tests your movement on the screen. Use the Esc key, or select the Stop icon to take you back to the Direction Editor.

EIGHT DIRECTION MOVEMENTS

FIGURE *The Eight Directions icon.*
11.6

This movement (shown in Figure 11.6) provides you with the classic eight different directions that are used by a joystick. You can also use the cursor keys to control this movement. There are several basic controls. Speed, acceleration, and deceleration have been described above. The Possible directions option allows you to select or de-select the number of directions your object can move in. See Figure 11.7 for the Movement Direction dialog box.

To select or de-select a direction, simply click the relevant box. Possible directions are shown by having an arrow pointing to that box. In Figure 11.7, the only possible direction that the object could move in would be right.

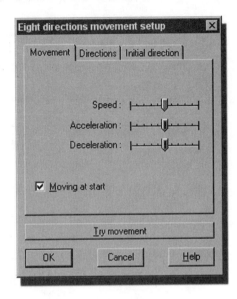

FIGURE The Movement Direction dialog box.
11.7

Race Car

Figure 11.8 simulates a birds-eye view of a car's movement; thus there are controls for steering, braking, and accelerating.

FIGURE The Race Car icon.
11.8

Action	Keyboard	Joystick
Accelerator	Up Arrow	Joystick Up
Brake	Down Arrow	Joystick Down
Turn Left	Left Arrow	Joystick Left
Turn Right	Right Arrow	Joystick Right

In addition to speed, acceleration, and deceleration settings, there are three more options.

Enable Reverse Movement

This option gives your object the ability to go backwards. With it turned off, you can only have forward movement.

Directions

Directions lets you decide how many different directions it is possible for the vehicle to move in. Selecting 4 will only give you left, right, up, and down; Selecting 32 will give you the smoothest possible direction changes.

You can easily create all the different animation tracks needed for each direction by using the Animation Editor. We discuss this later.

NOTE

Rotating Speed

Rotating Speed sets the rate of turn. Having a high value will allow tight corners to be turned; having a low value reduces the cornering ability.

PLATFORM MOVEMENT

This movement (See Figure 11.9) is used mainly to define platform game-type movement; i.e., characters who walk along a platform on the screen, viewed from the side, like in Commander Keen or Zeb. They are controlled by the cursor keys or the joystick. In addition to the usual acceleration, deceleration and speed, there are a large number of controls peculiar to platform movement.

You can make platforms and ladders that are obstacles out of backdrop objects.

You must still test for a collision with a backdrop platform object; otherwise, your active object will fall through the platform as if it weren't there.

NOTE

FIGURE   *The Platform Movement icon.*
11.9

Gravity
As it suggests, this option selects the effect of gravity. A high setting will have your object fall rapidly, allowing only short jumps.

Jump Strength
Jump Strength selects the jumping power of your character. Changing the gravity will also affect this parameter.

Jump Controls
Jump Controls are used to change the control system for jumps.

No Jump
Obviously, this option turns the jumping off.

Up Left/Right Arrow
This option makes the object jump when both the up arrow key and either the left or right cursor keys are pressed.

Button 1
Button 1 uses fire button one or the Shift key to control the jump.

Button 2
Button 2 uses the second fire button or the Control key to activate a jump.

Computer-Controlled Movements

There are two computer-controlled options: Bouncing Ball and Path Movement.

The first option is Bouncing Ball and, as the name indicates, this option is used to allow the computer to move or control the other objects in your games — from a simple bouncing ball, to an attack wave of aliens, or even a preset path on which a guard walks his patrol.

BOUNCING BALL

This movement option shown in Figure 11.10 is normally used to produce an object that will bounce around the screen, mimicking the movement of a bouncing ball. However, by changing several parameters and using the Event Editor, this movement can be used to control the movement of a host of aliens, or other enemies that will chase you around.

Speed

Speed is set as for all the other types of movement.

FIGURE *The Bouncing Ball icon.*
11.10

Ball Deceleration

When this option is set to zero, the ball will keep on bouncing around forever. Increasing this value gradually slows your object down until it eventually grinds to a halt.

Bounce Randomizer

As the name suggests, this option makes the bounces more random in their direction when this control is set high.

Bounce Security

This option jiggles your objects around to stop them from getting stuck in corners. But, as a result, the rebound effects are made slightly more random.

We will look at Bouncing Ball in a little more detail later.

PATH MOVEMENT

The Path Movement option (shown in Figure 11.11) sets your object moving on a predetermined path that you define; for example, a patrolling guard who walks a set distance, then turns around, or who has a preset walk around a corridor. With this movement, you can really script some neat effects since you can control many parameters, such as the looping and speed of different sections of the path as the object moves along.

FIGURE   *The Path Movement icon.*
11.11

Path Editor

You can see in Figure 11.12 that there are six different buttons for you to define your movement, plus the speed bar, which changes the speed at which the object moves along its path. A path-type movement is entered using your mouse to define the path (See Figure 11.13).

New Line

This function will add a single line to your movement.

If you already have a movement defined, New Line will be added at the end of this by default, unless you insert it by choosing the insertion point with the mouse.

NOTE

FIGURE
11.12
The Path Editor Menu Window.

 New Line

 Tape Mouse

 Pause

 Loop Movement

 Reverse at End

 Reposition Object at End

FIGURE
11.13
The individual Path Editor option buttons.

Tape Mouse

This function allows you to set a very complex path movement. By holding down the left mouse button and dragging it around the screen, you set the movement you want.

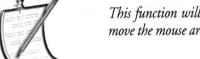

This function will change the speed of the object, depending on how fast you move the mouse around.

Pause

This function stops your object at its current position for a pause that you define in seconds.

Loop the movement

This function will run whatever movement you have defined over and over.

This will reposition the object to its original starting position to continue the loop, so try to ensure that your path finishes at the object's start point, or it will jump around the screen.

NOTE

Reverse at End

This function simply reverses an object's movement and sends it back along the original path, backwards. This function is good for a guard patrolling the grounds.

Reposition Object at End

This function replaces your object to its original starting position when it has completed the movement.

Try Movement

This function allows you to try the movement before finally deciding upon it.

Editing a Path

Once you have added a movement to your object, you can edit it very easily afterwards from the Level Editor, by selecting the object, then choosing the Edit Movement option. This will open the Path Editor again. You can select individual points of the movement, or whole sections by dragging a box around them. You can then manipulate these selected pieces by either deleting them, or using the Cut, Copy, and Paste options from the Edit menu (the drop-down menu at the top of the screen). You can simply drag one of the points that you select using the left mouse button.

INSERTING A CONDITION

By using the right mouse button on one of the points, you can insert one of
the previously defined conditions at any point along a path; e.g., set a pause,
tape mouse, new line, etc.

Bouncing Ball Movement

The Bouncing Ball movement is normally used to provide a ball-like movement that will bounce off other obstacles on the screen. However, by setting
all the parameters to zero, you will have a movement "blank page," which
you can then manipulate entirely from the Event Editor. This is useful for
enemy movements.

When you first select the Ball movement setup option, you will see a
three- layered dialog box. You can change the layer being shown by clicking
its tab (See Figure 11.14).

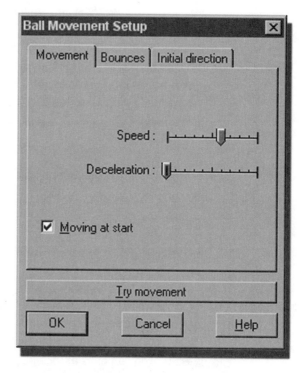

FIGURE *The Bouncing Ball dialogue box — Movement tab.*
11.14

MOVEMENT

Speed
This option sets the maximum speed at which your object can move.

Deceleration
Deceleration sets the rate at which your bouncing object will slow down. Having this option set to zero will bounce your object around endlessly.

Moving at start
The Moving at Start option will set off the movement in one of the directions you choose, right from the start of the game. Having it set off means that the object will remain stationary until it collides with another object.

BOUNCES

Number of angles
This option (See Figure 11.15) sets the number of angles that it is possible for your object to bounce in. Having it set to 32 will result in the smoothest, most realistic effect. Having it set to 8 will result in an object that can only move left, right, up, down, and diagonally in-between, and would not suit an object that is supposed to bounce like a ball.

Randomizer
This option gives your object a chance of bouncing off in a different direction from what you would normally expect. The higher the setting, the more unpredictable your bounces will be.

Security
This option jiggles your objects around to stop them from getting stuck in corners. As a result, the rebound effects do become slightly more random.

Initial Direction
This option allows you to choose one or more directions for your object to move in when the game begins. Having more than one direction selected will result in a random choice being made between the directions that you have selected. You can select and deselect the directions individually by clicking the box at the end of each direction arrow. A selected direction will show an arrow in that box; deselecting a direction will remove the arrow.

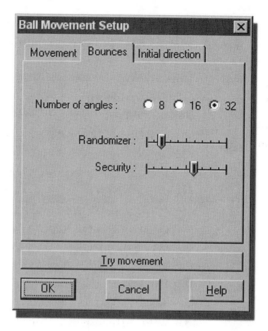

FIGURE   *The Bouncing Ball dialogue box — Bounces tab.*
11.15

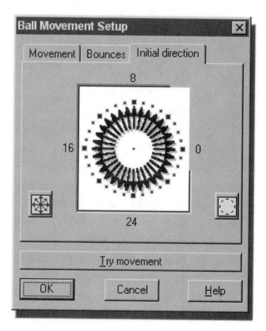

FIGURE   *The Bouncing Ball dialog box — Initial Direction tab.*
11.16

You can select all the possible directions using the icon on the bottom left, or deselect all directions by using the icon on the bottom right.

Backdrop Objects and Quick Backdrop Objects

All the following parameters apply to both backdrop and quick backdrop objects, except that quick backdrop objects can be constructed without using the Picture Editor, if their appearance is going to be relatively simple. This option is discussed in the next chapter.

Backdrop objects are normally used to "set the scene" in games. They provide backdrops for your players to move over, or even to interact with. You cannot move backdrop objects or change their appearance when the game is playing, as you can with active objects. But you can change their position on the screen, as well as their size, shape, and color, from the Level Editor.

You can either select one of the many backdrop objects from an object library or create your own backdrop and quick backdrop objects using the icon from the toolbar at the top of the Level Editor screen.

Most of the changes that you make to the actual appearance of the backdrop object are done using the Picture Editor (see next chapter). You only use this when you have selected the Mosaic option when using a quick backdrop object.

All the other changes to backdrop objects are done from the main menu that you pull down when you right click the actual backdrop object from the Level Editor screen. The pop-up menu from the backdrop object can be seen in Figure 11.17.

OBSTACLE

You can change the way that other objects on the screen will interact with a backdrop by turning on or off the menu options here. There are four options:

No

This option means the backdrop object will not be an obstacle to active objects. You will not be able to detect a collision with an active object when this option is turned on.

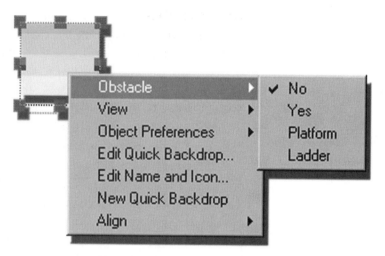

FIGURE *The Backdrop Object pop-up menu in the Level Editor.*
11.17

Yes

This option means it will be possible to detect a collision with an active object. You must test for a collision with a backdrop object in the Event Editor and insert a stop action.

Platform

This option means that the backdrop object will act as a platform for active objects controlled by platform-type movement. This is not the same as the Obstacle option because you will not be able to detect a collision from an active object that has been assigned a platform-type movement.

Ladder

This option will treat the backdrop object as a ladder when you are using a platform-type movement.

For those animated objects that have a relevant animation sequence, the animation will automatically be changed when they are climbing a ladder. If not, you could change the animation via the Event Editor. We discuss Active-Actions-Animation later.

EDIT PICTURE

The Edit Picture option allows you to change the appearance of the back-drop object using the Picture Editor. We will look at this in the next chapter.

NEW OBJECT

The New object option is available for both backdrop objects as well as active objects, and it means that you can produce another object that looks exactly the same as the original object, only it exists as either a backdrop, quick backdrop, or an active object. You can then place this object on the Level Editor screen and, although it looks exactly like the original backdrop object, it takes on all the qualities of whichever object type that you selected. We used this in the last chapter, if you will remember, to create the walls that were indestructible and destructible.

NEW QUICK BACKDROP OBJECT

This is only available from the menu of a quick backdrop object. It produces a clone of the original, but with a different name, one up in numerical order.

For example, if you created a quick backdrop object and it was the first one that you had produced in that game, The Games Factory would call it Quick Backdrop 1. If you cloned that object using this method, even though it would take on all the same parameters as the original object, it would be called Quick Backdrop 2.

NOTE

This differs from using the right mouse button to lay down multiple copies of the same object. Using that method results in producing genuine clones with the same name. If you made a change to one, that change would occur to all of them.

Resize

Resize allows you to resize your object by using the pick points on the box that will appear around the object.

Align

This option will correctly align your backdrop object. You can push it up against the left-hand or right-hand edge of the playfield, or center it horizontally using the Horizontally option. You can align it against the top or bottom, or center it vertically using the Vertically option from the menu.

SPECIAL OPTIONS FOR QUICK BACKDROP OBJECTS

The reason that there are two different types of backdrop objects is that for many purposes, it is only necessary to produce a block of color, or a gradient of color.

For example, to produce a plain black backdrop, it is very easy to simply select a block color for a quick backdrop and then stretch it to fit the screen, rather than go into the Picture Editor and fill a picture. Simple structures, like platforms and ladders, are very quick to produce.

You have several options within the Quick Backdrop Editor, as shown in Figure 11.18.

FIGURE *The Quick Backdrop Editor.*
11.18

Solid

The Solid option will fill your object with a solid color, selected from the palette.

Mosaic

The Mosaic option will take you to the Picture Editor. We will discuss this more in the next chapter.

Gradient

The Gradient option will produce a smooth gradient from one color to another. To use this function, click the Gradient button, then click the From button. Now choose your first color from the palette. Then click the To button, and select the second color from the palette. You will see a smooth gradation of color from one to another. You can change the orientation of the gradation using the Vertical and Horizontal buttons.

Pattern

The Pattern option uses a crosshatch to grade the colors from one to another rather than smoothly fading the color.

TEXT OBJECTS

Only the options related specifically to text objects are described in this section. All the other options available have already been described for the majority of the other active objects. You can see the options we describe in the pop-up menu in Figure 11.19.

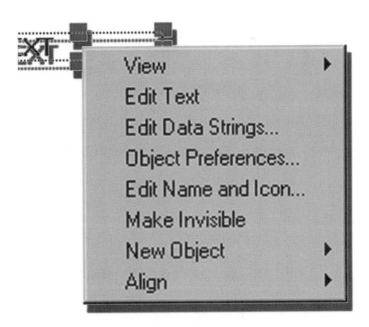

FIGURE   *The Text pop-up menu.*
11.19

Text objects are used to put text on the screen. You can use them for instructions, comments, end of game displays, or just about anything where you need to place text on the screen. There are some texts already in the object libraries, but you will no doubt be wanting to make your own.

To make your own text objects, select the Create New Object icon from the toolbar at the top of the Level Editor screen, then click the Text icon. The mouse pointer will be replaced with a cursor. You place this cursor at the point where you want the text to start.

You will also have a dialog box, which is where you select your fonts, and size and color of text, as well as the justification style you want to use (See Figure 11.20).

FIGURE   *The Text Options dialog box.*
11.20

Selecting a Font, Size, and Color

Clicking the Font icon will take you to a dialog box where you can choose the size, style, and font that you want to use for the text in your text object, as shown in Figure 11.21.

To change the parameters, simply click each text box. All the text boxes have scroll bars so that you can view all the options available. The Sample box will give you a preview of the style you have chosen.

The Color Selector

This option is merely a shortcut to changing the color of the text via the Font Editor, and brings up a palette from which to choose the text color.

Left Alignment

When you have more than one line of text, this option will align it all so that each line starts evenly from the left-most margin.

Center Align

This option will align all the text centrally, so the length of the lines will be mirrored about a central line.

FIGURE   *The Text Formatting dialog box.*
11.21

Right Align
This option aligns all your text to butt up against the right margin.

Import
This option allows you to load up .txt files and place them into your text object from disk, rather than typing them into the window. This allows the creation of text in a word processor where things like spell-checking and organized storage of the text can take place.

Edit Data Strings...
The Edit Data Strings... option allows you to have one text object used to display several different paragraphs of text during the game. When you select this option, you will be presented with a dialog box like the one in Figure 11.22.

This screen shot was taken with three paragraphs entered: "One paragraph," "And another," "And the last one."

You can edit or clear the selected paragraph, or change its order, using the up and down arrows on the right of the dialog box.

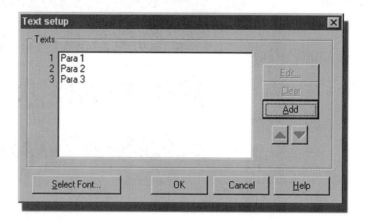

FIGURE *The Edit Data Strings... dialog box.*
11.22

You can add more paragraphs using the Add button, which then takes you to a text box where you enter the text for your new paragraph.

On the left of each paragraph is a number. This number is used to identify the paragraph when you display it in the Event Editor.

For example, an action you could insert under the text object on the Event Grid would be Display paragraph 1, which, in this case, would display "One paragraph" on the play area during a game.

Once you have placed your text object onto the play area, you will be able to right click it to produce its menu and edit it as you can the other active objects.

These were the most common active objects in TGF, and the ones you will be working with the most. In the next chapter, we will look at asset creation using the Picture Editor and Animation Editor. These tools will round out your ability to make your own games and productions with TGF.

12

WORKING WITH PICTURES AND ANIMATION IN TGF

I n our final dealings with TGF, we are going to look at the way you create and manipulate assets for your games. Some of the most useful tools for the game developer that come with TGF are buried in the Animation and Picture Editors. These tools make it easy to import and deal with your assets in the game, and they offer functions for animation that previously required you to manually work in another application like Photoshop, such as copying, rotating, and other tedious operations.

First we will look at the Animation Editor.

The TGF Animation Editor

Animation is a word that still strikes fear in the hearts of many who want to develop games, but TGF makes animation a lot easier with this tool and some of the features it contains. For example, if you have an animation of a creature facing one direction and want to make it walk in the opposite direction, you can click one button in the Animation Editor and create a new animation of the creature walking in the opposite direction. We will look at that function later in this chapter.

There are two methods to edit or create an animated object using TGF:

1. You can go to the Level Editor and open a library of objects from the pull-down bar in the menu, and then pick an object from the Object Shelf on the left of the Level Editor;
2. Or you can create a new active object using the New Object icon on the toolbar at the top of the screen.

See Figure 12.1 for the two methods of accessing an active object.

Only active objects can be animated from the Animation Editor.

NOTE

For this exercise, we will open an active object that already exists to analyze how the tools have been used to animate it. As we do this, you will see the steps required to create your own animated object. An animation can often be done using one image or a few versions of one image.

Start by opening a new blank game, going to the Level Editor, and then opening the Dragon Flight game library with the pull-down menu.

Now that the objects are on the left-hand bar, select the dragon object and place it in the middle of the play area of the Level Editor screen.

Right click the object and this will pull down a menu of options. Move the pointer to the Edit animation... option and click the left mouse button.

You should now have a screen similar to Figure 12.2.

CHAPTER 12 WORKING WITH PICTURES AND ANIMATION IN TGF   231

FIGURE *The pull-down menu for libraries of objects and the New Object icon.*
12.1

FIGURE *The Level Editor with only the dragon object on it.*
12.2

Some of the things you can do with the Animation Editor are: change the name of your animation; run a preview of what it actually looks like when all the images are run together; create a different animation depending on the direction your character is moving in; or create a different animation for any situation your character may get into, such as climbing, running, etc.

NOTE

To select all the frames of an animation, use the Alt+A keyboard shortcut. This will allow you to move or delete a whole sequence of animation at one time. You can also hold the Ctrl key to select multiple animation frames, and you can hold the Shift key to select all animation frames in between two selected frames.

Let's explore this screen a bit more (See figure 12.3).

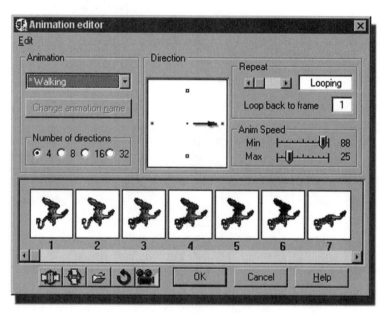

FIGURE *The main screen of the Animation Editor.*
12.3

ANIMATION SPEED

At the top right of the window are the controls for the speed of the animation, as well as the number of times it will repeat itself before it stops (See Figure 12.4). You can select Looping by moving the Repeat slider below 1 with the arrow pointer. This will repeat the animation sequence over and over.

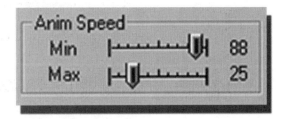

FIGURE   *The animation speed control on the main screen of the Animation Editor.*
12.4

You can also change which frame number the animation loops back to in the Loops Back to Frame box. This could be used to deal with a longer animation of which you only want to play certain parts. Say you are working with an animation of a man getting up from a crouched position and then running away. You may only want to play the first couple of frames of him being crouched down, then loop the animation back to the running sequence only for the running portion of the animation.

NOTE

For some animations, there are two sliders for the control of speed. There are only two controls for when the object would normally be moving; e.g., the walking animation of a character. If the character was stopped, then there would only be one slider, which controls the speed of the animation regardless of movement.

Minimum speed

This controls the speed when the character is not moving. Setting this to zero will halt the animation when the character is not moving; having it set higher will have the animation running all of the time, which may look unrealistic if your character is running frantically without moving!

Maximum speed

This controls the maximum rate of the animation when the character is at full speed. Note that the rate of animation will be proportional to the speed of the character, in between the Minimum and Maximum settings. To create a realistic running action, you may need to change the Maximum setting to a similar value as a character's speed across the screen.

For example, if you were to set a character's movement speed high and the animation speed low, it would appear as though the character was being dragged across the screen. If you had the animation speed high and the actual movement speed low, it would look as though the character was trying to run fast on an icy floor.

ANIMATION DIRECTION

This is a very useful feature that can seem hidden at first. If you look at the Direction box you will see that when you click a different direction square of the Animation Direction Clock Face, you will have the option of creating a different animation for each direction the character may move (See Figure 12.5).

FIGURE *The Animation Direction Clock Face.*
12.5

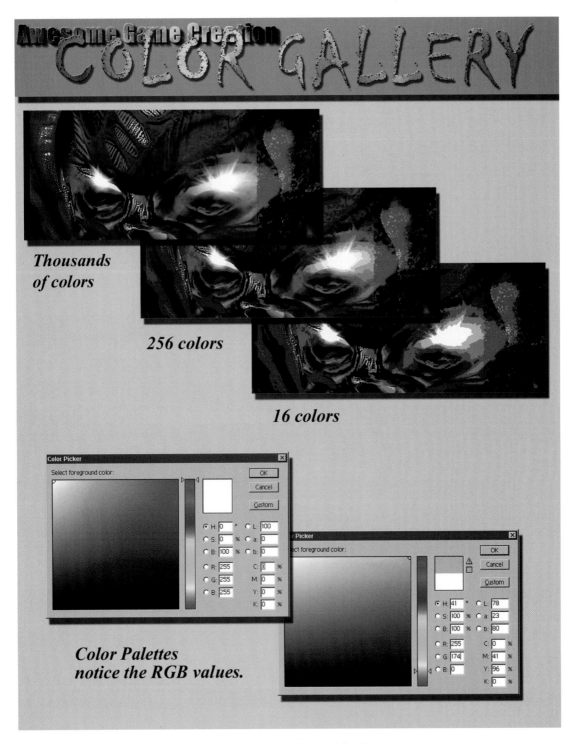

Awesome Game Creation
COLOR GALLERY

Thousands of colors

256 colors

16 colors

Color Palettes notice the RGB values.

Images from Part One of the book.

Awesome Game Creation
COLOR GALLERY

*Creating a ghost using a
transparency mask and opacity*

Creating a ghost in an image using techniques from the book.

COLOR GALLERY

Awesome Game Creation

A high color image

SHOOTING STARS

256 color reduction

16 color reduction

A high color image reduced to various color modes.

*Games made with
The Games Factory*

Games made with The Games Factory in this book.

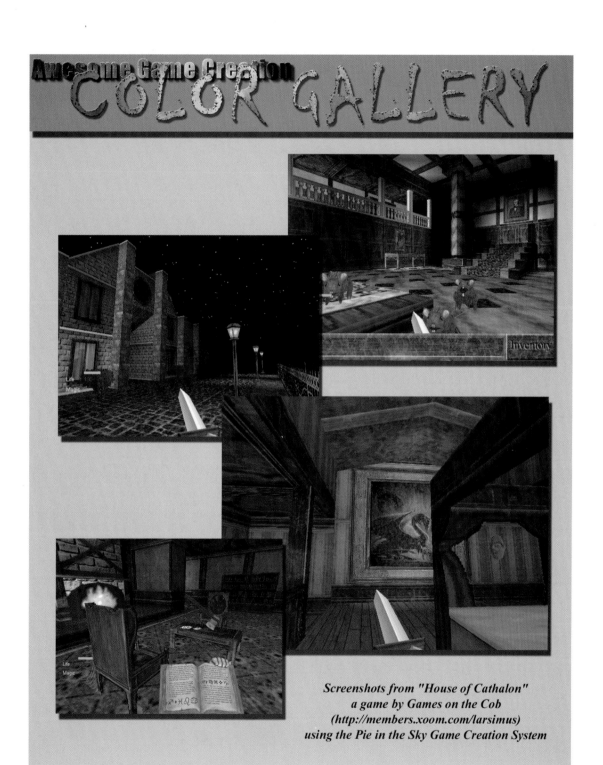

Screenshots from "House of Cathalon"
a game by Games on the Cob
(http://members.xoom.com/larsimus)
using the Pie in the Sky Game Creation System

A 3D Game made with the Pie GCS

Awesome Game Creation
COLOR GALLERY

The 3D RAD Interface

0050600

3D RAD	Current project: UFOATTK (53 elements)	
Editing Camera	Ed MoveHere Info B	Open Project (F1)
Light (ambient)	Ed MoveHere Info B	Save Project As (F2)
Light (directional)	Ed MoveHere Info B	Load Resource (F3)
Scenery (visual)	Ed MoveHere Info B	Save Resource (F4)
Scenery (ground)	Ed MoveHere Info B	Clone (V) · Delete (Del)
Scenery (volume)	Ed MoveHere Info B	Group (G) · Ungroup (U)
Ufo A	Ed MoveHere Info B	Collisions Map (M)
Ufo B	Ed MoveHere Info B	Test Project (Space)
Bombing Ufo C	Ed MoveHere Info B	Build Self-Executable (X)
Spot Light	Ed MoveHere Info B	Options (F9)
Spot Light (source)	Ed MoveHere Info B	Tools (F10)
Bomb (handle)	Ed MoveHere Info B	Register 3D Rad
Bomb (counter)	Ed MoveHere Info B	
Bomb (1)	Ed MoveHere Info B	
Bomb (expl. fire 1)	Ed MoveHere Info B	

U.F.O. Attack

FIVE MINUTES!

We just spent five minutes to make this action game level sample!

PROCEDURE

We used pre-made elements from the 3D Rad resource library

We added a player controlled tank and three intelligent U.F.Os to the scenery

Then we assigned the IR Rockets to the tank and the bombs to one U.F.O. Yes, characters automatically detect and use any weapon!

Finally we enabled collision processing for the elements (rockets/U.F.Os, tank/bombs, etc), and added minor details like counters and indicators.

The 3D Rad engine did all the rest!

Understand all basic concepts in just a few minutes, by following the quick-start tutorial (see help file, 3drad folder), and enjoy the creative power of 3D Rad!

F1, F2 - view mode
F, V, C, B - tank controls ALT - fire

©1998 Studio Biplane
http://www.3drad.com
3D RAD
CLICK FOR MORE

0004500

HEALTH

The 3D RAD interface.

COLOR GALLERY
Awesome Game Creation

Textures by Nick Marks on the ROM

Textures on the CD-ROM in this book.

Various 3D Games made with The Pie GCS.

For example, if you look at the dragon animation for Dragon Flight, you can select the walking animation from the scroll list and you will see that on the clock face, the 3 o'clock and 9 o'clock positions have smaller solid black *x*'s, which indicate that an animation is assigned to those positions. So when the dragon moves backward, a different animation will play. To add realism here, you can have the dragon go slower and fly differently as it goes backward. In other words, you can have up to 32 different animated sequences for the walk direction of a character. While 32 directions will look smooth, it will also be a real resource hog on your machine and is overkill for most purposes. A standard platform game has only four animations for walking.

NOTE

An easy way to create several different directions from one animation is to click the Create Other Directions By Rotating This One button. This will copy and rotate the current animation and will likely turn your objects upside down for some of the directions. But you can correct this using the controls we discuss next.

Number of Directions Radio Buttons

You can select the total number of different directions or animations by clicking one of the buttons shown in Figure 12.6. Obviously, the higher the number of different directions, the smoother will be the turning effect. This is particularly useful for race-car movement, but four different directions will be fine for a platform character.

FIGURE *The Number of Directions radio buttons on the Animation Editor window.*
12.6

You can manually fill the other directions using Cut, Copy, and Paste from the Edit pull-down menu (on the Animation Editor). It is recommended that you use Copy and Paste; otherwise, you will simply move one frame to another location rather than copy it.

MANIPULATION ICONS

These icons (See Figure 12.7) are used to manipulate all the frames of the animation being displayed on the Animation Editor screen. Be careful when you use them, since you may mess up your animation. The View Animation icon is safe, since it merely previews the whole sequence of images together and shows you what your animation looks like when running.

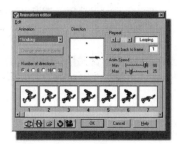

FIGURE *The Manipulation icons on the Animation Editor window.*
12.7

Horizontal Flip

The Horizontal Flip function reverses all the images from left to right. This is useful when you have a character going one way and you simply want to turn all the frames to face the other way. This saves a lot of time and effort. An example of this is shown in Figure 12.8.

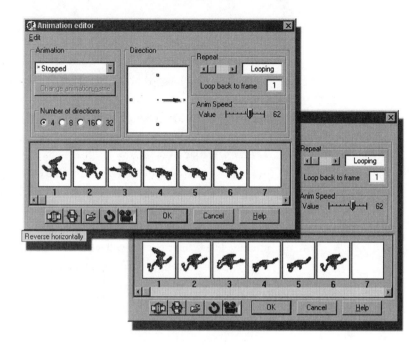

FIGURE *An example of an animated sequence being reversed using the Horizontal Flip*
12.8 *function.*

Both the Action Point and Hot Spot will also be moved when you use this function.

NOTE

Vertical Flip

Like the Horizontal Flip function, this function turns all the images upside down. This is useful when you have created several new directions from your original animation, and some of the sequences are the wrong way up. You can even use this to make a character walk on the ceiling. This also moves the Action Point and Hot Spot as well.

IMPORT

Import is a very important and useful function that grabs one or more graphic images from the disk and loads them into the Animation Editor. Then you can manipulate or process them in the Animation Editor.

You can load images stored as PCX, LBM, GIF, TIF, or BMP formats. You can even load FLC and FLI files, but beware: These files are normally very large, since they contain many images — usually more than 50 separate images — and will therefore use up large amounts of memory and storage space.

NOTE

Capture Style

Once you have entered the Import function, you will be asked to select a drive and the types of files to look for, which can be any of those described above. Once you have selected the file that you want, you will be asked to select a Capture style. This decides the method by which you grab one or more images from the file you are looking in.

Transparent Mode

Transparent mode will make the background color of the images that you pick transparent, rather than the actual color on the original image.

For example, if the background color of the images that you select is red, and you have Transparent mode on, instead of pasting them with a red background, The Games Factory will paste them into the Animation Editor with a transparent background. If Transparent mode is off, then the background color for the frames you grabbed will be transferred as well. So, if the background color was red, then it will be pasted into the Animation Editor as red, as shown in Figure 12.9.

FIGURE *The images in the Animation Editor with the transparent and non-transparent*
12.9 *backgrounds.*

Box Image Mode

Box Image mode imports a series of images from a disk using a single operation. Box Image mode is ideal for creating animation sequences.

NOTE

The format and layout of this image file is important to the capture procedure. The first point in your picture should be set to the color used by your background (usually zero or transparent). The second should hold the color of your box (usually 1). Each image should now be surrounded by a one-point thick box.

Box Image mode grabs all of the images that are within boxes — the selected areas that you have defined with the mouse — and pastes each boxed image into its own animation frame, in order, from top left to bottom right.

If, for example, there are ten boxed images on the screen, and you drag a selection area that completely encloses nine of them, but only half crosses the tenth, only nine of the images will be taken. If Box Image mode was off, one image comprising the entire contents of the selection area would be taken and pasted into only one animation frame.

Full Window Mode

Full Window mode will grab the whole area inside the Capture window (not just inside your selection area) and paste that into your animation frame. This only produces one frame of animation, comprising the entire contents of the window.

NOTE

If you have Box Image mode on at the same time you try to use Full Window mode, all the boxed images in the window will be grabbed and treated as separate frames of animation.

CREATING DIFFERENT DIRECTIONS

As mentioned above, the Animation Editor allows you to quickly and easily create many different directions from only one animation direction. Be aware, though, if you have several animation frames and 32 different directions, you will be using a lot of memory space. Also, it literally just turns your object around. So if you start with an object that faces to the right, when it is rotated to the left, it will be upside down.

Let's look at a frame of animation and then copy it to fill several frames, creating an animation.

Creating and Editing a Single Frame of Animation

You should still be in our new game file and in the blank Level Editor, with only the dragon object on the playfield. Right click the dragon active object to bring up the pop-up menu, then select the Edit Animation option to enter the Animation Editor.

When you are in the Animation Editor, click the middle of frame number one with the right mouse button. This will pull down a menu. Select the Edit Frame option. You can also double click the frame to automatically pop up the Picture Editor.

Once you are in the drawing screen, or Picture Editor, for the animation, you can decide the color, size and, shape of your animation frame. We will talk more about the Picture Editor later in this chapter.

In the Picture Editor, you can modify each frame individually to suit your own requirements. To save you from laboriously copying each frame, you can return to the Animation Editor and use the following commands, which are selected from the menu produced when you right click the frame you want to modify.

Adding Animation Frames

You can create most animations easily by creating several frames that are slightly different from one another, based on one original image. When they are run quickly together, they will give the impression of fluid movement. Whether you are starting from scratch, or using one initial frame, it is far easier to copy each frame and then modify it as you go along, than it is to draw each image for each frame, or modify each image by hand in a paint program.

First, click the first frame of your animation with your right mouse button, and then select the Insert option. This will insert an exact copy of your first frame into frame number two. You can also do the same thing using the left mouse button. Simply select the image that you want to copy with the left mouse button, hold the button down, drag the image to the frame you wish it to be copied to (in this case, frame number two), and let go of the button.

You can enter the Picture Editor for that frame and modify it slightly. When you are ready, you can insert a copy of that frame into frame number three, which you can then modify further, continuing the process until you have a finished animation. You can check on your progress at any time by using the View Animation icon.

Resize Zoom

The Resize Zoom option allows you to automatically create several frames of animation that will gradually shrink or grow in relation to the frame that you start off with. When you select the Resize Zoom option, you will see a dialog box that looks like Figure 12.10.

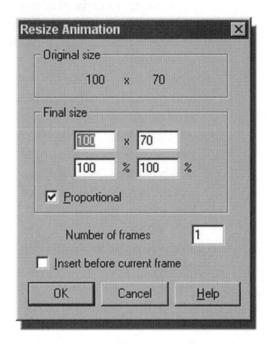

FIGURE   *The Resize Zoom dialog box.*
12.10

This option was used to create the fireball powerups for the Dragon Flight game. We will recreate the fireball animation here.

Start by opening a new and blank game file. Go to the Level Editor, click the New Object icon in the toolbar, and then select the New Active Object option. Now you will see the Create New Active Object Editor.

Double click the first blank frame and go to the Dragon Flight directory. From here, select the fireq.bmp image file, and then capture it. Click OK and then place a copy of the fireball on the play area. Notice how it does not move.

You may want to create a quick backdrop object, make it solid, and choose the color black. This will give you the full effect of the animation we are creating.

NOTE

Once you have the fireball on a black field, right click to open the Animation Editor. Right click the first frame and select the Resize Zoom option. Now you will be in the Resize Zoom window, as shown in Figure 12.10 above.

Under the Original Size heading of the window, the size of the frame that you are zooming from in pixels is displayed. Under the Final Size heading, you can select the size of the frame that you want to end up with. You can either enter the actual size of the X and Y dimensions of the final frame (i.e., the number of pixels wide and high that the final frame will be) or you can enter a percentage ratio. For example, 50% would shrink that particular dimension by half.

If the Proportional radio button is selected and you change any of the values, then the other dimension will be changed proportionally. For example, if you changed the width to 50%, then the height would also be changed by 50%. With the Proportional radio button deselected, you can change the dimensions independently.

The Number of frames option allows you to select how many frames will be between the original image and the grown or shrunken final image. The higher the number, the smoother the effect will be.

The Insert before current frame option will grow/shrink the object before the current frame. For example, if you had selected the first frame of an animation to shrink by half, and you were using ten frames to do so, which you inserted before the current frame, then when you had finished the process, the first frame would be the smallest, with each of the next ten frames getting gradually bigger until you arrived back at the original frame.

You can also perform the function both before and after the image so it appears to shrink and grow, rather than simply shrink then reappear the same size, then shrink again.

Rotate

The Rotate option can be used to insert several frames of animation that gradually rotate either clockwise or counterclockwise from the initial frame. You can choose the number of frames used to perform the rotation, ranging from 4 to 32. Obviously, the higher the number of frames used, the smoother the rotation effect will be. The rotation frames will be inserted after the initial frame.

Morphing

The Morphing function allows you to change one frame into another, allowing for stunning transformations. You can use this function to make a human face morph into a monster or a space-ship smoothly change into another spaceship, rather than simply having the images snap from one to the next. You may well have seen advanced versions of this technique in Hollywood movies. Now you can do it on your PC!

To morph an object, you simply need to set up the Animation Editor with the first image in frame one and the "morph to" image in frame two. Right click the first image and you will be taken to the Morph Editor, as shown in Figure 12.11.

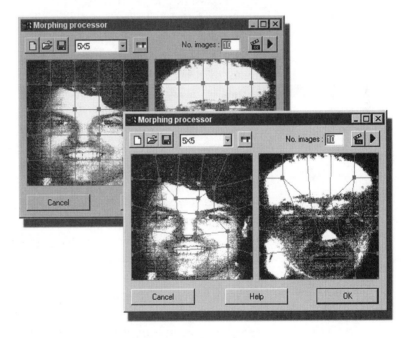

FIGURE   *The Morph Editor before and after adjusting the morph points.*
12.11

The easiest way to do this is to select your second (destination) object first, enter the Animation Editor, select the frame you want, copy it using the Edit function from the Animation Editor (top left), then exit the Animation Editor.

Now select the first (start) object, enter the Animation Editor for that object, and paste the finishing frame after the frame you want first. You may have to enter the Edit mode and deselect the Remove all option, which will remove all previous animation frames if you try to paste a new frame into that animation sequence.

NOTE

This function works best when there is only one frame for the original object. If there is more than one frame, delete the redundant frames so that you are only left with the start frame and the finish frame. You can leave part of the original animation if you want, but bear in mind that the morphing part of the animation will not start until the original animation has run. This can also use a lot of memory.

Using this Morph Editor screen, you can select the number of frames used to morph from the original frame to the final one. This is done by clicking the No. Images box. The more frames that you have, the smoother and more realistic the end result will be. However, this is also time-consuming and uses a lot of memory. By default, The Games Factory uses ten frames, which is a compromise between smoothness of the effect and speed of execution. You can also choose the definition of the change in the grid box at the top of the Editor (by default, set to 5 X 5). Having a higher number here will raise the number of fine changes that are made in between each frame, although again, be aware that a very high definition combined with a large object will take a long time to do, and may use up lots of memory.

The icon actually starts the whole process off. When it has finished you will be presented with a whole new animation strip, morphing smoothly from the first image to the last. I used this function for the dragon wings to give the wings a nice blur effect as they moved. This was also easy, since I had two images of the dragon — wings up and wings down — rather than ten separate images.

Use of the Morph Grid

You can change the color of the Morph Grid using the icon, which you may find very useful, depending on the color of the images that you are morphing. The grid is used to define common points between the two images that you want to move. The grid is composed of a number of "elastic bands" that you can stretch to fit various strategic points on the objects that you are morphing.

For example, if you were to morph from one face to another, you would stretch the grid so that

each point corresponds to an eye, nose, edge of mouth, etc. Make sure that the same grid point on the other object is used to correspond to the same feature. For example, if the point one from the left and one from the top is placed on the eyebrow on the first object, the very same grid point (one from the left, one from the top) must be used on the eyebrow of the second object, even if it means stretching the point right across the image window.

NOTE

Try to ensure that you do not get grid points "crossing over" each other, since this will spoil the effect.

SETTING THE HOT SPOT OF AN OBJECT

The Hot Spot is an invisible handle, or anchor, used to drag your images around on the screen. It is used as a reference for the X, Y coordinates of your object. Each image can have its own separate Hot Spot. As a default, when you create a new active object, the Hot Spot is automatically positioned at the top left corner of each image (See Figure 12.12). You can, however, move it anywhere you like.

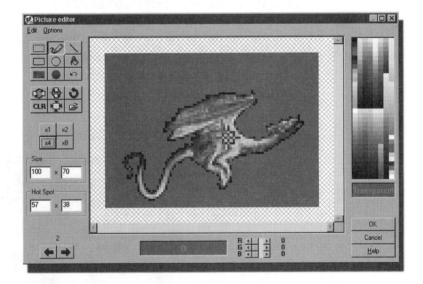

FIGURE   *The Hot Spot on an object.*
12.12

You can view the Hot Spot by going to the Options heading and selecting the Show-Hot Spot option. Try to position it centrally if your object is going to have several different directions; otherwise, it will 'jump' when you change direction.

SETTING THE ACTION POINT OF AN OBJECT

This is the point where things like bullets are fired from objects. If, for example, you had a large spaceship with a gun mounted aboard, you would want to set the Action Point to the end of the barrel of the gun. This means that this is where your bullet would first appear. You can show the Action Point by going to the Options heading and selecting the Show-Action Point option.

The Hot Spot and Action Point can look the same, so double-check the menu to be sure the right option is selected.

NOTE

THE PICTURE EDITOR

The Picture Editor is used for creating your own animation, background objects, icons, and quick backdrop objects. Because many of the features are identical for all these types of objects, they are summarized in this chapter.

We have already visited the Picture Editor, but Figure 12.13 shows the Picture Editor window for your reference as we go through the specific functions of the editor.

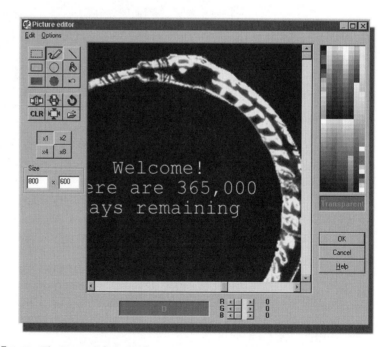

FIGURE *The Picture Editor window.*
12.13

In the center of the screen is the drawing area where you will be drawing/editing. If the area is too large to fit in this screen, you can either scroll around it, zoom in or out using the zoom control buttons, or maximize the window using the Window Manipulation icons on the top right of the window.

Zoom Icons

On the left of the screen are four buttons: x1, x2, x4, and x8. These simply mean that you can view the image at one times its size, twice its normal size, etc. This function does not actually change the size of the image, only the viewing of the image.

The Color Palette

To the right of the screen is the Color Palette, which allows you to pick and choose the colors you draw with. You can select whether you draw with the transparency color as well as a solid color.

You draw with any normal color by clicking a color on the palette. The selected drawing color is shown in the box immediately below the drawing area, with the letter "D" in the middle of the box. If you click the color, you will see the color of this box change.

To draw with the transparency color, click the Transparency color box below the Color Palette. When you draw on your picture, you will, in effect, be making that portion of the image clear, making them transparent in the game.

The transparent areas of an image are denoted by a specific color (See Color Masking in Chapter 2), which is normally green-blue, but you can change this by using the Options menu at the top of the Picture Editor.

Go to the toolbar of the Picture Editor, click the **Options** menu and then select the color you like. Any color you select to be transparent will be transparent, or "show through," for the entire image. This is very useful for leafless trees, or large animated objects that have gaps in the structure. Anything in the background will be seen through the transparent areas.

The drawing tools

The drawing tools include the most-used feature of the digital artist — Undo. Also included here are the Pen, Fill Bucket, and solid and outlined forms and shapes.

The Pen Tool

This tool is used to either draw one pixel at a time or to draw a freehand line. Note that if you are drawing a freehand line and you move the mouse too fast, you will end up with a dotted and broken line.

To create a grainy effect, use this tool with several different colors and go over the drawing area very fast. This will lay down pixels of color spaced apart. Doing this over a gray background with brown, black, and white will give the effect of a brown, stone tile.

The Line Tool

This lets you draw perfectly straight lines using the mouse. Simply click the point where you want the line to start, hold down the mouse button, and notice that when you move the mouse it "drags" a line behind it. Move to the other end of the line (where you want to end the line), let go of the mouse button, and you will have drawn a line between the two points.

The Rectangle and Filled Rectangle Tools

These drawing tools allow you to draw rectangles and squares more easily than by trying to construct them out of four separate lines. After selecting the icon you want, place the pointer at the place you want the top left corner, press and hold down the mouse button, then drag the rectangle to the shape you want.

Performing the same procedure and using the Filled Rectangle icon will do exactly the same thing, except that it will produce a solid rectangle of the color you have selected.

The Ellipse and Filled Ellipse Tools

These tools allow you to create ellipses and circles, both filled and empty.

To create a circle, select the icon you want, and place the mouse pointer at the place where you want the center of the circle. Holding down the mouse button, move the pointer *away* from the center of the circle. You will notice that an ellipse is drawn in proportion with how far you move the pointer from the center point. Moving sideways from the center will stretch out the ellipse horizontally; moving it up (or down) from the center will stretch it out vertically.

The Fill Tool

The Fill icon fills an area with a solid block of color. The area to be filled should be completely enclosed. If there is a gap of even *one* pixel, the color will "leak" out into other areas of your frame.

The Undo Tool

This tool is used to undo the last step that you performed. It will only undo the last thing you did, though. Clicking it again will undo what you have undone, in effect redoing it!

The Selection Tool

This tool defines a rectangular block, which can be cut or copied from your image. When it is selected, you can move the mouse to where you want the top left corner of your block and then drag a box down around the area you want. If you make a mistake, click once on another part of your image and try again.

Once you have selected a block, you can save it into memory using the following commands from the Edit menu (top left of the Picture Editor):

Cut. The original area will be cut out and replaced with a block of whatever the transparency color currently is.

Copy. This tool will do the same thing as Cut without affecting the original image.

Paste. After you have grabbed your area, you can copy it onto the image using the Paste command. This provides you with a rectangular box which can be used to position your block over the image. You can fix it in place with a single click of the mouse button.

Horizontal flip

This tool reverses your image from left to right, just like a mirror.

Vertical flip

This tool turns the whole image upside down.

Rotate

This tool allows you to rotate the whole image very finely. When you select this function, you will be asked to select an angle by which to rotate the image. The arrow will point to the current direction. Simply click a new direction on the clock face, then click OK, and the image will be turned by the angle you have specified.

Clear

Caution! This option will clear the image window, so you can start from scratch. If you accidentally clear all your work that you wanted to save, you can undo the Clear command from the menu, or with the Hot Key combination Ctrl Z.

CAUTION

Shrink

The Shrink tool removes any unnecessary transparent border areas from the image, reducing its size. This is very useful for saving memory and will speed up your game by removing overly large images, trimming them to the minimum required.

Import

This tool loads an image from disk. This works very similarly to the way the Import command works in the Animation Editor, except in the Picture Editor, you will be working with individual images.

MOVING ON TO 3D

Well, we are at the end of our time with TGF. In this section, you learned a lot and applied many of the technologies and techniques we discussed in Part 1. As you continue to work with TGF, you will discover many uses for it and many creative ways to use TGF that have simply not been thought of yet. In the next chapter, we start a new part of the book, Part 3, Making a 3D Game. You now have a solid foundation and will be ready to step easily into the next dimension of game development.

P A R T

3

AWESOME 3D GAME CREATION

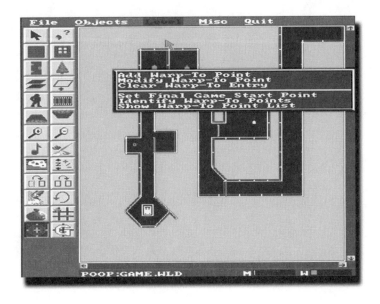

13 INTRODUCTION TO GCS

The GCS is copyrighted commercial software. Copying, distributing, or selling this program without written permission from Pie in the Sky Software is illegal.

INSTALL · Cancel

I n this part of Awesome Game Creation, we will make a 3D game using The Pie 3D Game Creation System. We will refer to it as GCS from here on out. Special thanks goes to Pie in the Sky Software (See Figure 13.1) for releasing the GCS free to the readers of this book. Please visit their Web site for information on the forthcoming version of GCS.

Pie in the Sky

FIGURE *The Pie in the Sky logo.*
13.1

The best thing about GCS is that it allows you to create an entire game without doing any programming. You will see how much you can do with GCS using your own imagination to create 3D games that are comparable to *Doom*. Although you will not be doing any programming, things will get a bit more complex as we start to look into the third dimension. We will learn a new set of tools and techniques. But the basis you have from the first two parts of the book will serve you well, since you will still be using the vocabulary and processes you have already learned.

While there are several 3D game development tools on the market, I chose the GCS package for the following reasons:

- It was FREE! Totally free. The good people at Pie in the Sky Software released the GCS free only to the readers of this book. They did it in large part, to support the community, but also because they have a newer, more powerful version of the GCS coming out. I hope you check out the screen shots on their site.

- It has a large and helpful online support community. Hop on over to www.GCSGames.com and join the mailing list.

- It was the easiest to use. The last thing you need is to be overwhelmed by a lot of complexity when you are first learning the process of building a game. Once you get your feet wet with GCS, you can move on to larger and more complex 3D game systems and learn them more rapidly. This product has been designed from the ground up with the intent of making an easy-to-use program for nonprogrammers to use, so the program is very much mouse- and graphically based.

- It required a minimal system to run it. There are still a lot of older systems in schools and homes out there and it is frustrating to use tools and games that require increasingly higher specifications to run an application. GCS has very minimal requirements since it is a DOS application. It requires a 386 or better computer with a VGA graphics card.

- You can freely sell and distribute the products you create with it. A barrier to many is not only the cost of an application, but the cost of selling products made with a specific application. With GCS, there are no complex license agreements or royalty payment schedules.

Installing GCS

To install this version of the Pie 3D Game Creation System, put the CD-ROM from the back of this book into the drive, find the GCS folder, and click the Setup icon. The installation procedure will install everything you need and will also include an Uninstall option.

The first step in the installation procedure is to agree to the terms of using the software, as shown in Figure 13.2.

Next you have to select the location where you want the software installed. It is usually a good idea to use the default directory, since many of the examples and instructions given later in this part assume a normal installation.

Then comes the critical step — validating your software. You only have to do this once, when you first install the product, and not every time you run it. Type in the information in the validate.txt file (in the GCS folder of the CD-ROM), as shown in Figure 13.3.

Terms of Use

FIGURE *You must agree to the terms in order to use the software.*
13.2

Owner Validation

FIGURE *The Owner Validation screen.*
13.3

The last step asks you if you want to have a shortcut to GCS in either the Windows Start menu or on the desktop (See Figure 13.4). It is a good idea to select at least one of these options so you can find GCS later on. Whatever you select here, later you can delete, move, and create shortcuts in Windows.

Start Up Options

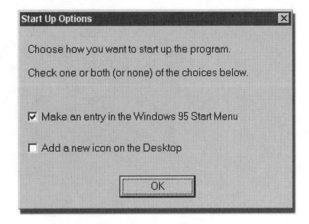

FIGURE   *This option will create a shortcut on your Windows Start menu or your desktop.*
13.4

The Main Parts of GCS

The Pie 3D Game Creation System consists of the following three main areas:

1. Layout Editor
2. Paint program
3. Smooth-scrolling 3D game engine

THE LAYOUT EDITOR

In the Layout Editor (commonly called the Map Editor or Mapping Utility), you will handle almost all aspects of creating your games. You will work on one game level at a time, from a top view, using the toolbar icons to do the most common functions like copying, rotating, placing walls, etc. In addition, there are standard pull-down menus across the top of the screen.

NOTE

There are some similarities to TGF in the terms and terminology we will be using, but in GCS, you are laying out a 3D world in two dimensions and can't see one entire dimension. You will have to mentally visualize what you are laying out, whereas with TGF, you could see exactly what was going into your game.

From the Layout Editor, you can click **test level** to drop into the 3D world to test your layout and game play. The Layout Editor interface can be seen in Figure 13.5.

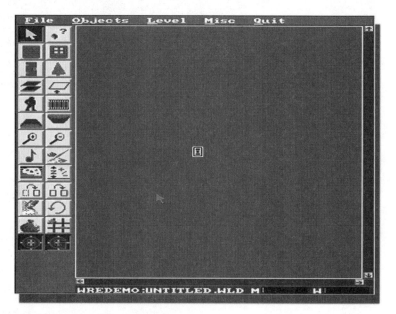

FIGURE *The Layout Editor interface.*
13.5

GCS PAINT

The second part of GCS is the Paint tool for creating or retouching images for GCS games. The GCS Paint tool has a set of features which allow the important control of image resolutions, contrast, and pixel-blending. If you have trouble with these concepts, you should go back to Part 1 and read up on Image Manipulation. The GCS Paint interface can be seen in Figure 13.6.

FIGURE   *The GCS Paint program interface.*
13.6

THE GAME ENGINE

Ironically, you can't see the most important part of GCS — the game engine. And that is what we want in a book that has "no programming required" on the cover. The term *game engine* is a rather generic term that is used to describe the core application that runs a game. This engine is the software that runs when the user is playing the 3D game — you never actually touch it in GCS. You simply build the levels and create the game on one end, and then the engine runs it on the other. Following are some of the things the engine does:

Visibility Testing. The engine must decide which parts of the world are visible and which are hidden behind other walls or objects and not to be displayed on the screen. Visibility testing is not only important for how well the game looks, but also how well it operates.

If this testing was not done, you would see objects through walls and other errors. Undoubtedly, you have played a game where you could see an object through a wall or other similar errors. If the testing was not done and objects were displayed, even if you did not see them, it would affect the speed and performance of the game. As you work with GCS, you will begin to get a feel for how you have to balance the amount of art you use, and you will become more sensitive to the way the engine will handle your world when it runs it.

Sounds. The engine must also play sounds and control the volume and the way the sounds are played back. As we mentioned previously, sound is very important and can make or break the "spell" of your game, or how immersed the player is in the game experience. A game engine typically will mix sound for depth and direction, on cue, and juggle the number of sounds, prioritizing the order in which they are played and canceling them, if necessary.

Collision Detection. The engine must also make sure that the player and the enemies can't walk through the walls. It must detect a collision between the two and dictate the behavior of the objects that have collided.

Artificial Intelligence and Behavior. It must control all the moving objects in the game, from the burning torch to the sliding doors, up to the enemy characters with their AI and very complex behavioral routine.

And all of the above — and a lot more — must be done in "real time," or as you are playing the game. And those are just a few of the things a game engine must do and still keep up a decent frame rate.

NOTE

You will often hear the term frame rate, referring to games — especially 3D games. Frame rate is quite literally the rate at which frames are created and displayed on the computer screen — just like the frames of a movie. One critical difference, however, is that when a movie's frame rate suddenly drops to half speed, the film itself is playing half speed. In a game, when the frame rate drops, the world is still moving at the same speed — you are just seeing half as many frames. So the movie you are watching is still running at the same speed, but it is choppy.

Figure 13.7 is an illustration of traditional film frames and the frames of a computer game — if they could somehow be put on film. Keep in mind that while film is static, or the way it is forever, a game's frames can potentially be different each time. Figure 13.7 is only to illustrate the effect of a frame rate drop in a game.

GCS First Look

Once you have GCS installed on your system and running, you need to be aware of a few unique things about GCS. When you edit levels and build games using GCS, you will be in a full-screen DOS window, but the game will be a 100% Windows game. We will discuss a few specific things you will need to be aware of so you won't lose any work when switching between the DOS editor and the Windows engine.

Film Strip

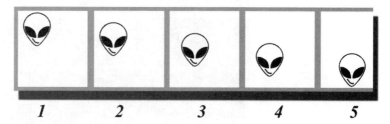

1   2   3   4   5

Game Frames

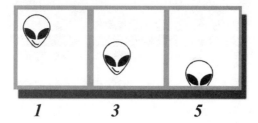

1   3   5

FIGURE *Film frames and computer game frames during rate drop.*
13.7

RUNNING GCS

Click the Start button on the lower left of your Windows screen. Then choose the Programs menu, and select the GCSWE group. From that group, choose GCSWE to start up GCS.

A DOS window will open on your Windows desktop that says "Type any key to start the DOS editor" as shown in Figure 13.8. At this point, the world editor is ready to start. Just press the space bar or any key to begin.

When GCS first runs, you will be prompted to select a project file from Windows, as shown in Figure 13.9. This is a good time to remind you of the distinction between a project and a level.

The Project folder is where all the level files are stored. Once you select the WRDEMO project, you can store multiple level files within it.

Click the Show List button, and then click WREDEMO. Click the Accept button and open the WREDEMO project.

A red box will pop up, warning you that the colors are going to change on your screen. This is normal and is only GCS adjusting itself to use the same colors that the WREDEMO game will use.

NOTE

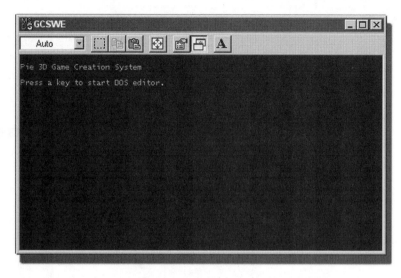

Press a key to start DOS editor.

FIGURE *The DOS window that pops up when you start GCS.*
13.8

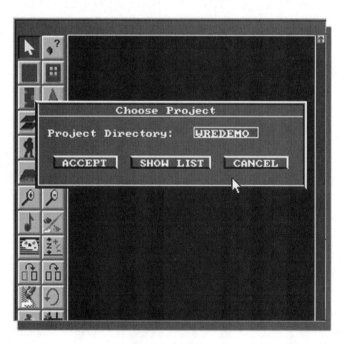

FIGURE *The Select a Project window.*
13.9

THE GCS MAIN SCREEN

Now you should be looking at the GCS main screen (See Figure 13.10). There are pull-down menus across the top of the screen, icon buttons on the left side of the screen, and the viewport window in the middle. There is one white layered square in the center of the screen. You are looking at an empty level named UNTITLED.

Just as a word processor usually opens a document called untitled when you start it up, GCS starts with an untitled level as well. To load the demo level we want to look at, click the File menu in the upper left part of the screen and then select Open Level.

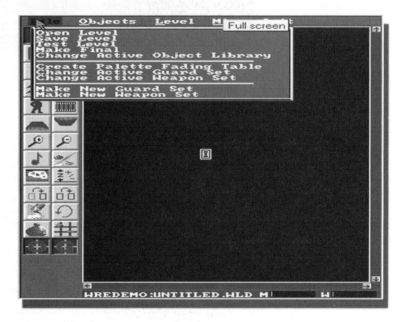

FIGURE *The main screen of GCS.*
13.10

Now you are back to the box that says Choose Project. The word *WRE-DEMO* should already be typed for you, so just click the Accept button. Next you will be asked to select a level from a scrolling list. Click INTRO.WLD, then click the Accept button (See Figure 13.11).

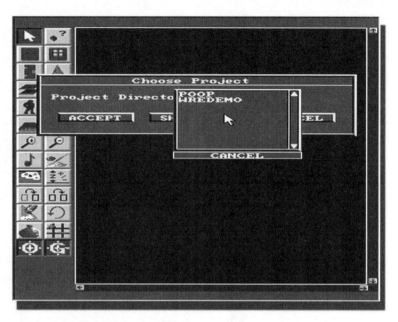

FIGURE *Opening a level that is stored in a project folder.*
13.11

When the level opens, you will see in the viewport a top-down view of the level, like the plans of a house. The yellow lines are walls and the blue squares are inventory items. The little yellow squares are enemy guards.

View Mode

If you want to see what each wall actually looks like, click the icon on the top row that looks like a question mark and a little box (See Figure 13.12). Then move the mouse pointer around on the level. As the little white line jumps around from wall section to wall section, a picture of that wall appears in the lower left of the screen. This is one way around the fact that you are looking down on your level and can't actually be in it to see the third dimension.

Now click the right mouse button to get out of View mode. Notice that when you are in View mode, the question mark icon stays depressed, letting you know that you are in View mode. When you click the right mouse button, you will leave View mode and enter Selection mode. The big arrow icon is now depressed. You can use the arrow keys to scroll the top view around. The keypad + and - keys zoom in and out.

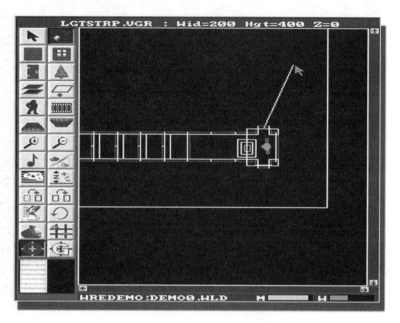

FIGURE *The View mode while looking at the walls in your level.*
13.12

Test the Level

Before you modify the level, it would be fun to jump into the 3D world to see this level in 3D. To do this, pull down the File menu, and select Test Level. A red box comes up, asking if you want sound. If you have a sound card, click Yes.

Then another box comes up that asks if you want to test the game in God mode. God mode is a term used to mean that the player is impervious to damage. This can be useful for testing purposes. Click either Yes or No.

Now the screen should change back to the Windows desktop as the Windows game engine starts up. Since the game engine will use Microsoft's Direct X/Direct 3D, the program must select which Direct X drivers and which video mode to use. The first time you start up the game engine, the program will try to choose the drivers and best mode automatically. Sometimes it cannot, and you will be prompted to make selections. Once those are answered, you should have a dialog box on your screen with your name and address on it, like Figure 13.13.

In the next chapter, we will talk in greater detail about choosing drivers and screen resolutions for optimal performance.

NOTE

FIGURE *The Options screen that you see the first time you run the 3D engine.*
13.13

In addition, there will be three buttons available. Right now you want to click the Test 3D World button. The 3D game engine will then start, and you will be in the 3D world. If you get an error message, or something else goes wrong, the problem is probably quite easy to fix. See the Troubleshooting section in Chapter 19.

Entering the 3D World

When you first run GCS, it will choose a screen resolution for you that will most likely work, but may not be the best your video card can do. If the 3D world screen appears to be low-resolution, don't worry. Later we will look at how to run and fine-tune your setup.

NOTE

Once you are in the 3D world, you can move around with the arrow keys or the keypad arrow keys. Press the space bar to fire your weapon, or press the Escape key to exit the 3D world.

F1 puts up a Help screen. The mouse can also move you — move it left or right to turn; move it down to go backwards. You can press the left mouse button to fire the weapon, and the right mouse button moves you forward at a fast rate. If you press Escape, or get killed, the 3D world will end. Depending on how the game play ends, the game engine may exit altogether, or you may just return to the desktop, with the game engine program open on the desktop.

Returning to the Level Editor

When the game play ends, you get back to the world editor by finding the DOS prompt window which will be blank or have the words "Press a key to start DOS editor" in it. If the title bar at the top of the window is gray, click it to make it the top window again, and then press the space bar to go back into the Level Editor.

NOTE

*Whenever you come back to the game engine after testing a level, the Level Editor will always be waiting in a DOS prompt box. It is **very** important that you restart the Level Editor rather than start up GCS again using the Start menu (or desktop icon), because then you will have two copies of the GCS Level Editor running, which will lead to a crash, and possibly the loss of your level. If you are not sure if the Level Editor is already running, look on your task bar at the bottom of your Windows desktop. A GCSWE button with the MSDOS logo on the left means that the Level Editor is already running. Click it to bring it up so you can press the space bar and return to the Level Editor.*

Now that you have poked around GCS a little bit and you have it installed on your system, let's look at getting it to run as effectively as possible on your system. In the next chapter, we will look at and learn more about the technology behind the GCS 3D game engine and your computer.

C H A P T E R

14

RUNNING THE GCS GAME ENGINE

GCS 3D Game

pie in the sky

Game Creation System

Game Creation System

The GCS is copyrighted commercial software.   Copying, distributing, or selling
this program without written permission from Pie in the Sky Software is illegal.

INSTALL   Cancel

Now we will spend an entire chapter looking at all the options there are for setting up and running the GCS 3D game engine on your system. Simply setting up the engine to run at its best on your system can get complicated, with all the options presented and all the different technologies referred to, so we will look at those options and technologies in great detail here. Don't let this chapter overwhelm you. Maybe the best way to use this chapter is if you really need (or want) to use it to speed things up. If you are happy with the default settings of GCS and it runs well on your system, then skim this chapter and come back to it later.

NOTE

The mose important thing for you to learn from this chapter is the details of working and moving between the Windows and DOS environment.

As we have said, GCS is a Windows program; however, the rest of GCS is based in DOS. When we switch from the DOS Editor to the Windows 3D Engine, we are switching operating systems — literally making a big move in terms of how we should work on our computer. In The Games Factory, we were always in the same territory and no matter how complex things were, we could always do a consistent operation to return to the main screen, or exit the application. In GCS, we have to always be mindful of the fact that we are jumping from DOS to Windows. You will always have to start the Level Editor from the DOS box or window, and you will return to it this same way. If you ever close the DOS window instead of going into the Level Editor to save your work, you will lose your work.

Starting Up the GCS Windows Engine

Run GCS as we reviewed in the last chapter: From the Start menu click Programs, select the GCSWE group, and then select the file GCSWE (See Figure 14.1).

Use the Level Editor commands to open the WREDEMO project, and then open the INRTO.WLD level. Go to the File menu and select Test Level. At this point, the DOS Editor will close and the GCS Windows Engine will start up.

NOTE

If the Windows Engine does not seem to start up after ten seconds or so, it is possible that Windows decided to start the game engine behind your DOS prompt window, in which case you must bring the window to the top by minimizing the other windows on your desktop.

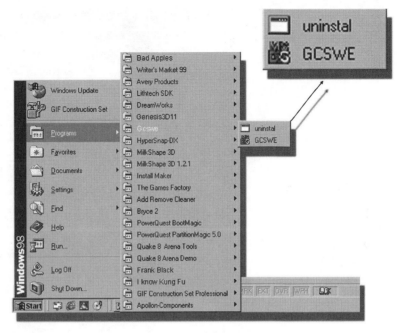

FIGURE   *Shows the Windows Start menu and the GCSWE group.*
14.1

IMPORTANT DOS BOX NOTES

The DOS boxes, when running in Windows, can operate in two modes — full screen or in a window. The Level Editor always runs full screen. What we are concerned with now is how the DOS prompt box looks when the Editor halts temporarily to display the message "Press a key to start the DOS Editor." If your DOS prompt box is running in full screen mode when displaying that text message, press Control + Esc (hold down the Control key and then press the Escape key) to return to the desktop. Then right click the MS-DOS prompt task bar button on the bottom of the screen to change the screen properties to Window. (See Figure 14.2).

If you are still in full screen DOS mode after selecting Test Level, and you are staring at a message that says "Press any key to start Level Editor", then you will need to change a setting in the properties of the DOS prompt box as described above.

FINDING THE BEST SETUP FOR THE 3D ENGINE

When you run GCS for the first time, you will see a Windows option, window as shown in Figure 14.3.

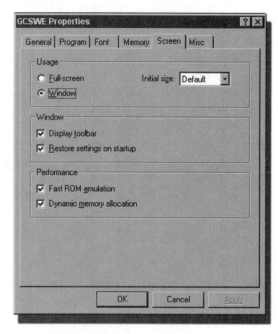

FIGURE *The GCS Properties — Screen tab.*
14.2

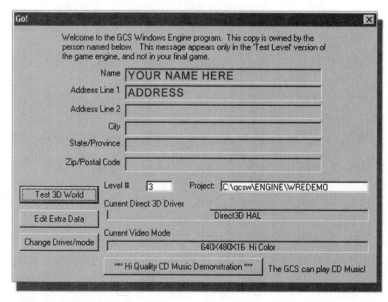

FIGURE *The Windows option window that comes up the first time you run the GCS 3D*
14.3 *game engine.*

Let GCS select what it thinks is best and run the world.

Once you enter the 3D game world, you will notice a yellow number on the upper part of the screen. This will appear only when testing levels, and not in the final game. This is the fps number, or frames per second display. Anything over 10 fps is pretty good, and the game will play pretty well. If the fps dips below 5 fps, then it may start to get a little difficult to control your motion. We want to get this number as high as possible.

We will look at all the options available to you to make the GCS game engine run at maximum efficiency on your system. You should try a variety of video modes and 3D Direct (D3D) Devices to find the combination that works the best for you.

A good portion of game design and development — level editing, specifically — is spent balancing the technology, user base machines, amount and size of the art and world geometry, and other factors to make the best game possible. Some games call for huge worlds with little geometry, while still others may call for small rooms with high-detailed art and models.

NOTE

The Setup Options

The Pie 3D Game Creation System relies heavily on Microsoft's Direct 3D. This means Microsoft developed a set of pre-written code libraries that perform certain functions which are repeatedly used by games — drawing geometry, handling the textures and art, etc. When any of these redundant tasks are needed by GCS, they are "called" by the program. Since GCS relies on D3D, we will be looking at the several different modes of operation, full screen modes, and the best setup for all these options. The GCS Windows Engine tries to make these selections for you, when the game is run for the first time, based on what is most likely to work. However, in some cases, the program cannot decide which is the best, or perhaps you want to experiment to get the best performance.

Selecting a DirectDraw Device

To select a DirectDraw Device start up GCS by using the Test Level command on the WREDEMO Intro level.

When the game engine dialog box comes up with the three buttons, choose Change Driver/Mode. This button just makes the dialog box go away so you can have access to the program's pull-down menu. You can now change the Direct Draw Device (See Figure 14.4).

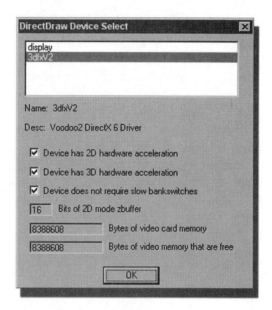

FIGURE *The Select DirectDraw Device Menu.*
14.4

Go to the File menu of the game engine, and choose Select DD Device. On most computers, there is only one choice, so it should be rather simple. But the selection box does let you see some of the features of your video card, such as whether or not it has hardware acceleration, and how much video RAM Direct X thinks the card has.

On computers which have a Piggyback-type hardware accelerator, there will be two choices. Some 3D accelerator cards, such as the Diamond Monster and Monster II, connect to your old video card without replacing it. If you have such a device, you will see more than one listing in the DD selection box. One will be your old un-accelerated card, usually called Display. The other will be the accelerated device, called 3DFX or something else. Choosing the accelerated device is usually the way to go. The only time you might want to try the Display device, is if you are having troubles with the accelerated device and you want to try slower software emulation to isolate a problem. You can also use this option when testing your game to see how it will run on a slower system without 3D hardware.

When you make a change to your DD Device, your options for the other choices will probably change as well. Therefore, after you change your DD Device, you must then change the D3D Device and the video mode.

NOTE

Choosing a Direct 3D Device

Microsoft's Direct 3D Device allows you to select from a list of 3D drivers. Even though the game engine tries to make the best decision for you automatically, you may want to change it. Go to the File menu and choose Select D3D Device. The number of options you get here depends on your computer and your video card (See Figure 14.5).

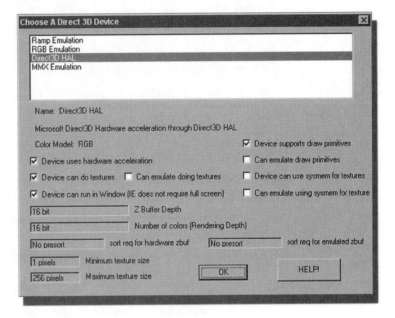

FIGURE *The Select D3D Device menu window.*
14.5

Following are the most common choices:

HAL. This device represents your 3D acceleration hardware. This will usually (but not always!) be the driver which will give you the best performance. However, it is also the most likely to suffer from incompatibilities. If something seems wrong with the graphics, give the RAMP driver a try. Also, some 3D accelerators (like the S3 Virge) will actually run slower than the software drivers. If the software drivers mentioned below work fine, but the HAL driver fails, send an e-mail to Pie in the Sky Software, with your exact video card, and they will try to resolve the incompatibility.

RAMP. If you choose this device, all the 3D graphic computations will be done in software, and your hardware acceleration will not be used. Microsoft seems to be phasing out the RAMP driver, and if you have Direct X 6.0 or higher installed on your machine, it might be better to try the MMX or RGB software drivers if your HAL driver will not run correctly.

MMX. This device uses multimedia extensions built into your CPU to accelerate the 3D graphics. If you have no HAL driver, try both this driver and the RAMP driver to see which one works better for you. If you have Direct X version 6.0 installed, the MMX driver may also use the 3D acceleration.

RGB. This device is a software 3D graphics device like RAMP and MMX. Try this one out and compare it to RAMP and MMX on your system.

The full screen video modes that are possible change when you change the D3D Device. Therefore, you will automatically go into the Video Mode selection box if you change your D3D Device.

Choosing Screen Size

Your video hardware has the ability to change the resolution of your screen, as mentioned in Part 1. If you remember, the more dots, the sharper the image; and the more dots, the larger the image, which takes more resources to display those images and more RAM and computer time to draw the 3D graphics. While high-resolution screens are great-looking, they may cause your computer to fail if it runs out of video memory or if it becomes too bogged down because there is too much information for the computer to handle. Images that have low resolution are block, but require less work from the computer. See Figure 14.6 for the Screen Size Selection window.

You will remember that screen resolution is measured in width and height. A screen with a resolution of 640 x 480 has 640 dots from left to right, and 480 dots up and down, the total number of pixels being (640*480=307,200).

We are also concerned with color depth here. The lowest number of colors which GCS can work with is 256. This is called either 256-color mode or 8-bit color mode. GCS can work with 8-bit color, but in some cases, the colors won't look exactly right. The best choice is probably 16-bit color. It gives you 65,535 colors, which is plenty for excellent graphics, and it only uses twice as much video RAM as 8-bit color.

The most common mode to use GCS in is 640 x 480 x 16, which means a 640 x 480 resolution screen with 16-bit color. Keep in mind the difference between the art and images for the game and the display mode. We are talking about display mode here.

NOTE

There are also 32-bit color modes, which offer 16 million colors, but in practice this won't look any different than the 16-bit color modes and it will use twice as much video RAM. If you have a video card with lots of RAM (12MB or more), this shouldn't be a problem, however.

FIGURE *The Screen Size Selection window.*
14.6

It is actually a bit of a mystery as to which video modes Direct X will make available. With some video cards, there are more than 50 modes to choose from, while on others there will be only three. Try to stick with the most common ones at first. The most likely to work are the following:

640 x 480 x 16

320 x 200 x 16

You can experiment with the other modes if you are inclined to, but working with the above common modes should cover your bases well.

NOTE

Although GCS will run in 8-bit color modes (256 colors), you may have trouble with certain colors being drawn incorrectly. The 16-bit color modes are better if you can use them. The 8-bit color modes have the advantage that they use much less video memory.

The top selection of the video mode list is the Windowed option. If this is selected, GCS will run in a window on the Windows desktop. In this case, the color depth is not adjustable from within GCS. If your Windows screen is set to 256 colors, then GCS will have to run in 256-color mode. If you really want to run in a window on the desktop, you can change the resolution and color depth by exiting GCS and the Level Editor, and then right clicking the desktop and choosing Properties from the menu. From there you can go to the Settings tab to change the main screen resolution and color depth (See Figure 14.7).

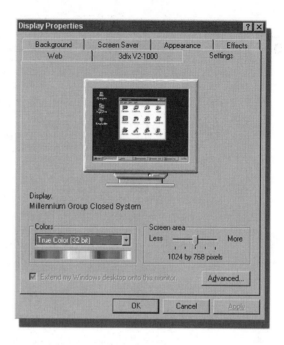

FIGURE *The Windows Properties dialog box with the Settings tab showing.*
14.7

NOTE

Using the windowed screen mode with 256 colors is not recommended. Direct 3D does not appear to do such a great job with the palette management, and most of your colors will be inaccurate. This appears to be a Direct X weakness because Microsoft's own demos exhibit this behavior when running windowed in 256 colors.

If Performance is Terrible in All Modes...

Since Pie in the Sky Software has made sure that the frame rate is decent on an old 120Mhz Pentium with no hardware acceleration, you may have a problem with your system if it is a better one than this and it still runs poorly, or you may have over-designed your game. The next suggested step is to consider a new computer or a 3D hardware card. The best bet is probably a new 3D card. If you are running an older Pentium class computer without a 3D card, you'll be surprised when you see how much it improves your performance. Of course, more RAM will help as well, as we discussed earlier in the book.

For a list of video cards that work well with GCS, see www.pieskysoft.com.

WINDOWS ENGINE GAME OPTIONS

When you test your level and the Windows Engine starts, you have access to a Options menu that allows you to make changes which affect the control of the game and the graphics quality.

To use these options during 3D game play, press and release the Alt key and then use the mouse or arrow keys to choose the option you want. When you press Enter or click the desired option, you will automatically return to the 3D game play. See Figure 14.8 for the pull-down menu of options.

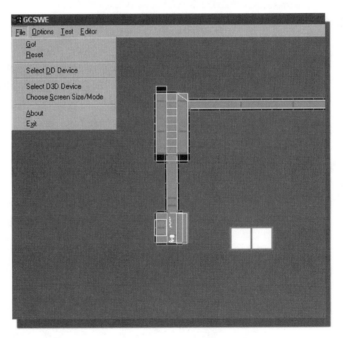

FIGURE *The Pull-down menu of options for the Windows Engine.*
14.8

Some menu options, including changing screen size or driver, will not operate unless you pause the 3D game first by selecting Reset from the File menu. To resume your game, select Go from the File menu after you are finished using the menu.

Horizon Bitmap

The game engine can display a horizon bitmap or a sky bitmap in the distance when you start using the Extra Features Editor. This option can enable or disable the horizon you have set. Turning it off can increase performance.

Wall Bumping (Collision Detection)

Ordinarily, walls are treated as solid by the game engine; i.e., you can not pass through them. But with this option, you can make the walls so that you are able to walk through them. Even though in the game you will probably want most walls solid, during the testing of your level it is convenient to turn off wall bumping so you can go directly through walls to get from place to place quickly.

Frames Per Second (FPS) Display

This option turns the frames per second display on and off (the yellow number in the upper left of your screen). Some people find the number very distracting when trying to see how the game will *really* look to the end user.

Correct Orientation

Leave this option off! This option was for the DOS game engine.

Bilinear Filtering

This option will do a smoothing operation on the pixels in your screen's image. This can make a level look much nicer, but on some video cards this can cost you significant performance; on many others it will have no measurable effect. Also, on some video cards this will tend to make dark outlines around the enemies and other shaped objects. So you will have to experiment to see what works on your card the best.

This option can be turned on and off before or during 3D game play.

Dithering Enable

Just like the above option, this can change the quality of your graphics, but at a potential price. Try turning it on and off, to see which way you like it better.

Object Presort

Some video cards (only some hardware accelerated ones) will draw black rectangles around enemies, objects, door frames, and other objects that use transparency. Turning on Object Presort should eliminate the problem, if it arises.

Brightness

If your monitor is too dark to see walls and textures very well, you can use this option as a last resort. It only works when you change the setting *before* you start up the 3D world. Many video cards today come with their own utilities for boosting brightness that work very well, so only use the GCS option as a last resort. It will increase the brightness, but at a price, since your colors will become washed-out.

Joystick

This option allows you to select or enable a joystick device. To calibrate your joystick, use the Windows control panel, and adjust the properties.

Mouse

This option allows you to select or enable mouse control. In the unlikely event there are two or more mice on your system, you can select the one you want to use with the Select option. You can also change the sensitivity in the x and y directions. You can hold down the right mouse button for forward motion, which is more convenient than walking forward by pushing the mouse forward.

STARTING UP THE 3D WORLD

After you have selected your devices, video mode, and the options that work best for you, start up the 3D world by going to the File menu and selecting Go. In the process of making all these choices, you will do this a thousand times.

Returning to the Level Editor

The Escape key will exit the game engine when you want to return to the Level Editor. If you are using a nonstandard mode (not 320 x 200 or 640 x 480), you may get asked if the video mode worked OK or not. This is so GCS can keep track of which modes don't work well on your system and remind you if you try to use it again.

When you exit the game engine, Windows should return you to a DOS prompt box, and there should be a message that reads "Press any key to start the DOS Editor." Now that you are returning from using the Windows Engine, press the spacebar to start up the Editor once again.

If you exit from the Windows Engine, and you don't return to the Level Editor like you would expect, and you don't see the level editor window on the desktop, then check the task bar that runs along the bottom of your screen. Each program that runs in Windows has a little block on the task bar, as shown in Figure 14.9.

🏁Start   ⬚ 🌐 🅰 🕸   💼 Microsoft Word - ch 14 ...   📦GCSWE   📦GCSWE

FIGURE *The Windows task bar and the running applications.*
14.9

One of those blocks should be your Level Editor. It is still running, but it is halted until you restore it to full screen by clicking the space bar.

If the window with the message "Press a key to start DOS editor" is on the screen, but it ignores your key presses, then probably that window is not the active window. Click the title of the window once with the mouse to make sure the window title is blue, not gray. Then try pressing the space bar again.

NOTE

Warning! Whatever you do — don't go to the Start menu to start up GCS again, if you still have a copy of the Level Editor running! This will crash your computer, and you may lose your level design! Make sure you don't already have the level Editor running, by looking at your task bar on the bottom of the screen before you try to start up a new one from the Start menu!

CAUTION

TIPS FOR USING GCS

Accessing the Menu When the Game is Running

If you are running the game engine in full screen mode, there is no mouse pointer. However, if you would like to access the menu, you can press and release the Alt key. The game play will halt and a menu will appear. After you make your selection, the menu will disappear, and the 3D game play will continue.

Some menu commands require that the 3D game be paused first with Reset on the File menu.

NOTE

Getting Back to the Desktop Temporarily

If you are in full screen mode, you can go back to the desktop while halting GCS, by pressing and releasing the Alt key, and then selecting Reset from the File menu. When you wish to return to the game play, select **Go** from the File menu. Sometimes this will fail, because Direct X cannot get control of the keyboard back.

Changing Screen Mode During Game Play

It is possible to change the screen mode during game play. First press the Alt key and release it to bring up the menu. Then select Reset from the File menu. This will stop GCS. Next select Choose Screen Size/Mode from the File Menu. Select a new video mode, then click the OK button. At this point, you can then select Go from the File menu to restart the 3D world where you left it.

Well, that was the whirlwind tour of probably the most tedious part of GCS. Now we can focus more on making the game world. While these aspects are a bit tedious, they are very important to the overall quality of your game — how well it looks and runs. The effort spent here will ensure that you can make a game that pushes the limits in terms of quality and performance. Further, knowing all the terms and technology described in this chapter will be very useful if you plan to move up to a more complex development environment in the future.

In the next chapter, we will look closer at the 3D Game World Editor.

CHAPTER

15

LOOKING DEEPER INTO THE 3D EDITOR

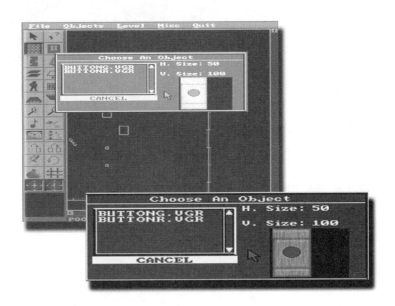

I n this chapter, we will take a closer look at the various options of the Level Editor. While there will be figures illustrating, you may want to start playing with the icons and changing a level around. This is often the best way to learn. If you do this, make sure to make a copy of the level first. Click the Save option in the File menu. But instead of just accepting the name level, you can save it as another name. Then feel free to modify it without the worry of losing the original level.

In general, the right click should get you out of most active functions.

NOTE

Level Editor

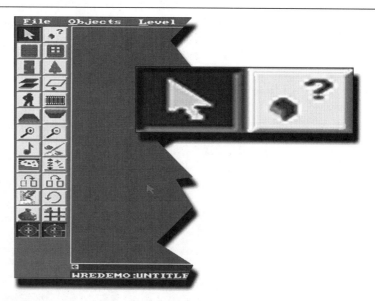

FIGURE *The main screen of the Level Editor and the Select and View icons.*
15.1

THE SELECT AND VIEW ICONS

The Select icon is the arrow button (See Figure 15.1). When you select this, you are ready to select objects from the viewport to move, copy, elevate, rotate, etc. This is the top level of GCS. This means that upon completion or cancellation of most commands, you automatically return to this select mode.

The view icon is the one with the question mark. When you click this icon, you go into View mode. Then, as you move around on the viewport, you can see what the walls look like by watching the lower left corner of the screen (See Figure 15.2).

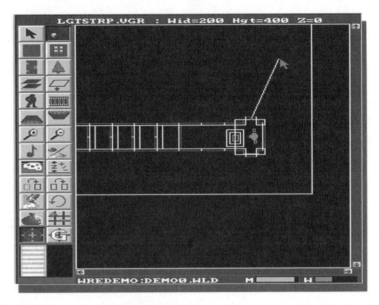

FIGURE   *The View mode of the Level Editor.*
15.2

OBJECT PLACING ICONS

You click these icons when you want to add a new object to your 3D level. The Object Placing icons can be seen in Figure 15.3.

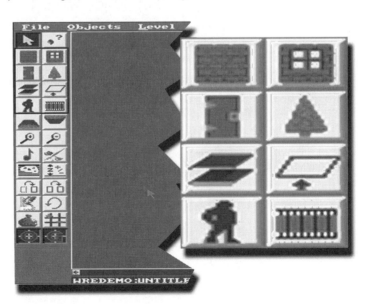

FIGURE   *The Object Placing icons.*
15.3

The **Brick Wall** icon adds walls to your levels.

The **Windowed Wall** icon is for walls that have black pixels. The black will be treated as clear, or invisible, in the 3D world (color masking). If you make a wall with a black rectangle in the middle, the wall will have a window cut out that the player can see through.

The **Door** icon is not really a placing icon. It operates on walls you have already placed. If you select a wall and then click this icon, it will assign to that wall the properties of a door. We look at doors in much greater detail in a later chapter.

The **Tree** icon is for placing stand-up objects like trees or lamps in your level. These are taken from a library.

The **Flat Squares** icon is for solid-color floor/ceiling polygons.

The **Wire Frame** icon is for placing platforms.

The **Person** icon is for placing enemies from a library.

The **Film** icon is for placing animated objects that you have already created and put into your library.

We go into much greater detail about these icons in a later chapter. Each of these icons has further options and properties that allow some really cool design control in your game.

MAGNIFY ICONS

The Magnify icons (See Figure 15.4) are for zooming in and out on your top-view layout. The + magnifying glass zooms in. The - magnifying glass zooms out. When you click one of these icons, you enter Magnify mode. Each left click zooms you in (or out) again. The location of your mouse pointer when you click the button is where the new screen center will be.

FADING TABLE ICON (FOG)

First the bad news — you must choose the color black.

Normally you would click this icon (See Figure 15.5) to set the fading color for this level, a color that your level will fade to as the light recedes. Choosing white would look like fog and choosing red would not work, but currently you have to choose black. With the DOS game engine, it was possible to change the color which the level faded to with distance, but this is not possible with the Windows game engine because of the limitations of Microsoft's Direct X/Direct 3D 5.0.

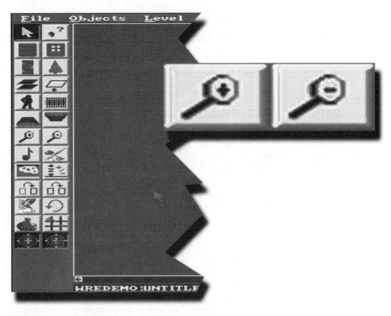

FIGURE
15.4   *The Magnify icons.*

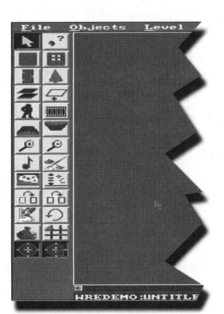

FIGURE
15.5   *The Fading Table icon — you must choose black.*

EDITING ICONS

These icons all perform their operations on items that you have selected while in Select mode. (See Figure 15.6).

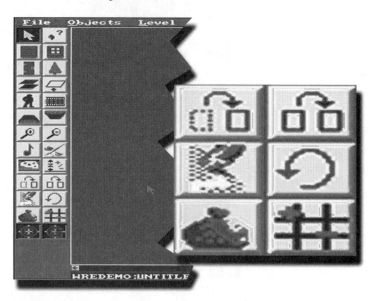

FIGURE *The Editing icons — objects must be selected to be affected.*
15.6

1. The top icon is the Set Elevation icon. This icon is for moving your walls up and down.
2. The next icon is for moving groups of objects.
3. The next icon is for copying objects. It works the same as the move icon, except that it leaves the original objects where they were, and makes a copy somewhere else.
4. The Eraser icon is for removing objects.
5. The Circular Arrow icon is for rotating groups of objects by 90 degree increments.
6. The Bag icon is not really an Editing icon. It belongs with the Object Placing icons. It is used for placing inventory items. As for why it isn't in with the Object Placing icons, when asked, Pie in the Sky defers to Ralph Waldo Emerson: " A foolish consistency is the hobgoblin of little minds." We will discuss Editing icons and inventory items later.

FLOOR/CEILING ICONS

Do not use these! These icons were for creating a floor or ceiling in the GCS DOS version, (See figure 15.7). The floor/ceiling capabilities of GCS have been greatly improved and extended, and now these buttons are obsolete. We will look at how to put down floors and ceilings later in the Extra Features Editor.

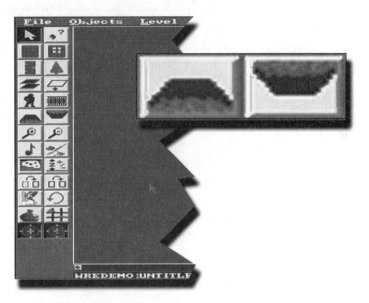

FIGURE   *The Floor/Ceiling icons - do not use these in the Level Editor.*
15.7

GRID ICONS

The grid will be covered in more detail later. The icon that looks like a tic-tac-toe board (See Figure 15.8) sets the grid spacing, usually 100, 200, or 400. This setting doesn't affect wall-placing grids, but it will affect grids for placing trees and other stand-up objects. It will also set the grid for the editing commands.

The O icon toggles the snap-to-object features.

The G icon toggles the snap-to-grid features.

MUSIC ICON

You can add music to your level by clicking the Music icon (See Figure 15.9). You can specify a suitable .midi file that exists in a directory, or there is a way to play .midi music off a CD. Later we will talk about making sound.

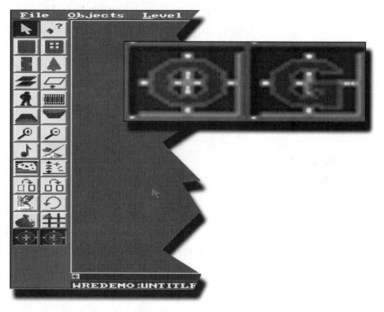

FIGURE *The Grid icons.*
15.8

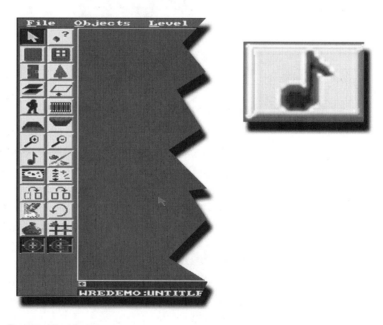

FIGURE *The Music icon.*
15.9

Now that you have been introduced to and looked around GCS (you even entered a 3D game world and then came back to the Level Editor), we can move on to the next step, creating game project files. This is important to understand so you will not be confused as to where certain files may be and how things work in GCS. You will prevent many problems from happening if you set up your game files correctly.

Creating Game Project Files

When you create new games in GCS, they are all kept in separate directories. These directories are called your project directories. Each project is an entire game and can have multiple levels. For example, you might have a project or game that features a haunted house and call it HAUNTED, and then have many levels like cemetery, floor-1, dungeon, and attic.

The first thing you do when you create a new game is to tell GCS the name of your project or game. A project directory will then be created for you. If you would like to start a new project, start from the DOS command line, and run GCS. The first dialog box that comes up asks you to select a project. If you want to make a new one, just click the name box, and make up a name for your new project that is eight or fewer characters. Then either press the Enter key, or click the Accept button.

NOTE

*For those of you not familiar with DOS, you are limited to **eight** or fewer letters or numbers in all of your file names.*

When you click the Accept button, GCS then creates a directory on your hard drive filled with files that the 3D game engine needs for the 3D world you are about to detail. This directory will have the same name as your project name. So if you made a project called myproj, then a new directory would be created. Assuming you installed GCS in the directory c:\p3dgcs, the full name of the project directory would be. c:\gcsw\engine\myproj.

Many files are put in this project directory. These include the picture files for your game's background, the damage indicator artwork, and so on. At the beginning, these files are stock, or default, entities. Once you have created your directory, you may edit these files to customize the game. We will look at how to do this in a later chapter.

Next GCS asks you to pick a palette for your new game. A palette is a set of colors. $rp9a.pal is the general purpose palette. For most applications, $rp9a will probably suit your needs.

In GCS, each set of artwork is kept in a separate directory on your hard drive. All the object libraries and enemy directories are specific to certain palettes, or color sets. If you tried to mix images from different palettes, then the colors simply come out all wrong, and the enemies, walls, or whatever, will come out looking like fluorescent soup. This is because GCS uses 256-color artwork for efficiency.

You will remember from Part 1 of this book that we discussed the various color palettes, and this is where you will need that knowledge the most. The images in GCS are not only limited to 256 colors, they are limited to the same 256 colors for the entire level. Pretty limiting, but it helps the engine run faster. While you are limited to 256 colors, the engine actually uses thousands of colors as it creates shades of the colors you have selected for your world.

You may want to think about your palette a bit before building all the artwork. Since you will be limited in colors and shades of colors, you will want to decide if you will use a lot of reds and oranges for a volcano, blacks and browns for a haunted house, or blues and whites for an icy level. This sort of planning and color scheming will allow all your artwork to have lots of subtle variation in color.

To keep artwork together that all uses the same palette, there is a separate master directory for each palette. The enemy directories, and object libraries are all kept in directories that are inside the master palette directory on your hard drive. Once you choose a palette for a project, there is no way to change it. Since you cannot change a palette without re-matching every piece of artwork in your game, it would always be easier to start a new project.

Your new palette directory name should appear when you click the Show List button when choosing a palette. Since your palette file has nothing in it, the first thing you must do is create a new weapon set, and new guard set, and a new library directory. All of these need to be in your palette directory in order for you to make a game that uses your new palette. Note also, that your new palette directory will have no artwork in it at all, so you will have to either copy some .VGR files into your newly created library file, and import them, or palette-match some from the other palette directories, and import those.

Once you have selected which palette you want to use for your project, you are asked to choose an object library. Unlike the palette choice, you can switch libraries anytime. Object libraries are just what they sound like. They are directories filled with artwork images. Object libraries also have a system for storing the sizes of objects.

Choose any library from the list. You can browse through the libraries in your palette directory easily, adding a wall from one library, and then switching to another. After selecting the library, you are left facing a blank world from the top view. The little box thing in the middle of the screen is the default player starting position, in the exact middle of the level.

GCS rejects a project with no levels. Therefore, when it creates a new project, it will create an empty level named UNTITLED. You can start editing right away. When you think you've created something you want to keep, use the Save button to save the level with a real name. You cannot save your level with the name UNTITLED, so make sure you give your level a new name.

PUTTING WALLS AND OBJECTS IN A LEVEL

All the trees, enemies, and wall pieces that make up the 3D world are called objects. Rooms and hallways must be made from fixed-length sections of textured wall. It is easy to predefine the sizes of textured walls or other objects, but that will be discussed later. The point is that doing your 3D layout is simply a matter of selecting the object you want to place, and then placing it.

You must have at least one solid wall in your level, or you will get an error message when you test the level. Be sure to place at least one wall section before attempting to run the game engine.

NOTE

Putting Walls Into Your Layout

Now we are ready to start laying out a test room. To get started right away, just click the Brick Wall icon. Then select a wall texture from the scrolling list. As you move the mouse over the items on the list (without clicking), pictures of walls will appear to the right of the scroll box. When you find one you like, click the name in the scrolling list. When you click the name, you are then in Place mode. The menu bar at the top of the screen goes away, and a text message appears, telling you to choose an anchor point for your wall. In addition, a grid will appear in the viewport to help you align your walls. As you move your mouse around on the viewport, you will be dragging your wall around. See Figure 15.10 for the Wall Selection menu.

Unlike other programs, you do not hold the mouse button down to drag things. As you drag the wall around, it will always hang in an east-facing orientation. You first must click to fasten the lower end of the wall to the grid. Now you will see another wall section is now there. It is following the mouse. It is attached to the first wall you put down.

NOTE

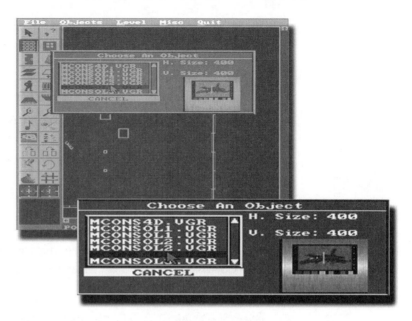

FIGURE   *The Wall Selection menu — notice the wall in the lower left.*
15.10

After placing a wall, you have the following three options:

1. Get out of wall-placing mode with two right clicks. This leaves your first wall, but cancels that second one that is pending placement.
2. Detach the new wall section with one right click. Then you are dragging it around, ready to place a new wall somewhere else in your level.
3. Choose a direction for the new wall, and click to make it permanent. After doing this, you have placed two walls that are attached.

When you are starting a new layout, you will want to make big rooms and hallways with all the same wall type. Thus, you would choose option three above. You can always go back later, delete a wall here and there, and replace it with another type for variation and customization.

Move Around in Zoom Mode

A thing to remember about Place mode, is that you can scroll up, down, or side to side by clicking either of the Magnify icons. If you want to move your view of your level, click one of the Magnify icons. The cursor will turn into a cross. Clicking the left mouse button will zoom you in or out, depending on which Magnify icon you selected. The + zooms you in, and the - zooms you out.

When you are in Magnify mode, the Magnify icons remain down. You can also use the cursor keys or the keypad + and - keys to zoom in and out. You can leave Magnify mode by right clicking the mouse. Then you will be put back into Place mode.

Putting Up Trees and Other Stand-Up Items

The Windowed Wall icon is used for walls that have holes in them, such as a wall with a window or a fence with a rough top. Placing these objects in your level is the same as placing the solid walls.

The Tree icon is for drawing stand-up objects like trees or floor lamps, etc. These are shaped objects that look the same from every direction. When you click the icon, you are presented with a list of object names (See Figure 15.11). Moving the mouse pointer across the list will show the images in the lower left-hand corner of the screen. Choosing one item puts you in Place mode.

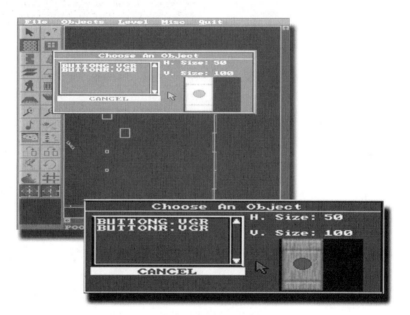

FIGURE *The Object Placement window.*
15.11

This Place mode is a little different, though. The direction doesn't matter for these stand-up items, since they always rotate to face you. Therefore, there is no reason to anchor one end first, and then swing it to the proper direction. These are called anchored sprites.

To place the stand-up objects, drag the square to the place you want, and click to place it. The square shows a rough representation of the horizontal width of the stand-up object. This is so you can judge its distance from walls. Once you click to place the stand-up object, another potential stand-up square appears attached to your mouse pointer. You can drag and place this one, or you can right click to get out of Place mode.

NOTE

You usually want to turn off the grid before you decide to click the Tree icon. When placing things like floor lamps, wastebaskets, and other things, the grid is usually more of a hindrance than a help. You can click the Grid icon to toggle the snap-to-grid feature on and off.

Solid-Color Horizontal Panels

The Pie 3D GCS can have texture-mapped floors and ceilings, and we will discuss those when we talk about the the Extra Features Editor. For the situations where you want to make a horizontal surface that is not a floor or a ceiling (like a tabletop), use the Flat Squares icon.

Click the tool icon that looks like two purple sheets suspended in the air. Choose a color from the color box that pops up. Click twice to specify the corners of the rectangular floor areas that you want covered. You can also adjust the elevation of this surface.

Platforms

Platforms are rectangular areas in the 3D world that sense the presence of the player. One of the most common uses of a platform is to raise the player when he steps on one. Another function is to use the platform as a trigger for a teleport device to another level. In fact, this is how most level-switches are implemented with GCS.

NOTE

The rectangular platforms are, by default, not drawn; they are completely invisible. Usually, they are placed right in front of tunnels or staircases. When the player walks up to the staircase, the game switches levels as if he or she had traversed the staircase.

As mentioned above, another common use is to raise the player. Let's say you create a box out of wall panels, and you want the player to be able to jump up on the box and stand there. Without a platform, the player would sink right down into the box instead of standing on top of it. The box needs to have a platform over it so that when the player is within the platform's boundary, his feet are lifted to the height of the platform's z value.

Creating a Platform

To create and place a platform object, you click the Wire Frame icon
(See Figure 15.12).

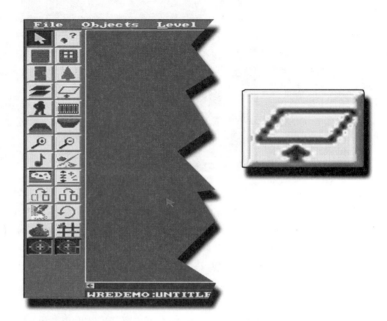

FIGURE *The Wire Frame icon.*
15.12

A dialog box comes up with some options. You can set the platform to be
visible. This actually just makes a floor polygon in the same place as the platform. If you choose to do this, you will be asked to pick a color. In addition,
you will have to choose the function of the platform. Warping to a different
level is a common one. If you select this, then you will have to know the entry
point number of the destination level. Don't worry if you don't know what an
entry point is at this point. We will discuss them later as well (See Figure
15.13).

Putting the Bad Guys In

Placing enemy characters is as easy as placing stand-up objects. You get a dialog
box of options for each enemy and when you are finished, you click the OK
button and you are put into Place mode. You are then asked to choose a direction for the enemy to face (north is toward the top of the screen). After you decide on the facing direction, you click where you want your enemy to be in
your level.

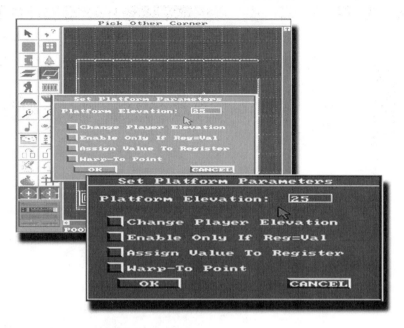

FIGURE *The Platform Options dialog box.*
15.13

You will usually want to turn the grid off before placing enemies. Otherwise, the Layout Editor may place your enemies in the middle of walls when attempting to align your enemy with the grid.

After you place them, the enemies can be copied, moved, and rotated like any other object, using the normal Copy, Move, and Rotate icons. However, there is a maximum number of 32 enemies on any one level.

As you learn more about the characters in GCS, you will be able to control how the enemies patrol (randomly or centered in one spot) and other behaviors by setting their parameters. Enemies will also notice players and start shooting and chasing them and other neat behaviors. You can also change their appearance by editing their artwork files. We will look at all these options later.

If you have not done so already, you may want to run a test on a level. Drag out a few walls, select one wall, and click the Door icon to assign the door properties to it. Go with all the default settings and then run your world. If you are unable to get your test level running, then you may need to go back and try the options in Chapter 14 on running the 3D game engine. It may not be set up properly on your system.

Once you are comfortable with that, turn to the next chapter, where we will start laying out a game level.

CHAPTER

16

MAKING A 3D GAME LEVEL

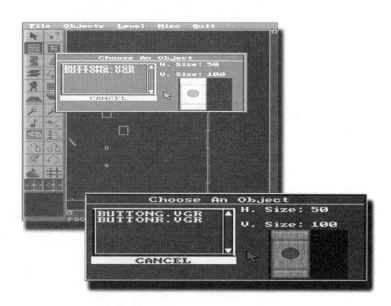

Laying out a good game level is really easy with GCS. In fact, you can lay them out in minutes. This chapter will take you through your first basic game level.

For this chapter, we will lay out the most basic of game levels. We will start by placing the player's starting point, then we will set up the walls that make up the hallways and chambers of our level, and then we will add a door or two. Finally, we will populate the level with the enemies. Once you have gone through this basic process, you will see that you will be able to make larger and more complex game levels that are almost endless, since you can attach them to each other for a large and complex game.

Designing The Level

First we will do a basic level where you enter through the front door (which will be sealed behind you), and then you will have to proceed through the level and kill a few guards and open a few doors to get to the last room.

PLACING THE FIRST WALL

Next we will select the Wall icon and this will bring up the Menu where we choose the art that goes on the wall we are about to place, see figure 16.1.

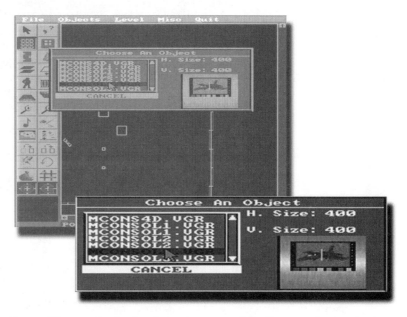

FIGURE   *The menu for choosing the art that goes on the wall you are about to place in*
16.1   *the game level.*

We will use this first selected wall for the outer walls of the level. Most of the level will have the same walls. I selected a mossy rock wall, since it will make the level look like it has been hewn out of solid rock on the outer walls. I selected a brownish brick wall for the inside walls, so the player will get the feeling that the base was cut out of the rock and the interior walls were finished in stone. This is also a design device to help the player feel orientated when wandering the level. I will use these two basic walls for most of the level, and you can start filling in the floor plan by laying out walls when you are comfortable (See Figure 16.2).

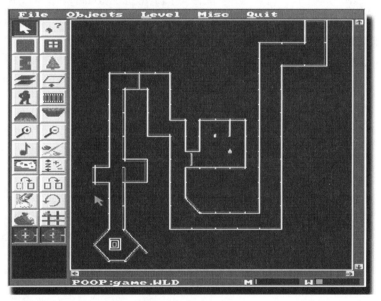

FIGURE *The floor plan of our test level.*
16.2

Using grid snap, we will be able to make our level very quickly and all the walls will line up and close beautifully.

NOTE

Each level can contain a maximum number of 700 total objects.

You can see that our level has a few twists and turns and can seem complicated, but the first thing that was done was simple. One huge room was built and the complexity was added after the second (finished stone) wall was selected.

WORKING WITH RAM LIMITS AND NUMBER OF OBJECT LIMITS

On the bottom of the Level Editor screen are two meters: the "M" meter and the "W" meter. These are two horizontal bars at the bottom of the screen. These meters monitor the limits of your level size in two ways.

The RAM limitation (while working with GCS) is that all your artwork must fit into the video memory, depending on the hardware accelerated video card that is used. The more pixels in your artwork, the quicker your texture RAM will be used up. The "M" meter on the bottom of the GCS screen shows how much texture RAM you have left. Note that the amount of texture RAM left is based on a typical customer with a 4MB HAL card. It does not reflect your own video card, since you'll want your game to run on everybody's computer, not just your own.

The "M" Meter

Each time you add a new wall, you will see your "M" meter increase. When the meter increases to the end, you cannot add any more different objects to your game without hearing warning beeps. Due to technical issues, the "M" meter is most accurate right after you come back from a test. If you have been adding and removing many objects, it can get inaccurate, thus requiring another Test command.

NOTE

If GCS starts beeping at you, it is trying to warn you that you may have loaded too many unique pieces of artwork. You may ignore this warning if your target machine will have more than 4MB of video RAM. Currently, there is no way to turn this beeping off.

The "W" Meter

The "W" meter measures the number of objects you have placed in your 3D world. This is very different from the "M" meter, because the "W" meter doesn't care whether you are placing a wall you have used before on the current level. Any object placed into a 3D world counts as one object. A tiny key on the floor counts as one object, the same as a huge wall panel. Adding an enemy or a platform or a solid-color floor panel also counts as one object.

You cannot have more than 700 total objects on a level. When your "W" meter hits its limit, you cannot add any more objects to your 3D world without removing another object.

EDITING YOUR 3D LEVELS

Once you have started laying out the walls of our level, you will undoubtedly want to start manipulating and editing the level to a greater degree. The following tools and functions will take you farther than the introduction when we discussed the basics of the Level Editor. You read how to place walls and other objects; now we look at editing your layouts.

Grid Snap

In making a room, it is very important to get your wall panels to butt up against each other perfectly. Gaps even 1 cm wide can result in unsightly bright lines between walls. This is the reason for grid snap. When using grid snap, your walls will naturally line up along the grid. You don't have to worry about misalignment.

The only problem with grid snap is putting a wall in a position that is halfway between the grid lines. Here, you need to go to the Misc pull-down menu, and use the command that aligns the grid to an object. This is very useful when working with walls of different sizes. Sometimes it is better to turn the grid off and use object snap, as described below.

NOTE

When using very fine grids like 50 units or smaller, you will have to turn off object snap, or the two effects will interfere with each other.

Object Snap

Object snap is very similar to grid snap. However, this feature snaps new objects to existing walls, rather than to a fixed grid. This is very handy when you need to join walls not aligned along a grid snap line. This may seem to make grid snap extraneous, but in reality, grid snap is better because you can always close your rooms and hallways with grid snap. If you mix different-sized wall sections, you can still manage to connect the walls with no gaps by using object snap instead of grid snap. However, you may have a problem when it comes time to close a room. When you mix wall sizes, you may find there is no wall section that will fit nicely in the leftover gap. If you use walls of 400 cm width and 400 cm grid spacing, you will never have this problem.

CAUTION

Warning! You can always turn both grid snap and object snap off, and place your walls free-form. You can actually get quite close by operating zoomed in all the way. However, you will find that if you try to make rooms and hallways this way, your errors will pile up as you place long strings of walls. Eventually, you will be faced with so many nasty gaps between your walls that it will be next to impossible to repair.

Selecting Objects

It is very common to put down walls that you decide to remove later. This process of trying to make something better than what you first created is called tweaking; all the pros do it. There are several things you can do to walls that have already been placed. These include moving, deleting, copying, rotating, and raising and lowering. Like many Windows programs you may have used, these functions are implemented in a two-step process. First, you select which objects you want to operate on, and then you press the tool icon to make the action happen.

Select objects with the selection tool, the big arrow icon in the upper left corner of the screen. If you aren't in the middle of placing a wall, or doing something else, you are probably already in selection mode. When you click existing walls or objects while you are in selection mode, red x's appear on those items. The little red x means that an object is selected. If you want to select a whole area of objects at once, you can click the center of each object, and "x" them one by one. Or, you can click where there is no object, and "rubber-band" a rectangle around a whole region. See Figure 16.3 for selected and de-selected objects.

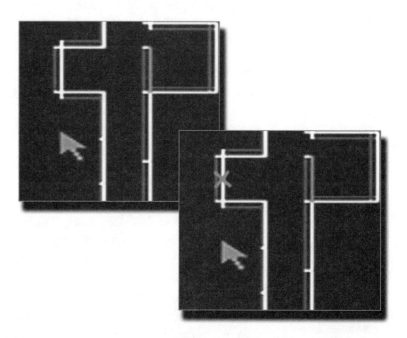

FIGURE *A selected and deselected object in the Level Editor View window.*
16.3

NOTE

Object selection in GCS works differently than in many other graphical programs you may have used. In many other programs, clicking a second object after already selecting another will cause the first one to become deselected. In GCS, the more objects you click, the more are selected. Also, in many other programs, you hold the left mouse button down and drag the mouse (while holding the button down) to make your selection rectangle. This is NOT the way GCS works. To get the rectangle in GCS, you simply click once in a spot where there are no objects nearby. A rectangle is started. Click again at the opposite corner of the selection rectangle.

The real beauty of this selection system becomes evident when you want to pick and choose a few items that you *don't* want selected. If you click again on an object that already has a red x on it, the red x will vanish, thus showing the object as deselected. To move or copy nearly all the objects in a room, draw a box around the whole room to select everything. Then simply go through and deselect the few objects that you didn't want included.

A right click will cancel all the selected items. Most of the editing tools will leave the items selected. The right mouse button is great for quickly deselecting, in case you don't have any further editing to do on those items. The tools that need selected items are the icons in the bottom third of the toolbar. The most commonly used icons are the Move, Copy, Delete, and Rotate icons.

Moving Walls or Whole Rooms

To move some objects from one spot to another, first select the things you want to move. Then click the Move icon. Now you will be asked to pick a reference point. Pick an endpoint of one wall that you have selected. The point you pick will be the "drag point" of the cluster of objects that you selected. When you then click the new grid position, the "drag point" will be put exactly where the mouse is.

Take, for example, the layout of a secretary's cubical in a large office room. To move the secretary's cubical 400 cm down the wall, use the selection tool to draw a box around the desk, plant, partition, and wastebasket. Then click the Move icon. For a reference point, click the point where the partition meets the office room wall. Then move the mouse pointer down 400 cm. Click a different spot on the same wall. GCS moves all the objects down, and puts them in just the right spot, relative to where the partition meets the wall.

If, in the above example, we had chosen the center of his desk as a reference point, then it would have been harder to click the right spot when choosing the move destination. We would be looking at the layout, trying to figure out where the center of the desk would have to be to get the partition to butt up against the office wall perfectly. We could easily misjudge and wind up with the partition sticking through the wall or leaving a gap between the wall and the partition. One problem you may encounter is that the grid does not let you move your objects exactly where you want. You can easily make the grid spacing finer with grid snap. You can also turn grid snap off, but that might be undesirable when trying to match up walls. Of course, if you are just moving symmetrical objects, the grid is not really needed. If the grid is really preventing you from putting a wall just where you want it, the object snap feature should allow you to join walls perfectly, even with grid snap turned off.

Copying Groups of Objects

The Copy function is identical to the Move function, except that the original objects stay in their original positions. A copy is placed at the new position.

Erasing Groups of Objects

The Delete function should be obvious. Select whatever objects you want to discard. Click the Erase icon. All the objects that had the little red x's on them are gone forever.

Rotating Groups of Objects About a Point

The Rotate function is really fun to use. Select your objects and click the Rotate icon. Once you pick a rotation point, all the objects rotate counterclockwise 90 degrees. If you wanted a different rotation angle, just click again to go another 90 degrees. To exit rotate mode, just click the selection tool, or right click once. The objects remain selected after a rotation because you frequently want to move them after rotating.

NOTE

You can't rotate in 45-degree increments because that would involve changing the sizes of the wall sections. If you zoom in and measure the wall lengths on your screen, you will notice that the diagonal sections of your walls are longer than the right-angle sections.

Adjusting Altitude

The elevation adjustment tool also operates on selected objects. You can raise a whole cluster of objects by a certain amount, or you can move them all to the same new elevation. Those two functions may sound the same when you read the sentence, but they aren't.

If you want to raise a cluster of many objects up by 50 cm, select all the objects and then click the Elevation Adjust icon. Put a 50 in the text box, and click the OK button. If you don't click the Absolute button, the objects would just move up 50 cm from their initial heights. This raising function preserves the fact that one object may be at a higher elevation than another. To move the objects back down, you would perform the same steps, but you would type in an elevation of -50 cm. The negative number would move them back down.

Following the same steps as above, only this time clicking the Absolute button, will move every object to the same height. All the objects, no matter what their original elevation, will be placed at the level entered in the options box. See Figure 16.4 for an illustration of this concept. Please note that the figure is not from GCS, but only an illustration of the concept.

Group moved up

Group moved up to an absolute elevation

FIGURE *The difference between Elevation Adjust with and with out the Absolute option*
16.4 *checked.*

Changing a Placed Wall Into a Door

To turn a wall panel into an opening door, select the wall, and then click the Door icon. You can actually make multiple doors at once by selecting several walls. Usually, though, you will want your doors to open in different directions, and to have different keys, etc. We go into more detail on making doors later.

Find All Function

When using GCS, sometimes you will want to eliminate all instances of a particular wall. Instead of having to find them all one by one, GCS can whip through your level and find all instances of a particular wall and select them for you. To use this, just select one wall object, and click the Find All option in the Object pull-down menu. All objects of that type will be selected.

NOTE

An idiosyncrasy of this feature is that it only finds up/down copies of the object, or diagonals, not both at the same time. So in general, to delete all instances of a wall, you need to first find all the up/down and side-to-side walls and delete them, and then find all the diagonal versions, and delete those.

Invert

Frequently, it is necessary to flip a wall 180 degrees. Although you can do this with each wall individually with the Rotate function, it is more convenient to select a whole bunch of walls, and press Control+I. The usefulness of this feature is illustrated in the next section.

Editing Object Attributes

Each wall in your level has various attributes. These attributes alter the way the wall is drawn by the 3D game engine and how the wall interacts with both the player and enemies. First select a wall. Then select Edit Attributes from the Object pull-down menu. You will see a list of settings for the wall (See Figure 16.5). The default is for all these settings to be turned off.

CAUTION

Warning! It is not advisable to set the attributes to groups of selected objects. This practice leads to serious errors. Select objects and set their attributes one at a time and test your level frequently. While this makes your level-building seem to go slower and is tedious, you will save yourself a lot of frustration and time in the long run.

Don't Draw Backsides

Each wall has a front and a back side. This is great when making a room within a room, where you want to see both sides of the wall. This makes level design easier for reasons discussed below.

But the 3D game engine doing 3D calculations to draw both sides of a wall can be a waste if the player would never have occasion to see the back of the wall (the outer wall of our dungeon level, for instance). Thus, the Don't Draw Backsides option speeds up the frame rate, since the 3D game engine will not have to draw the walls that are not seen.

FIGURE *The Wall Settings menu.*
16.5

NOTE

Pay attention to your walls and which side is their front and back. Since both sides are drawn, the walls appear normal when you test your level. However, when you turn on the Don't Draw Backsides attribute, walls will appear invisible when looking at them from their backs. The walls are still there, but you just can't see them from the back.

If you are using this feature and a wall seems invisible, select the wall and use the Invert command (Ctrl+I) to flip the wall. Now the front of the wall will be facing you and it will reappear.

Warning! Only use the Don't Draw Backsides attribute with walls! You will run into serious and critical errors if you use this feature with any other object.

CAUTION

Don't Fade With Distance (Full Bright)

This attribute is used with lights, torches, glowing keys, and other objects that seem to have their own light sources. This attribute turns off fading and shading for the particular object that you selected.

Don't Draw If Far Away

You can speed up the frame rate of your level by setting this attribute with small objects. Why slow down your computer by having it do the calculations necessary to draw objects that are too far away for you to see anyway? This also applies to objects inside buildings or rooms that are way on the other side of your layout. Use this feature to tweak your finished level to make it run at the optimal frame rate by not drawing objects you can't see.

Can't Bump Into Object (Collision Detection Off)

By setting this attribute, you allow the player to pass through the object as if it were a ghost or hologram. This is great for making curtains, for example. This is a feature that you will need to use when making door frames; otherwise, you won't be able to get through your doorways. You might also want to use this feature to cut down the frustration level of players who get stuck in dense areas of foliage or in crowded rooms.

Set Wall Lighting by Angle

You can enhance the 3D look of your level with this feature. Walls with a north/south orientation are shaded differently than walls with an east/west orientation. You'll see that corners look especially good.

Object Won't Show up on Radar

The name for this attribute is a holdover from a previous attribute. Originally, GCS had a radar device and this data was also used for the wall-bumping and detection of the guards. The radar was not very popular, so it was removed when the Windows version came out. But the name lingers on. Now this attribute simply controls whether enemies can walk through the wall or not.

You have to use this feature when constructing door frames that you want enemy characters to walk and shoot through.

Set FTC (Floor-To-Ceiling) on Solid Walls

This attribute is used to create barriers that tell the 3D game engine to forget about drawing any object that would normally appear behind the selected wall, because the wall definitely extends from the floor to the ceiling and cannot be seen through. This is used to maximize the frame rate. You should be careful when using this feature, and it should be used last when your level is complete and final.

Warning! Never use this attribute with a windowed wall, fence, or any other wall panel that the player can see through, since everything behind the wall would be invisible. For best performance, make sure you set this attribute on every solid wall that goes from floor to ceiling.

ADDING DOORS TO YOUR GAME

Knock and the door shall be open . . . actually you need the green key card.

Doors add so much to a game — interactivity, the feeling of suspense, the opportunity for exploration. Doors are a great tool for the designer to work with — *The player will need the green key card to get through this door, but the green key card is beyond a room full of sleeping guards, suspended over a pit of lava and behind an electrical force field (hehehehehehe, evil designer laugh).* Also, locked doors force players to search through your beautiful level and to make sure they look carefully at every texture you created for keys.

Doors are extremely easy to make. In short, the whole process consists of selecting a normal wall section, clicking the Door icon, and then setting a few parameters.

Look at your layout and decide where you might want to place a door. Then click the Brick Wall icon and place a wall section where you want your door. It doesn't have to look like a door. You are free to make "secret" doors out of any solid wall. You can make a secret door part of a continuous stone wall or a bookcase.

You cannot make doors out of symmetrical objects like trees — only walls.

After placing the object, return to selection mode by right clicking your mouse button, or by clicking the selection tool icon. Then click once on the center of the door-to-be. When the little red x is on the door, click the Door icon on the toolbar.

A door menu will come up with some text boxes and buttons. Fill in the numbers, or use the defaults. Click the buttons to choose the sliding direction, and then click the OK. Your door should now be functional (See Figure 16.6).

Warning! Doors will fail if you make them too wide. Walls greater than 600 cm wide may fail, and walls 1200 cm or wider will certainly fail when you test your level.

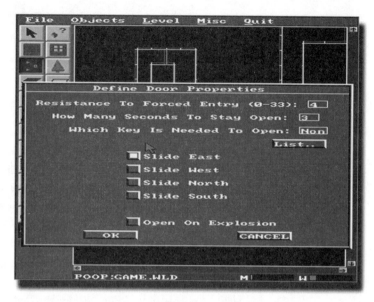

FIGURE *The Door Properties menu that pops up after you click the Door icon.*
16.6

Door Parameters

Resistance to Forced Entry

This number determines how hard it is to open or break the door.

0   A value of 0 means that merely bumping the door breaks it, and then stays open forever.

1   Putting a 1 in here makes it open by shooting or kicking. Increasing this number increases the difficulty of breaking the door.

2 - 8   If the player bumps the door while shooting his weapon, the door will only be weakened by repeated attacks if the resistance is lower than eight.

Up to 31 If the door is set to resistance 31, the door is only damageable by jump-kicking. This takes some practice by the player, but it is a fun action to master. Please note that on levels where you have a texture-mapped ceiling, the player cannot jump for technical reasons. Therefore, it is best to leave doors like that for outside areas or for those indoor areas with high ceilings.

Higher than 31 May as well be a wall. Doors with resistance set higher than 31 will not be affected by the player at all.

Number of Seconds to Stay Open

When the door is opened by enemies, or by the player, it stays open for a while before automatically closing. Doors will not close on the player. They will stay open until the player gets about 800 cm away.

Key Value

The key value number selects which key will be needed to unlock the door. The player must have this key in his inventory to get through. If the player does not have the right key, an icon of the needed key will show up in an inventory window on the game play screen. The keys are coded by color.

CAUTION

Warning! If you have changed the default inventory item pictures, then these colors might not be accurate. If you are modifying the picture images for the keys, it is up to you to keep track of what color keys you have modified.

Open Upon Explosion

The Open on Explosion button on the Door dialog box makes the door open if an explosion from a hand grenade, or other source, occurs close to the door.

Tips For Placing Doors

Door Frames

You need to set certain object attributes to make your door frames operate properly.

1. First, select the wall your door frame is on.
2. Then select the Edit Attributes option from the Object-pull down menu.
3. Click the Can't Bump into Object button. This allows the player to pass through the wall the door frame is on.
4. Next, click the Object Won't Show up on Radar button. This allows enemy characters to pass through the doors. It also allows enemy characters to shoot through the doorways.
5. Finally, select the Don't Draw Backsides option. This will help with 3D game engine performance. Remember that once you set this option and the door frame is gone in your game, you may have the wall object it is on reversed, and you will need to go back to the Level Editor and flip the wall so the door frame is visible.

How to Avoid Graphical Problems With Doors

The normal door movement is to slide sideways, into the wall on either side of it. And this can cause problems if you aren't careful. When the door and the art-work slides to the left or right, the wall section that is moving does not stop at the door frame. It remains the same size and will pass through space and walls without discretion. In other words, the wall/door panel comes out through the side of a wall when it opens, and you, as game designer, are responsible for making sure the door panel is hidden when it slides sideways.

The easiest way to deal with doors is to put your doors in hallways. Make sure that the hallway has some inaccessible space on the side the door panel slides into (See Figure 16.7). Otherwise, the player may be in a room at a time

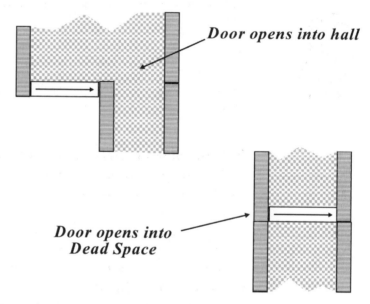

Door opens into hall

Door opens into Dead Space

FIGURE *The proper and improper placement of a sliding door.*
16.7

when an enemy unit opens the door, and the door panel will slide through the supposedly solid wall of the room and ruin the atmosphere of the game.

Another problem that can frequently occur is that the door slides out along another wall panel lengthwise, and can be partially seen through the wall it is in. Here, the door and the wall panel are exactly overlaid in the 3D world and are fighting to be displayed, since they are each in the same exact location. The graphics then break down and you will see a shimmering mess of vertical strips.

This is easily avoided by recessing your door into a door frame a little bit. By door frame, we mean that you build a square of dead space on either side of the door. Then you place your door at the entranceway. However, if you set the object to be a door, and leave it here, you will run into the same effect described above. Offset the door 200 cm, so it will not be aligned with any other walls when the panel opens. The snap-to-grid feature will make this offsetting impossible if the grid is set to the standard 400 cm. You will have to change the resolution of the grid or turn the snap-to-grid feature off.

Click the grid tool and change the grid setting to 200 cm. Then select the door with the selection tool, and click the Move icon. Move the door one 200 cm grid line back, so that the door is now centered in the frame. Now when the door opens, the panel will slide safely into the dead space. Of course, you can set your grid spacing to as little as 50 cm to inset the door just enough to keep the "scalloping" from occurring. It's best to be zoomed in before setting your grid to such a fine spacing.

NOTE

If you make a door, but you can't go through it when you test your level, read the previous section on door frames. Likewise, if enemies won't walk through or shoot through your door, the section on door frames will explain the attributes that must be set to make the door function properly.

PUTTING ENEMY CHARACTERS IN YOUR GAME

No 3D action game is complete without enemies. You can place up to 32 enemies in a level. Placing them is as easy as placing trees, but with more options. To place an enemy, click the Person icon. This creates an enemy in your game level. The kind of enemy that will be created is controlled by the selection of the Active Guard Set option in the File menu.

After you have clicked the Person icon, a big dialog box appears filled with options, as shown in Figure 16.8.

First, you must determine the properties of the enemy unit. The following parameters adjust their strength and behavior:

Quickness. This property determines the quickness of the enemy's movements.

Step Size. This property determines how fast the enemy moves by adjusting the distance traveled in each walking step.

Resistance. This property sets how much damage the enemy can sustain before succumbing.

Attack Strength. This property controls how much damage is inflicted on the player when the enemy strikes or fires upon the player.

Attack Accuracy. This property controls how often the enemy will hit you with his weapon.

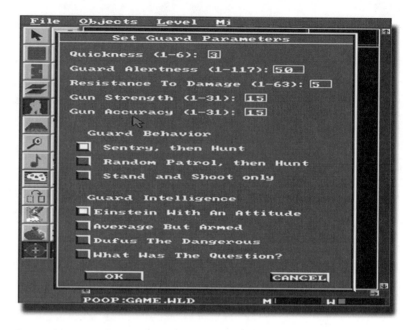

FIGURE *The Guard Options pop-up menu.*
16.8

Range. This property sets how close an enemy must be before his attacks harm the player.

Enemy Character Behavior:

Sentry, Then Hunt
The enemy stands still until he sees the player, then chases after the player in attack mode.

Random Patrol
The enemy walks about at random and then chases the player when he or she is finally seen.

Stand and Shoot
The enemy stands still. If he sees the player, he will remain in current position, but he will shoot.

Enemy Artificial Intelligence:

Einstein with an Attitude
The enemy is highly alert.

Average but Armed
The enemy is somewhat alert.

Dufus
The enemy is not very alert.

What was the Question?
The enemy is so oblivious, he will almost never attack a non-shooting player.

The basic behavior of the enemies is always the same. They ignore the player until alarmed, and then they hunt the player down relentlessly. What causes them to become alarmed is a complex calculation.

What Alerts an Enemy?

Initially, all enemies are in casual state. The only event which can cause enemies to become alarmed is seeing the player. However, not all enemies will become alarmed right away upon seeing the player. Whether or not they recognize the player as hostile depends on the intelligence setting, the viewing angle, and what the player is doing.

The most intelligent enemy units will recognize the player on sight from any angle, and become alarmed. The least intelligent will not become alarmed even if the player is standing in front of him, blasting his pal. All enemy units will become alarmed if they take a hit from the player, however.

The view angle is very important in being recognized. If the player is directly behind an enemy, the chance of alarm is much less. Also, for the most part, the enemies can't see through walls.

If an enemy comes near a slain fellow enemy, alertness can also be raised.

The player's chance of being detected depends on the player's actions. Certainly, if the player is running around shooting weapons, he is much more likely to be spotted than if he is standing still. All this information about the player's running, jumping, or shooting is boiled down into one number, called the profile.

The bigger the profile, the easier the player is to spot. Running or moving quickly will raise the profile. Shooting a weapon raises the profile drastically. Being wounded will also raise the profile.

How Enemies Behave

Enemies shoot when they are alarmed. If the player is out of range, enemies will not continue shooting, but will serpentine towards the player. At the halfway point, enemies will stop and take at least one shot. If within range, enemies will shoot repeatedly before venturing closer.

These steps will be repeated until the enemies are so close that there is no point in coming any closer. Then they will just stand and attack continuously.

If an enemy gets hit by the player's weapon, the enemy's shooting is interrupted for a moment. How much damage is done to the enemy is dependent upon many factors. The range and accuracy of the player's weapon are very important. These parameters are adjustable by editing the text file weapons.txt in the game engine directory.

In addition, the resistance to damage setting determines how much damage is absorbed by the enemy unit when hit by the player's weapons. If the enemy is damaged enough, he will attempt a retreat. If he runs into a wall as he flees, he will turn and fight to the death.

If the enemy actually gets very far away from the player after running away, he may return to the non-alarmed mode, but this is very infrequent.

Once you have laid out the basics of a level and ran a test, you should be able to play in your own 3D first-person shooter. But it is not yet your own, really. In the next chapter, we will look at using the paint program that comes with GCS (GCSPAINT), and we will start learning how to use the tool that will allow you to customize and change the objects in order to make your own game.

17 GCSPAINT AND ARTWORK IN YOUR GAME

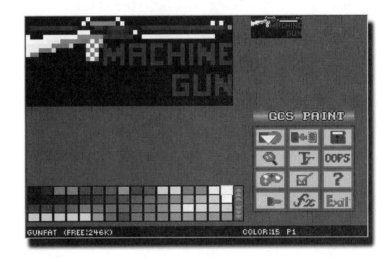

Ve will now depart the Level Editor for a while to look at the paint program that comes with GCS and some technical facts you will need to know about dealing with images in GCS. The paint program is called GCSPaint. With GCSPaint, you can import and edit images for use in the Level Editor and your game. We will look at GCSPaint in greater detail toward the end of this chapter.

GCSPaint was automatically installed when you installed GCS. You can access it from the Level Editor, as shown in Figure 17.1, or you can run it by finding the icon to launch it from Windows.

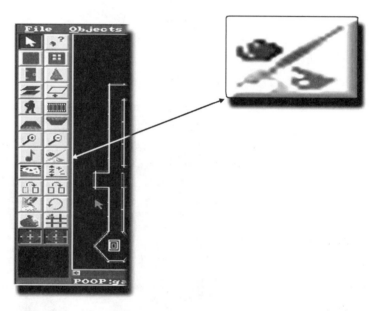

FIGURE   *The icon in the Level Editor to launch GCSPaint.*
17.1

To find the icon for GCSPaint outside of the Level Editor, do the following:

1. Go to My Computer and look on your C Drive.
2. Assuming you have performed a standard installation, the EXE for GCSPaint will be in the folder called GCSW.
3. Click the EXE and it will launch GCSPaint.

NOTE

There are two different color depths we will be discussing in GCS. One is the color depth of the original artwork. In GCS, all the artwork for your game must be in 256-color VGA files (we discuss making the VGA file later). But you can run the game engine with the color depth of your system set to 16-bit or 24-bit color. Although all the artwork on the walls and floors are 256-color, the fading to black with distance requires thousands of new colors to represent the continuous fade to black. Thus, there is a graphical advantage to using a 16-bit or 24-bit color video mode, even though all the original artwork is 256-color. This is because the game engine is taking every color —pure red, for example — and then creating hundreds of colors to fade from red to black. So in order to fade red (RGB 255,0,0) to black (RGB 0,0,0), the game engine must display colors such as the following:

> RGB 255,0,0
> RGB 254,0,0
> RGB 253,0,0
> RGB 252,0,0

Notice that the amount of red decreases as it approaches black.

It should be mentioned here that in the upcoming version of GCS, you may use 24-bit color artwork in your levels, as well as colored light sources and colored fog effects. In fact, the next version of GCS is going to be a major jump upward.

Memory and Image Resolution Concerns

We will look at GCSPaint in greater detail toward the end of this chapter. Right now, we will look at some of the technical aspects.

We discussed in the first part of this book the fact that each pixel of a 256-color piece of artwork takes up one pixel's worth of RAM. Each pixel can take 1, 2, or 4 bytes of texture RAM, depending on the video mode that a user has chosen.

- 256-color mode requires 1 byte per pixel of storage.
- 16-bit color requires 2 bytes per pixel of storage.
- 24- or 32-bit color requires 4 bytes per pixel of storage.

Therefore, a 64 x 64 picture for a wall section would take 4,096 4k pixels, and that would take up 8,192 bytes of texture RAM when running in 16-bit color mode. If you wanted to make a game with no weapons, inventory items, or enemies, you could probably have 290 different wall images in your levels. This is because 290 8K wall panels will use up approximately 2.5 megabytes.

In your real game, you will, of course, want inventory items, enemy characters, trees, and weapons. This all takes up space. In a GCS game level, you will most likely have at least 20 or 30 unique wall sections in a given level. You can see that managing your resources is important.

Let's say you wanted high-resolution artwork for your wall panels. The engine can't take any image that has a dimension bigger than 256. The largest image that could work is 200 x 200. This image contains 40,000 pixels, or ten times more than our 64 x 64 image. This means ten times fewer unique art for the wall panels in your levels. In practice, you should never go higher than 128 x 128 for most games, but with the speed of computers today, you may want to push the limit. Just be aware of how the game engine works and what the limit is so you don't waste time creating a game no one can play.

Getting Image Files into the 3D World

In GCS, levels are made out of objects: Trees, enemies, ammo, and walls are all objects. In fact, as you have seen, the walls are built panel by panel, just like modular construction. Erecting another wall is nearly the same process as placing a tree or a health-pack. These objects are the 3D portion of the 3D world. Objects are geometry.

Almost every kind of object has an image file associated with it. These images are the artwork, called textures or texture maps, that is placed on the surfaces of the objects.

In GCS, all images have to be either VGR files or VGA files. If you want to use one of your GIF, PCX, or BMP images, then load those pictures into GCSPaint one by one, and save them in the VGR format.

NOTE

You don't need to know this, but for those of you who are curious, the VGA file format is the format of MVPPAINT, which was written by David Johndrow years ago, and is the format GCS uses. VGR is simply a rotated VGA file. This is because of programming issues that cause images to draw faster in different situations, depending on how they are oriented.

IMAGES AND OBJECTS WORKING TOGETHER TO MAKE A BETTER WORLD

The 3D world is empty at first and, other than the need for at least one wall, you can literally test an empty level with one wall in it and wander around in oblivion. In the Level Editor, you fill this void with walls and objects.

Each object has an image stretched over it by the 3D game engine. This stretching of the artwork or images you assign to the objects to fit the geometry is often called *texture-mapping a polygon*, or *adding art to your geometry*.

When you are using the 3D game editor, it is as if you are building a world constructed entirely of white wall panels. And each time you select a blank wall, you assign the image that will be stretched over it. Usually the wall object is larger than the image, so in order to get the image to fit the wall, the game engine must stretch it out. Since we are working with a digital image, you will see the pixels as the image increases in size.

You have to be aware that the game engine will stretch and compress images to fit the objects they are on. If you assign a square image of say, a person, to a very tall, thin wall, you will have a sideways-compressed image of a person on that wall. It would look like a fun-house mirror reflection.

So you can't just tell the game engine to put an image into the game. You must tell the game engine how big to stretch the image. For a brick wall section, this is fairly straightforward. Most typical walls are 400 x 400 units in size.

BITMAP IMAGE RESOLUTION VS. 3D WORLD SIZE

Inside the virtual 3D game world, distances are measured in centimeters, but the unit of measure really doesn't have any impact on world design. The bottom line is that a wall panel that is 400 units long, in the 3D world looks about 12 feet long. But the length of the wall has nothing to do with the resolution (or size) of the picture that the game engine paints on this 12 x 12 wall panel. We could stretch a 32 x 32 pixel image on there (it would appear blocky, though), or we could put a 64 x 64 pixel image on it, or maybe even a 104 x 64 (See Figure 17.2).

The typical wall is 400 x 400 centimeters big in the 3D world and the art on it is usually 128 x 128 pixel size or smaller. The 128 x 128 pixel limit is for the image artwork only.

NOTE

Warning! You can make the game engine stretch a tiny image, such as an 8 x 8 pixel image, across a huge 800 x 800 cm wall panel; however, it will look terrible (See Pixel Rip in Part 1). You may also cause a *numerical overflow* in the 3D calculations if you try to do a stretch or compression that is this extreme.

CAUTION

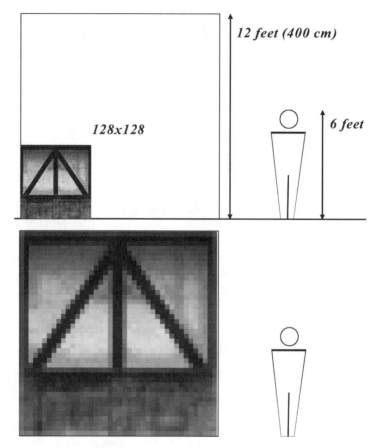

FIGURE *The average game wall is 400 cm long (about 12 feet); the typical 128 x 128*
17.2 *image stretched across it.*

Typical Dimensions

The typical wall panel is about 400 x 400 cm in size, and has an image on it
that is 64 x 64. In general, stick to the following dimensions:

- Images with horizontal or vertical dimensions of about 32-104 pixels
- Wall dimensions between 50 and 600 units wide

You will not encounter critical errors or overflows with these safe dimensions. You might also experience trouble when making very short, wide walls,
say 800 x 50. So be careful when making steps or guardrails.

NOTE

Having random wall dimensions like 477 x 613 cm makes it hard for you to match up the walls of adjacent rooms when laying out a level. The odd numbers do not affect the speed or smoothness of the game engine. On the other hand, it should be noted that there is no reason to keep these nice and neat dimensions in your image files, since they are stretched to the wall size and do not affect the layout of the level.

CAUTION

Warning! The above note does *not* apply to floor and ceiling panel artwork, which must be either 64 x 64, 128 x 128, or 256 x 256 pixels in size.

Walls with shapes and holes — Windowed Walls

Walls are not limited to rectangular shapes. In fact, you can have walls with a few large cutouts. Examples are walls with windows, doors with rounded tops, a prison cell wall made of bars, or fences with gaps you can see through. All these are as easy to do as solid walls.

Simply make the invisible parts black. If you want a brick wall with a big round hole in it, then load up your brick wall image in the paint program. Use the Circle tool to paint a big solid black circle on the image of the wall. Now the trick is that the black you use must be the first color of the palette. In GCSPaint, the first color is color 0. You can read the color numbers on the bottom of the screen when in GCSPaint. Choose your black from the upper left corner of the palette grid.

When the game engine draws this kind of wall object, it stretches the image exactly like a solid textured wall. The only difference is that it never paints the color 0 (black). So whatever was behind the wall shows through (color transparency again).

So, why bother having two types of walls?

There are two reasons.

1. You will want to be able to use black as a color on many occasions in your game without it always being treated as clear.
2. Windowed walls take more computer time to draw, because there are more computations involved. It is much more efficient to have two types of walls.

NOTE

You can use a lot of windowed walls in your levels. There is no real limit. In fact, you can define all your walls as Windowed Walls, but you might find that it will hurt the performance, and you will notice that the frames per second will drop off and the game will not appear as smooth.

Objects

Objects or symmetrical objects are things like trees, floor lamps, and chairs. Unlike walls, which are stationary and can be looked at from various angles, symmetrical objects always look the same. The viewing direction does not matter because they always rotate to face you. These stand-up objects are also called anchored sprites and will always turn to face the player (See Figure 17.3).

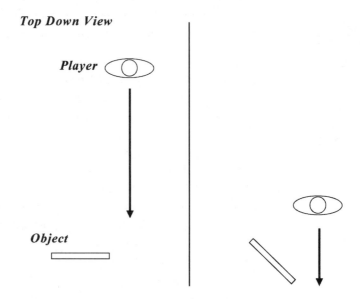

FIGURE *An object will always rotate to face a player.*
17.3

So to make a tree, you draw a tree on a black background. You put the size at 400 x 600 cm in the 3D world. The game engine draws that wall facing the player. It doesn't draw any of the black background between the leaves and around the outside edge of the image.

The important thing to remember about these objects is that they are stretched out over a rectangle, just like the images on the regular solid textured walls. The panels that these images are stretched onto have horizontal and vertical size in centimeters, just like the other walls.

Just like the shaped walls, the images you make are subject to the same hole restrictions. If you want to make your own shrub, don't try to have see-through areas between each leaf. You may have trouble. Most reasonable trees, chairs, and other objects will be nowhere near this limit. The transparent portion should be limited and not very complex.

Ceiling and floor images

Typically, you will use floor sections in repeating tile patterns which repeat in both the north - south and east - west directions.

Because your image will be repeated on the floor, the patterns you put on your image will be discontinuous as you go from one panel to the next. Sometimes this effect is desired, like when you are making floor tiles that look like square tiles. However, when making a dirt floor, you would like the user not to be able to see the tile boundaries. This means blending the color on the top of the image with the pixels on the bottom, and blending the left with the right side.

GCSPaint can handle this for you in the flx submenu. You can smooth the edges of your image to improve their appearance in your 3D world.

NOTE

VGA vs. VGR image files

Note that there are two types of image files that the 3D game engine can read: VGA files and VGR files. Typically, all your walls and other objects are VGR files, and all the big things, like the backdrop, are VGA files.

The file types are so close in format that they are interchangeable for the most part without a problem. For example, if you used the DOS Copy command to copy a 64 x 64 pixel WALLVGR file to WALLVGA, you could still read it as a VGA with GCSPaint. However, you would notice that the image was rotated 90 degrees on your screen.

This explains what a VGR file is. It is just a rotated VGA image. The 3D game engine can read artwork more efficiently if the images are rotated 90 degrees. So the VGR file format has the pixel data rotated 90 degrees internally. You never know this when you bring up your images with GCSPaint, because GCSPaint puts them up on the screen right side up, although the image is on its side in the VGR file.

The only files that need to be rotated with the game engine are those that are in the 3D game play world. Pictures of the hit point guys (HTPT0VGA), the game play screen (BACKDROPVGA), and the weapons identification fat files (GUNNONEVGA) all are put on the screen as regular flat pictures, not in the 3D viewport. That is why they are VGA files.

The wall panel artwork, however, needs to be rotated 90 degrees. You could do this by saving your artwork as a VGA file, but make sure that you rotate the picture onto its side before saving. Then rename the VGA file as a VGR file, so that GCS will let you import them.

There is really no reason to do this except to illustrate the difference between VGR and VGA files. This is necessary because, when using GCSPaint, you must be aware of which kind of file you want to load or save.

NOTE

An idiosyncrasy of GCSPaint is that it never asks you whether you want to save as VGR or VGA. If you call GCSPaint from the icon in the GCS program, you will always be saving as VGR, although you can read both VGR and VGA files. If you quit GCS, and run GCSPaint from the DOS command line, then all images you save are written to VGA files. This is good, because some bigger files that you might like to edit, like BACKDROPVGA or BACKG40VGA, are too wide to be saved as VGR files. So to change these large VGA image files, you need to exit GCS and run GCSPaint from the DOS command line.

GCSPaint

With GCSPaint, you don't need to hire an artist to create and edit graphics for your 3D project. GCSPaint is an image workshop containing all the tools and special effects you'll need to create original artwork or to manipulate existing images. At the beginning of this chapter, we looked at how to start GCSPaint. If you are in the Level Editor, click the GCSPaint icon. The Level Editor will suspend operation and the GCSPaint screen will pop up.

The main menu for GCSPaint is located on the lower right side of the screen. The current palette of 256 colors is located on the lower portion of the screen, as shown in Figure 17.4.

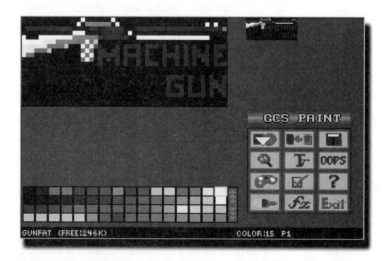

FIGURE   *The GCSPaint main screen.*
17.4

GCSPAINT HELP

Click the **?** icon for an introduction to GCSPaint's many features. The Help screens explain how to use each tool and special effect as you click the various buttons on the main menu.

DISK COMMANDS

Click the main menu's disk icon. You are presented with several options: Create New Image, Load Image, Save Image, Merge Image, and View as Tile. We will look at all these below.

Create New Image

Create a new image by dragging the size box to the desired dimensions. Please note the maximum image size in GCSPaint is 192 x 150. If you want to work on larger images, exit GCS and run GCSPaint from the DOS command line. Now you can work on full-screen 320 x 200 images.

Save Image

GCSPaint saves your images in the VGR format. Limit your file names to eight characters because of the DOS naming convention.

If you need to save your image in the VGA format, you will have to run GCSPaint from the DOS prompt (c:\gcsw\GCSPaint.exe).

This enables you to save large images like title screens and background images. Conserve RAM memory at game time by keeping your images small. Typical walls should be 64 x 64, and typical characters should be about 60 pixels tall. You can scale down large images with the Resize command. Try to maintain a reasonable balance between appearance and size when saving your images.

You should also avoid leaving a lot of unused black background in your images. Use the Move command to put your images in the upper left corner of the screen. Then use the Resize command to crop the excess black background.

CAUTION

Warning! You should also test images that will later become shaped and symmetrical objects to make sure that they don't have too many holes. Color 0 is not drawn by the 3D game engine, thus those areas are see-through. An abundance of see-through holes can sometimes cause critical errors when you test your levels. An easy way of testing for this pitfall is to use the color replacement feature to change areas drawn with color 0 to a bright color. Then you can clearly see how many invisible holes are in your image. Use color replacement again to refill those unintentional holes with a color other than color 0.

Merge Image

This command lets you combine two separate images. A problem arises when you try to import an image that is bigger than your current image. A warning will flash momentarily at the bottom of the screen, and the operation will fail. Use the Resize command, without scaling, to make your current image big enough to accommodate the imported image.

View as Tile

You will undoubtedly be working on wall, fence, or foliage artwork for your project. A common problem with artwork repeated or stacked in your 3D world is that distracting patterns appear. Edges look harsh and ill-fitting. This command gives you a preview of what your image will look like when it is placed side by side or stacked one on top of each other in your 3D world.

Hidden Main Menu

Large images sometimes cover up the main menu so you can't see it. To view the hidden main menu, move your mouse pointer to where the main menu normally appears and press the space bar. Once you select a command, the main menu disappears again and your image fills the whole screen.

Palette

GCS works with one palette of 256 colors. All the images that you use in your game must use this one palette. Each color has a number from 0 to 255.

The palette box displays 64 of the 256 colors on the lower portion of the screen. To see the other 192 colors, simply click the arrows on the right side of the palette box.

Select a Color

Move your mouse pointer over the desired color in the palette box. Click the left mouse button to select a color. You can also pick up a color from your image. Move your mouse pointer to a pixel in your image. Click the right mouse button to select that color from your image.

Hidden Palette Box

Large images sometimes cover up the palette box so you can't see it. To view the hidden palette box, move your mouse pointer to where the palette box normally appears and press the space bar. Once you select a color, the palette disappears again and your image fills the whole screen.

Load a Palette

Images do not always come with their own palettes. These images appear in wild colors when you load them, because they are drawn using a default palette. Remember that GCS uses only one palette of 256 colors at a time, so make sure that you are loading the same palette that will be used throughout your game.

Modify Palette

It is possible to customize your own palette. You can adjust each individual color by adjusting its red, green, and blue components. You can also work on several colors at once with the trend option.

Match Palettes

GCSPaint gives you the option of matching the palettes of imported images to the palette currently in use. This is particularly helpful when you are using scanned images for your game. This feature enables you to make all kinds of artwork compatible with the palette that you are using for your game.

Save Palette

You should always save the palettes of images before you try to match them to the master palette of your game. If the palette-matching operation doesn't turn out well, you will want to reload the image with its original palette and try again.

Warning! If you don't save the original palette, the original image will be ruined forever and you won't have a second chance.

CAUTION

Draw Tools

GCSPaint equips you with many powerful drawing tools: lines, rectangles, circles, ellipses, and polygons.

Interpolation

This command creates a morphing effect between two polygons. You can specify the number of intermediary shapes in the morph. You can also set the number of colors involved in the morph.

Warning! Be aware that the operation will fail if original polygons have too many sides.

CAUTION

Settings

You can set preferences for GCSPaint. Choose this command to specify the brush size. You can even design brush patterns. In addition, you can set prompt delays to suit your needs. Memory settings are also adjustable.

Text

Two CHR files come with GCSPaint, although you can put public domain BGI files in the same directory as well. Select the size and style of the text you want to put in your image. If your text operation fails, it's probably because the text was too big for your image. Try again with smaller letters, a more compact font, or a larger image.

Color tools

GCSPaint also comes with the following color manipulation tools:

Fill. You can fill areas of color with either solid colors or patterns.

Color Replacement. This tool lets you switch colors in your image. This is a big time-saver, since you don't have to add the new color to your image pixel by pixel.

Random Replacement. This handy tool lets you replace a percentage of a color in your image with a new color. This is especially useful when doing artwork that requires a haphazard pattern, such as dirt floors or carpeting.

Color Phase. This tool fills an area with a gradient. Pick a color and start the phase on that color.

Color Sunburst. This is similar to the Color Phase tool, except that it makes gradient fills in rounded areas. Pick a color, then start the sunburst on that color.

SPECIAL EFFECTS

Outline

Trying to draw borders around areas by hand can be tedious at best. Select this tool and your border is done in a flash! Your outline can be done with or without filled-in corners. Pick the color that you want to outline, then start the outline on that color.

Anti-Aliasing

This tool helps prevent the optical illusion that often occurs when two highly contrasting colors are butted up against each other. This tool also helps eliminate the sawtooth appearance of diagonal lines in low-resolution graphics.

Merge/Blend

This tool allows you to superimpose another image over your current image. You can control the transparency of the image that you are importing. Be sure that the image you are importing is smaller than your current image. If you try to import an image that is too big, the operation will fail.

Brighten/Darken

You can use this tool to brighten or darken lines or rectangles in your image.

CAUTION

Warning! Be sure to say NO to the prompt that asks you if you want the operation to affect the whole image and its palette. You never want to change the palette, since this would make the image incompatible with all the other images in your game.

Smooth Image

This is one of the coolest special effects that GCSPaint has to offer. You can smooth all the pixels in your image, or you can apply the tool to the edges of your image. You can control the intensity of the operation: light, medium, heavy, and extremely blurred. Other stunning effects include negative image, grainy glass, and double image. The pixel wrap-around feature is especially useful when working on wall panels.

Contrast

There are times when you want to adjust the contrast of your image. This tool is just about as easy as fine-tuning the contrast button on your TV!

Rectangle tools

These tools include Copy, Move, Overlay, and Erase. In addition, you can flip, rotate, and resize your image.

Zoom

There are times when you need to move in close to work on the details of your image. Zoom makes this possible.

The best thing about this tool is that most of GCSPaint's features can be applied while in Zoom mode. It is also possible to save the zoomed in part of your image as a separate file.

CAUTION

Warning! A prompt warns you not to save the zoomed section under the same file name as your original image, so you don't overwrite it.

Oops

You can cancel just about any operation in GCSPaint by selecting the Oops icon on the main menu. Usually prompts warn you that certain operations can't be undone. Another way to cancel an operation is to click your right mouse button.

Now that you understand the graphic formats, how they fit into the game, and how to use GCSPaint, we are ready to move on to the Advanced Features Editor, which is an extension of the DOS Level Editor in many ways. You will learn some of the additional effects and features of the Windows Engine to further tweak your game level.

CHAPTER

18

THE EXTRA FEATURES EDITOR

Level Options & Stats

Distance Fading
- Fade Start Distance: `0`
- Total Darkness Dist: `3200`
- Wall Fade Code 0 pt: `32`

Level Statistics
- Num Objects: `103`
- Num Bitmaps: `151`
- Num Floor/ceil: `120`
- 3D Art Bytes: `403899` Max `795320`

Graphics Options
- ☐ Fade to black with distance   ☐ Fade Lights with distance
- ☑ Use Zbuffer on Floors

Background
- red `0`   Green `0`   Blue `0`
- `None`
- [Remove Texture]
- [Change Texture]
- [OK]
- Xscl `0.200`   Yscl `0.500`
- left/right speed `1.300`   Up/Down speed `0.700`

Why are we forced to do all this jumping around from DOS to Windows and now into the Extra Features Editor? First be aware that the game engine that runs the game, the game editor, and the paint program are all separate programs. To develop even one of these applications is quite a bit of work. So when the game engine was rewritten and upgraded, several concessions were made so that the original DOS editor would not have to be totally rewritten.

The original GCS game engine was a DOS-based engine and was replaced by aptly named Windows Replacement Engine. This new Windows Engine was a great improvement over the original DOS-based engine, but in order to take advantage of the many features that have been added to extend the capabilities of the game engine, an intermediary editor had to be written. This was called the Extras Features Editor, since it edited the extra features of the new game engine. These features are obviously not available in the DOS editor, so we have to deal with them while we are out of the DOS editor and not yet into the Windows Engine. This section shows you how to access these features.

The GCS Extra Features Editor

In addition to the increases in graphics technology, there have also been some new features added to the game engine. These dramatically increase the visual impact of your game levels, and also increase the flexibility you have in controlling the appearance of your games. You can use these new features by using a part of the Windows Engine called the Extra Features Editor. This editor will make changes to a file called EXTRA??.TXT in your project directory. This is a simple text file which contains information about floor and ceiling tiles, as well as lighting effects and other things.

NOTE

EXTRA??.TXT is a file name where the question marks are replaced with a level number. In the real game, the file would probably be named something like EXTRA001.TXT.

HOW TO START UP THE EXTRA FEATURES EDITOR

You will remember that when we test a level, the first thing we get is the dialog box in Windows with your name on it and the following three buttons: Test 3D World, Edit Extra Data, and Change Driver Mode (See Figure 18.1).

We already looked at two of the buttons in great detail. Here we will look at the Edit Extra Data button that takes us to the EFE (Extra Features Editor). Click the Edit Extra Data button.

Go!   ☒

Welcome to the GCS Windows Engine program. This copy is owned by the
person named below.   This message appears only in the 'Test Level' version of
the game engine, and not in your final game.

Name   YOUR NAME HERE

Address Line 1   ADDRESS

Address Line 2

City

State/Province

Zip/Postal Code

| Test 3D World | Level #   3   Project: C:\qcsw\ENGINE\WREDEMO |

Current Direct 3D Driver

| Edit Extra Data | Direct3D HAL |

Current Video Mode

| Change Driver/mode | 640X480X16 Hi Color |

*** Hi Quality CD Music Demonstration ***   The GCS can play CD Music!

FIGURE   *The dialog box in Windows with the Edit Extra Data button.*
18.1

After clicking on the Edit Extra Data button, the client area will show a top
view of your game level, similar to that of the DOS Level Editor. However, you
will not be able to move or place walls or objects with this editor. They are on
the screen just for reference. Once the editor is running, you will be able to
place floor and ceiling panels down, and change various settings.

You can zoom in and out using the + and - keys on your keypad, and you
can use the scroll bars to move around on the image.

*If the + and - keys do not appear to work, then make sure that the main window is
selected, and not the little dialog box. What you want is for the main window's title
bar to be blue (or the active color) and the little dialog box's title bar to be gray before the + and - keys will function. You can make this happen by clicking the title of
the main window.*

NOTE

Placing Floor Panels

The floor and ceiling panels in the GCS are based on a 400 x 400 grid of
squares. You may control the size of the panels you put down, but the size must
be an even multiple of 400 units. The bitmap artwork that covers the panel will
repeat over and over again to fill in panels that are larger than 400 units. It is

more efficient to use large panels to fill in space, rather than many smaller panels.

To make a floor panel, just click once on your level. A small 400 x 400 floor panel will be created in your level at the default height of 0.

To make larger panels, click and hold down the mouse button, and then drag the mouse while holding down the button. The panel will grow or shrink to its maximum dimension as you move the mouse. When you let go, the panel will be created. When you enter the 3D world next time, your floor panel will be there.

Warning! You must exit the Windows Engine and start it again in order for your changes to appear in the 3D world. If you go directly from the Extra Features Editor to the 3D world via the Go menu item, your most recent changes will not appear in the 3D, world even though you have saved your changes.

CAUTION

Deleting Floor Panels

To remove a floor panel, click a panel that you already placed. An X will appear in the middle of the panel. It is now selected. Then go to the Editor menu and select the Delete Panel option. The panel will disappear, and will be deleted.

Choosing the Floor Image File

Just like when placing a wall, you must choose the artwork file to use for the current floor panel. You choose the image from a list before you create the panel. To choose your image, go to the Editor menu and select the Set Texture option. A dialog box will appear with a list of image files from which you can choose floor or ceiling panels. Select the one you want and click the OK button. All the images on this list will be loaded into memory when your level loads, regardless of whether they are actually used or not. If you would like to add to this list, you can press the Add more textures to list button that is located below the list of available textures.

Adding to the List of Available Floor/Ceiling Textures

Clicking the Add more textures to list button in the Set Texture dialog box will bring up another dialog box with two lists of image files.

The list on the left side is a list of VGA files in the FLCL_LIB (Floor Ceiling Library) object library directory. As you select different files in the list, the preview window in the center of the dialog box shows you what the artwork looks like. When you find a piece of artwork which you would like to add to the level's floor or ceilings, click the arrow that is underneath the preview picture. This will add the image to the level. You can add more images if you like. You may also remove images from the right-hand list with the button below the list (See Figure 18.2).

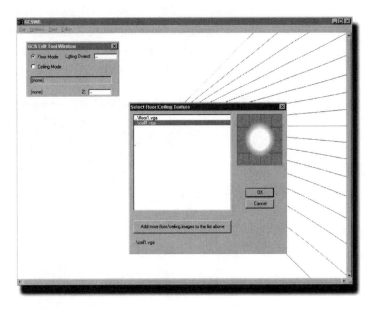

FIGURE *The window for adding more floor and ceiling images to the library.*
18.2

NOTE

There is a quirk of the EFE that requires you to save your changes and exit GCSWE after making changes to this list. When you return to the EFE again, the list will be updated with your changes.

Making Ceiling Panels

Making ceiling panels is the same process as making floor panels. It is just a matter of switching from Floor mode to Ceiling mode. The Editor menu has two items labeled Floor Mode and Ceiling Mode. If you wish to place ceiling panels, click Ceiling Mode. When that is done, the level will be redrawn without the floor panels, and you will be ready to place ceiling tiles. When you make them, they will be created at a default height of 400 units above 0.

NOTE

Floor panels will not be drawn on the screen at all when you are in Ceiling mode.

Gray and White Panels

You will notice that some panels in the drawing are white and some are gray. The panels that are the same texture as the current drawing texture are white. The panels that have a different texture than the currently selected texture are drawn in gray. For example, when you use the Set Texture menu item to set the current texture to Floor1.vga, all the panels that are already in your level that are Floor1.vga panels will turn white, and all those that are something else will turn gray (See Figure 18.3).

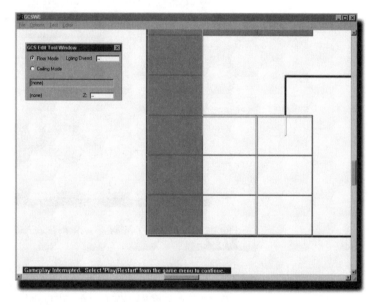

FIGURE *The white and gray floor panels.*
18.3

Another method for changing the Floor/Ceiling mode is to use the modeless dialog box that is constantly on the screen when you are using the EFE. There are two radio buttons called Floor Mode and Ceiling Mode. These can also cause the switch between Floor and Ceiling modes. See Figure 18.4 for the modeless dialog box.

This dialog box is useful in other ways, also. To use this box to get information about a floor panel, you must first select a panel. Do this by clicking a floor panel to select it. An X will appear on the panel. As soon as the panel is selected, notice that the name of the image file is now in the dialog box, and the height appears in the Z box. You can even select multiple panels by clicking several floor panels, one at a time. If all the panels you select have the same height, the Z box will contain the height. Otherwise, it will indicate "Various".

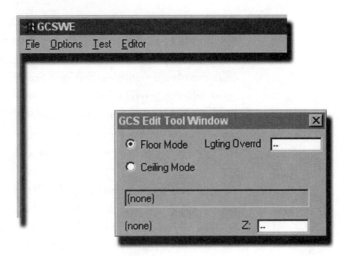

FIGURE   *The modeless dialog box used to switch between Floor and Ceiling mode.*
18.4

Adjusting the Height of Floor or Ceiling Panels

To adjust the height of a floor or ceiling panel, select it, and then use your mouse to select the height in the Z box of the GCS Edit Tool window. Type in a new height, and all the panels you have selected will move to the specified height. To deselect the panels after you change the height, just right click anywhere on the layout, and all selected panels will become de-selected.

Level Settings

Each game level can have its own settings. You can make changes in this dialog box, and if you select Save Extra from the Editor menu, your settings will stay set (See Figure 18.5).

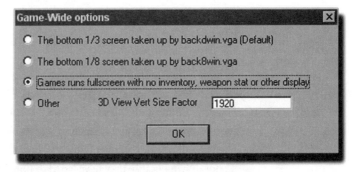

FIGURE   *The Game Level Settings dialog box.*
18.5

Fade Start Distance and Total Darkness Distance

If you wish, you can have the walls and floors fade to black as they recede from the viewport. The walls will be shown at maximum brightness until a distance from the observer equal to the Fade Start Distance. This is in regular GCS units, where one typical wall section is 400 units. Total Darkness Distance is the distance where the brightness has faded all the way to zero. No wall sections will be drawn that entirely darkened.

For example, say the Fade Start Distance is set to 1,000 units. Now say there is only one wall in your level. If you are close to the wall, it will be drawn at full brightness. Now as you back away, it will stay at full brightness until it is 1,000 units away; at that point it, will start to darken as you move even farther away.

Now assume the Fade End Distance is set to 3,000 units. If you keep moving away from that wall section, it will continue to darken until you get to 3,000 units away and it is faded all the way to black.

Sometimes you want to set the Fade Start Distance to a negative value. This will cause a wall to be somewhat faded even when you are right up against it. This is desirable when using special lighting effects because otherwise, the lighting effects wash out when you get close.

NOTE

In order for the fading with distance to work, the check box called Fade to blk with distance must be checked. However, even if it is NOT checked, the fade start distance and total darkness distance options do still set the Zero Point darkness. If you want all the walls to be at maximum brightness, make sure you make the Fade Start Distance a positive value.

Wall Fade Code 0 Point

The Wall Fade Code 0 point option sets the zero point for walls that have lighting overrides. The EFE will set lighting overrides according to the section on lighting effects. You can change the bias on lighting effects globally with this value.

Other Level Options

Fade Lights with Distance

The Fade Lights with Distance option lets you choose whether or not to have lighting effects diminish with distance. Sometimes this would be desirable when you don't want faraway lights to "show through" when surrounding walls are not drawn because they have faded to pure blackness. If this is not an issue, leave this option off for better realism.

Z-buffer

If you plan on having floors and ceiling panels at varying heights, you must turn this option on, even though it will hurt animation speed performance. If all your floor and ceiling panels are the same height, you can get a performance boost by turning this option off for the current level.

Background Options

Red, Green, and Blue

These boxes set the color of the background of the 3D viewport. This is the color that shows through between the gaps of the walls and floor panels. You can set this color using the RGB numerical mixtures we talked about previously.

Most of the time, you will want the background of the 3D world to be black, which would be the following settings:

Black = R0, G0, B0
White = R255, G255, B255
Dark Blue = R0, G0, B64

Horizon Texture

You have the option of using a horizon texture bitmap. This could be a wide mountain scene that moves as you turn in the 3D world. It is drawn behind all walls and objects and looks like it is far away because of its movement. This movement is called *parallax movement.*

The image must be a 256-Color VGA file. It is usually a very large one, maybe 1,024 wide or larger.

The XSCL and YSCL buttons allow you to stretch it in the horizontal and vertical directions. The left/right speed allows you to fine-tune how much it moves when you turn in the 3D world. It will take a trial-and-error process to get that right so the horizon does not appear to spin faster than the walls in your 3D world.

The same goes for the up/down speed, which is for when the user uses the A or Z keys to look up or down.

Setting of Game Wide Options

This dialog box allows you to change settings that affect the whole game, not just one level. At present, there is only one option, as shown in Figure 18.6.

FIGURE *The Game World Options dialog box.*
18.6

3D VIEW VERTICAL SIZE FACTOR

Originally, a full third of the screen was covered in the DOS GCS game engine. Here you get to choose the amount of the screen, as n/1920ths. This means that if you wanted the 3D view to use up half the vertical size of the screen, you would put the number 960 in here, because 1920/2 = 960. If you wanted the whole screen to be used for the 3D view, put 1920 in here.

The VGA file called backgwin.vga is stretched into the remaining portion of the screen. You may change the size of backgwin.vga as desired. It is not fixed.

SPECIAL EFFECTS WITH THE DOS LEVEL EDITOR

Adding Light Sources

By adding light sources to your levels, you can make stunning visual effects. A light source is an invisible object in the 3D world that emits light in all directions. In GCS, you can make rectangular light sources of any size and put them anywhere in the 3D world. This is accomplished in the DOS GCS editor.

A light source is really just a new kind of platform object. These are created using the Platform icon in the GCS Level Editor.

NOTE

Light sources are flat rectangles, as viewed from the top view. The area within the rectangle is illuminated at maximum intensity, and as you move away from the edges, the light will fall off with distance linearly when it gets outside the rectangle.

You will probably want to turn grid snap off when you make a light source. Usually, you do not want the edge of a light source to be on the edge of a wall; rather, you want your wall corners to be either decisively in the light rectangle, or in the fall-off area.

NOTE

Adding lights to the 3D world is relatively easy using the DOS GCS editor. To add a light source:

1. Make a platform object.
2. Specify that it is *not* visible.
3. Select the Assign Value To Register option. Click OK.

A new dialog box will open, asking you for the univ register and the value you want to assign. Here you must place a number between 192 and 223. For a light source of maximum brightness, put the value 223 in the top box where the univ reg number goes.

In addition to selecting the brightness of a light, you also need to specify how far away from the platform's edges that the light travels before fading out. After you decide on a fadeout distance, divide the desired range by 10, and put that number in the bottom box where the value goes.

For example, if I wanted a light source to reach 1,100 units, I would put the value 110 in there. The maximum range is either 1,280 units or 2,550 units, depending on if the DOS GCS editor can accept byte values greater than 127 or not.

You can also add negative light sources that suck light away. Any value less than 208 in the top box will suck light instead of adding it.

NOTE

Warning! The lighting effects are only calculated at the wall and floor panel corners. This means that to get smooth lighting effects, the range has to cover all four corners of a wall panel. Small lights that only include one corner of a wall panel will not give a very nice effect. Make your light sources large, unless you have small wall panels.

CAUTION

There can be up to 32 light sources on a game level. More than 32 light sources will cause some of them to be nonfunctional.

Lighting Effects

You can also modify the lighting on a wall panel. This can make a wall panel darker or lighter, or make it pulse or flash. To do this:

1. Place the wall in your level with the DOS Level Editor.
2. Use the Object menu to select Edit Attributes. This will bring up a dialog box with several buttons for selecting options for that wall object (See Figure 18.7).

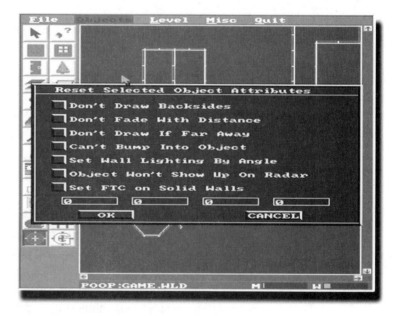

FIGURE *The Wall Options dialog box.*
18.7

If you only have one wall section selected, there will be four red boxes along the bottom of the dialog box. To make this wall object have special lighting effects, a number is placed in the *third* red box. If you want to modify the constant illumination on the wall section, put a number between 1 and 63 in the red box.

Put a 63 in the third red box if you want to brighten the wall by the maximum amount possible.

Put a 1 in the third red box if you want to darken the panel by the maximum amount.

The number that represents the zero point of illumination is a variable that you can set in the Level Options dialog box. This is called the Wall Fade Code

0 Point setting. All lighting effect values greater than this number will lighten the wall section; all values below this number will darken the wall section.

For example, if the Wall Fade Code 0 Point is set to 48, then any value greater than 48 that is placed in the third red box will brighten the wall section, and values less than 48 will darken the wall section.

In addition, you can make a wall pulsate or flash intermittently. To do this, you calculate a number based on a command code and an intensity value. First, choose one of the following commands:

- Command 2 Pulsate Phase 1
- Command 3 Pulsate Phase 2
- Command 4 Pulsate Phase 3
- Command 5 Flash Intermittently

Multiply that command number by 32. Then add an intensity value from 1 to 31. Most of the time you would leave the intensity value at 31 for the maximum effect, but it can be adjusted for milder effects.

Following are some examples of numbers to put in the third red box of a wall section:

- 63 for constant brightness added to a wall section's illumination
- 95 for pulsate effect using phase 1
- 127 for pulsate effect using phase 2
- 159 for pulsate effect using phase 3
- 191 for intermittent effect

Using Special Lighting Effects in Light Sources

You can also apply these pulsating and intermittent effects to lighting sources.

First make your light source, according to the instructions given above. Then select that platform object with the DOS Level Editor. Next open the Edit Attributes dialog box. Put a value in the *fourth* little red box. The value you put in the fourth little red box should be calculated according to the previous section on wall section lighting.

NOTE

When applying these effects to a light source (platform object), make sure you put your number in the fourth (the last) little red box instead of the third, like you would for a wall section. If you put it in the wrong little red box, the lighting source will not work at all.

USING CHEAT KEYS IN YOUR GAME

GCS has five cheat functions you can invoke during a game, using the following codes:

kill all - Kills all enemies on a level

invincible - Turns on God mode

magic heal - Brings the player to 100% health

open doors - Opens all doors on the level for a few seconds

teleport n - Teleports the user to entry point #n

To use a cheat code:

1 Hold down the left Shift key.
2. Press the c key.
3. You will then be prompted to enter the cheat code.
4. After entering the cheat code, press Enter.

Now that you can take advantage of the special features in the Extra Features Editor, we are finally ready to make your game final. In the coming chapter, we will complete our 3D game.

CHAPTER

19

ASSEMBLING THE FINAL GAME

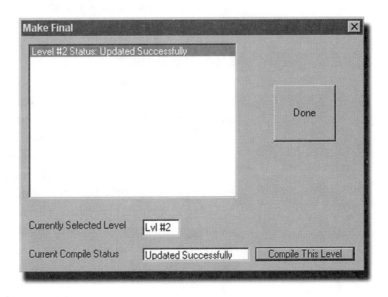

CAUTION

S o you've learned how to layout a 3D level, operate the paint program, and even enhance your level with the Extra Features Editor. Now you are ready to turn all those 3D levels into a game. The final step for all those levels in your project is to hook them all together with stairwells, transporters, or other devices. Then click Make Final to create the game.

Warning! *It is very important to read this chapter carefully. If you don't do these steps just right, your final game will not function properly.*

Connecting the Levels

To make your final game, each of your levels must have a unique level number. In general, it makes sense to set the level that the player starts in as level 0, and the next level 1, and so on. In more complicated level connections, it doesn't have to be linear. This means you might have level 0 connected to levels 3, 5, and 10. In this case, there really isn't a sequential progression of levels, since the user is going all over the place. Basically, each level needs to have a unique level number before you can make your final compiled game, and a linear progression is easiest for your first few games.

WARP-TO POINTS

Traveling between game levels is done through warp-to points. A warp-to point is merely a place where the player will appear. These points are set using the Warp-To Point Manager from the Level pull-down menu. You can put as many warp-to points in a level as you like. You assign a name to each warp-to point after you set it with the mouse (See Figures 19.1 and 19.2.)

Once a warp-to point is defined, then you can make the player travel to that level and position anytime. You can cause this to happen by using platforms, or by having an animated object execute the warp-to point command. Normally, the passageways between levels are done with a simple invisible platform placed around a stairwell wall piece. When the player walks within the invisible boundary of the platform object, he is whisked to a different level and position.

NOTE

The warp-to point is only a destination. It is the platform that makes the level switch happen. To make a connection between two levels, you must set both a warp-to point in the destination level, AND a platform in the original level.

CAUTION

Warning! This does NOT work in test mode. All warp-to platforms or animated object commands will be ignored in test mode. These will work only in your final game that you start with the GO.BAT batch file.

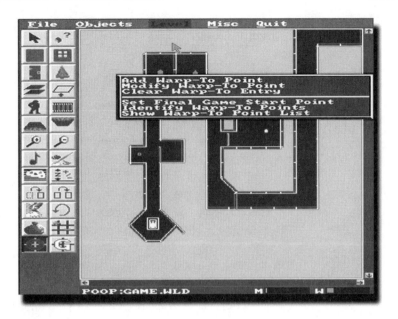

FIGURE   *The Warp-To Point Manager.*
19.1

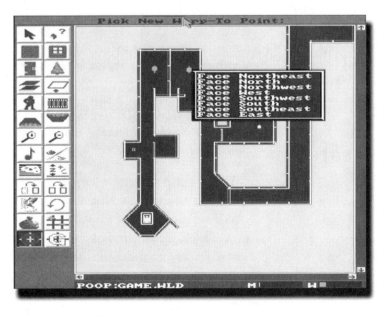

FIGURE   *The picking of a warp-to point and direction selector.*
19.2

You should keep track of all the connections between levels on pencil and paper. This is very important. Do not try to keep the level numbers and the warp-to point names in your head. List each of your level names, and write down the name and level number on a list. When you have assigned each level a number, and have written them down on paper, it is time to assign connections between the levels.

Internally, GCS makes a table when you use the Warp-To Point Manager from the Level menu. Each warp-to point has a name typed in by you. Warp-to points are a specification of a level number and a position.

For example, in a game I want the user to start in level 0, walk up to a staircase, and then do a level switch to level 7. Assuming you have already used the set current level number to each of your levels, then you can go about setting warp-to points.

Open level 7 of your game. Then click the Warp-to Point Manager menu choice in the Level menu. Next click Add, and then click the spot where you want the player to appear. A text box pops up asking you to choose which direction the player should end up facing (north is toward the top of the screen). Then it asks you to type in a reference name that you make up. Choose a descriptive name like "Back into the lobby from stairs," so you will know which warp-to point is what.

After you type in the name and press Return, you will see a red dot in your level. This is your warp-to point. It is not an object in your 3D world. This is only a marker on your screen to show you that there is a warp-to point. If you zoom in, you will see that the dot has a spike sticking out to show which direction you would be facing.

NOTE

Because it is not really a 3D object, the Box and Question Mark icon will not identify it. If you would like to see which warp-to point it is, then bring up the Warp-To Point Manager and click Identify Warp-To.

Thus, if a platform is set to warp the player to the lobby, he will be warped to level 7 in the final game. He will appear at the place you clicked upon.

So now you have set one warp-to point. To make it a functional passageway between levels, you must make a platform object in level 0, and place it right in front of the staircase wall. Make sure that the platform sticks out at least 150 cm from the wall. When you make the platform, click the Warp-To box. Then when you click OK, you will be given a list of warp-to points from which to

CAUTION

CAUTION

choose. Select the one you just made. You have formed the connection between level 0 and level 7 of your game.

Warning! Platforms can only do one function at a time, so only click the Warp-To button, and not any of the others. If you click more than one function for your platform, the platform might not work.

If you want the connection between level 0 and 7 to be a two-way connection, so the user can come back the same way, then you must make another level 0 warp-to point. You must make a platform which sends the user there in your level 7. To set a warp-to point in level 0, you need to open level 0, click again on the Warp-To Point Manager from the Level menu, and assign your new warp-to point a name.

Warning! A design challenge here is to make sure that you don't put the platform in level 7 where the user lands in the exact same spot as where he is teleported in from level 0. This mistake causes an endless loop. The perplexed user bounces back and forth between the two levels indefinitely.

IMPORTANT CONSIDERATIONS

No Level switches in test mode
The only way to test your inter-level connections is to click Make Final. Then exit GCS and run the game from the target directory. Level switch platforms and animated objects that give the level switch command will be ignored when trying out your levels in test mode.

Make Final Will NOT Work Unless You Have Specified a Game Start Position.
Bring up the Warp-To Point Manager, and click the command to set the final game start position. Don't get this confused with the Set Player Position command on the Level menu. That command is just for testing the 3D world.

After you specify and name the final game starting position, it will show up as a yellow dot with a spike. You can only have one game start position. This initial starting point can be on any of your levels. The player does not have to start on level 0.

Setting the Game Start Position
The Set Player Position command in the Level menu is only for using with the test command. This command does NOT set where the player starts in the final game. These positions are ignored in the final game. In order to set the starting position for the player in the final game, you MUST use the Set Final

Game Start Point command from the Warp-To Point Manager Menu. This will set the location of the player when he starts up the final game using the GO.BAT batch file.

Make Final Will NOT Work Unless You Have Tested All Your Levels.

When you click Test Level to try out your level, several files are created in your project directory on your hard drive. The Make Final feature uses these files to compile all your. VGR files and other files into compressed binary files. The upshot is that unless you have clicked Test Level for each level, the Make Final command will fail.

When you make changes to any level in your project, you must test the level in the 3D world. Otherwise, when you click Make Final, your changes will not be reflected in the final product.

If you change the level number of a level using the Set Current Level Number command, you must click Test Level, enter the 3D world, and come back. Otherwise, that level will not be stored correctly. If you make a mistake and give two of your levels the same number, it will get confusing. Only one of the two levels will make it to the final game. The level that you tested last is included. Its twin is bypassed. Then in your final product, any warp-to points that were meant for the missing level would take the player to inappropriate spots, since the warp-to points weren't meant for that level.

When you click Make Final, only levels that have warp-to points assigned to them will be included in the final product. This makes sense, because if there is no way for the player to get to that level, there is no reason to include that level in the final product.

The Correct Sequence of Preparing for Make Final

1. First go through all your levels and figure out where you want players to enter the levels.
2. Set the warp-to points, and write them down!
3. Then go through all the levels and put in the level-switching platforms. Use your list to get the *correct* warp-to point names.

Warning! If you set a platform to a nonexistent warp-to point, you will get a critical error when you go over that platform in the final game.

Don't forget to click Test Level after setting each warp-to point. If you don't test each level in the 3D world after changing it in any way, the changes don't get put into your final product!

CAUTION

Don't forget to set the final game starting point from the Warp-To Point Manager. If you forget, GCS will refuse to "make final."

After this, you are ready to make your final game. Open any of your game levels, and select Make Final from the File menu. The GCS game engine will start up, but instead of the normal dialog box, a different one will come up. All the levels in your game are listed in the dialog box. Select the first one, so it is highlighted in blue. Then click the Compile this Level button (See Figure 19.3).

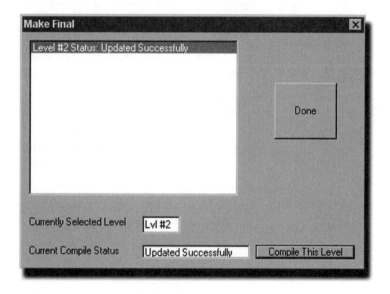

FIGURE   *The Levels dialog box during the Make Final operation.*
19.3

After this is done, exit the game engine and go back to the Level Editor. Then repeat this process for your other levels. When all your game levels have been "made final", your final game is ready for testing.

Trying out your final game

To try out your final product, exit GCS. Then change to the target game directory. The target directory should be in the root of your hard drive, and have the same name as your project. For example, if your project is named Blaster, and your GCS is installed on Drive C:, your final game target directory is named C:\Blaster.

Then you run the game by opening a DOS Prompt box, changing to your final game directory, and typing one of the following command lines:

GO.BAT Command Line Options

go	(for no sound)
go s1	(for sound; letter "s" and number 1, NOT letter "s" and letter "l")
go s1 j	(for sound and joystick control)
go s1 m	(for sound and mouse control)
go s1 m g	(for sound, mouse control, and God mode)

You will notice that the game loads much faster than Test Level does.

WHAT TO DO IF THERE ARE PROBLEMS

Make sure you typed "s1", not "s" and the letter "l" (sl). This mistake is the one most often made.

DON'T put slashes or dashes in front of the command line options as you may have done for other DOS applications.

If the level-to-level connections aren't working, then you can always redo them. Use the Box and Question Mark icon to tell you what each platform is set to do, and examine your warp-to points. You can overwrite their current values by erasing and replacing platforms, and using the Warp-To Point Manager to reset your warp-to points.

NOTE

If you feel that your warp-to points are messed up beyond repair, or you are simply confused and want to start with a clean slate (because maybe you didn't write them down), then exit GCS and delete the files WARP_TO.DAT and GAMESTRT.DAT, and then start putting your warp-to points in again from scratch.

CAUTION

Warning! If you remove a warp-to point, you must also remember to remove any platforms that direct the player to the now-absent warp-to point. Warping to a deleted warp-to point can cause unexpected results, or a critical error.

Common Problems in the Final Game

You might find it helpful to print the file THEATERS.TXT from your target data\ subdirectory. The first column is the warp-to point number. The third column is the level number. The next three numbers are the x, y, and z coordinates in the 3D world where the player should go to.

If weird things are going on, like levels are missing in your final game, or you are appearing in totally unexpected places, you may have given two levels the same level number. GCS will not complain about this, but the final game will never work correctly if you do this. This will not normally generate critical errors, but it can make level switches to unpredictable places.

Making an installation for Your Final Game

Once you get the final game running the way you want on your system, you'll want to distribute the final product for others to try. To do this, I suggest you use Install Maker by Clickteam. It is on the CD-ROM in the back of the book. You should install it and follow the Wizard that will take you through the process of building a professional installation routine. Install Maker allows you to have custom bitmaps and README files, and to create install directories. Best of all, it allows you to create an uninstall routine.

TROUBLESHOOTING

What to Do if the Game Engine Won't Go Into the 3D World

First of all, to isolate your problem, always try the original and unchanged WREDEMO level (remember, I suggested you make a copy if you altered it). If that fails, then you know the problem isn't with the level itself; it must be with the driver or mode selection. If the DEMO levels work fine, but your level won't work, then the problem must be with your new level.

If the WREDEMO level will not run, how do they fail? Normally, what happens when you click the Enter 3D World button is that text messages will be flashing in the lower left-hand part of the screen as the game engine loads the various components of your game level. When all the data is complete, the video should go blank for a split second while it changes to the new full screen mode. Then the game engine should start.

If it fails before the screen goes blank, then the problem is probably with the installation or something that is preventing the level data from loading correctly. If there is a critical error or a seterror, write the numbers down and contact Pie in the Sky at their Web site for assistance. Also, look in the ENGINE directory for a file called error.txt, which gets written when an error occurs, and send that along.

If the error or crash occurs directly after the screen goes blank, it could be a Direct X graphics type of error, in which case, switching the DirectDraw Device, the D3D Device, or video mode might solve the problem. The absolute most reliable settings would be using a DD Device of Display, a D3D Device of RAMP, and a video mode of 320 x 200 x 16. i.e.; start the game engine, but click the Change Device/Mode button instead of the Enter 3D World button. Then use the items on the File menu to change your settings to the following:

DD Device: Display   Use Select DD Device from File menu to set this.

D3D Device: RAMP   Use Select D3D Device from File menu to set this.

Display Mode: 320 x 200 x 16 Hi Color   Use Choose Screen Size/Mode from File menu to set this.

If this still fails, you'll have to contact Pie in the Sky at their Web site for assistance. Check the Web site www.pieskysoft.com for the latest support information. Perhaps your problem is one experienced by others, and there is already a solution on the site.

If these settings DO work, then you'll have to do some experimentation to find out whether it was the video mode that you had chosen, or the HAL driver, or which setting it is that seems to be causing the problem. Make sure you do your testing on the unmodified WREDEMO level, since that is known to be a functioning game level.

Debugging Your Game Level

If the WREDEMO levels work fine in the 3D world, but your level does not, first find out if all your levels fail, or just one in particular. If you only have one level so far in your project, try adding a new level with just a few walls in it which are close to the start position. Try setting the objdef library to Basiclib, the active guard to def_enem, and the level number to 30 or something you aren't using in your other level(s). If the WREDEMO levels test fine, but even this very simple level will not run in the GCS Windows Engine, then there must be something wrong with the whole project. Write down any error numbers and print out the error.txt file which gets created in the ENGINE directory when the game gets an unrecoverable error. Contact Pie in the Sky at their Web site for assistance, or check out the Web site www.pieskysoft.com to see if others have experienced your problem. There may be a solution there for you.

Troubleshooting Questions and Answers

1. I put platforms down in my level, and warp-to points, but it never works. I go there and stand right in the middle of the platform, but nothing happens.

Level-switching cannot occur when testing an individual level. You need to "make final," and then run the final game.

Also, make sure that you Test Level after setting any platform. If you forget to test your level after making changes, then the platform will not actually be in your final game.

Use the ? icon to check that your platforms are in the right place and are set correctly. If in doubt, delete your platform and replace it with a new one, but don't forget to click Test Level before making final again!

2. How do I put more than one kind of enemy on a level?

The Level Editor assumes you will have just one type of enemy on your game level. However, you may have several different types of enemies on your level. To add more types of enemies, you will need to use the Extra Features Editor and not the DOS editor.

3. When I save my files in GCSPaint, they don't get saved, or they are saved as the wrong file type.

There are a few different things that could be happening.

First, if you want to save your images as a VGR file, then you must have started GCSPaint from the icon that is on the GCS Layout Editor screen.

If you started the paint program by typing "GCSPaint," then your files will be saved as VGA files.

If you save your VGR file in the proper directory, it may not show up in your Import list in the Library Manager dialog box. Be advised that although things you add to the list usually appear at the end, this is not always so. This is dependent upon DOS file order on the hard drives, which is unpredictable. Look through the list carefully, and you can probably find it.

4. How do I change the damage indicator guy for my game?

CAUTION

Exit GCS and bring up GCSPaint from the command line. You need to load the VGA file called htpt.vga from your project directory. You will see that this image file is a tiled repeat of the damage indicator, with varying degrees of damage in each picture. Feel free to change your damage images.

Warning! Do not try to change the dimensions of the little damage boxes, or the size of the whole htpt.vga image. If you do, the game engine may crash.

5. Why does my sound not work in my final game? Why doesn't my joystick work?

The joystick cannot be used when testing levels. You need to add "s1" to the go command line (**go s1**). Make sure you use the number "1" and not the letter 'l' in your "s1" option!

You must also add a "j" if you want joystick support. When you actually finish your game, you will probably want to use GCSMENU to create a way for your customers to choose sound on/off, joystick on/off, etc.

6. When I try to define written text for memos and animated objects to use, it never works.

You need to edit the file pstr.txt in your project directory, and then you must run the program pstr.exe on it to actually make your new text messages available for your game. The Help file on Text Messages explains how to do this. Be very careful not to ignore the two periods and the backslash when you type PSTR! Also, make sure you understand how to give each message in your pstr.txt file a different number when you are editing the file.

7. When I try to load my .GIF, .PCX, or .BMP file into GCSPaint, the screen flashes, and it refuses to load my picture.

The most common cause of this is that you are trying to import a picture that has too many pixels in it. The largest image that GCSPaint can handle is 200 x 200 pixels in size. If an image is more than 200 pixels high OR 200 pixels wide, the image will refuse to load. 200 x 200 is too large for a practical object in the GCS game.

If you are absolutely sure that your image is small enough in number of pixels, but the image is still being rejected, then perhaps your .PCX or .BMP file is not the right type. Since the GCS artwork must be 256-color, all .PCX or .BMP files that you import must be 256-color also. 16-color files are not accepted, and neither are 16 million color versions of these files.

8. Why is the computer beeping at me whenever I do anything with my level?

You are close to, or have already added too much artwork to your level, and memory is full. See the explanation of the the M and W meters in the previous chapters.

And finally . . .

A Legal Notice of What You May Distribute

When you use the Make Final command, GCS makes a directory on your hard drive with the same name as your project. You may distribute all the files in this directory and the data\ subdirectory. These files comprise *your* game. The .EXE files in that directory are copyrighted by Pie in the Sky Software, but like shareware programs, you have implicit permission to distribute them in unmodified form. The same goes for all the other files that the unmodified GCS puts in that directory when you "make final".

When the user copies the game files from your floppies to his hard drive, make sure that he preserves the directory structure. This means that the Data\ subdirectory and its contents must be contained within the main game directory when he types the GO.BAT command line to start the game.

A P P E N D I X

WHAT'S ON THE CD-ROM

The **Awesome Game Creation's** companion CD-ROM is packed with everything you need to make all of the fully interactive games in this book – and more! Each of the folders includes useful tools for you to learn game creation!

General Minimum System Requirements: You will need a computer that can run Windows 95 with a CD-ROM drive, sound card, and mouse to complete *all* of the tutorials and play all of the games in this book.

- **The Games Factory and Install Maker by Clickteam** (www.clickteam.com)

There are two folders on the ROM (TGF FINAL 16 and TGF FINAL 32) and each includes either the 16 Bit (Win 3.1 and NT) or the 32 Bit (Windows 95/98/2000) install files for the respective version of *The Games Factory*. The proper file will install everything you need to run *The Games Factory*. As long as you can run Windows or Windows NT, you can run *The Games Factory* and *The Install Maker*.

This version of *The Games Factory* is a special demo version for the book and is *not* time limited. It is a fully functional shareware demo and is only limited in the following ways;

- You will see a Games Factory screen at start up.
- You will *not* be able to save stand alone games, screen savers, or Internet games. But you can save the .GAM data files created and when you

upgrade to the registered version your files will be fully compatible. Please got to www.clickteam.com for the upgrade price - it is a bargain!

- **The PIE 3D Game Creation System by Pie in the Sky Software (www.pieskysoft.com)**

With The PIECGS you can make your own stand alone 3D games with no programming. The (the 'PieGCS' folder on the ROM). Simply run the installer and you are in business. This application was designed to run on a 386 or better computer with a VGA graphics card. The best part of the PIEGCS is that it is free! The only limit being that there is no technical support, but on the web site (www.pieskysoft.com) there is technical support files and information. You can also join the mailing list at www.gcsgames.com and get all the help you need.

- **Professional Quality Game Textures by Nick Marks (www.freetextures.com)**

The textures in the folder 'NickMarks' on the ROM were created by Nicholas Marks and lots more textures can be found at the Free Textures site. If you use these textures you will need to give Nicholas Marks credit in your production.

- **3D RAD - 3D Game development tool by Bitplane (www.3drad.com)**

In the folder '3drad' is the file '3drad256.exe'. This file is the installation file for the latest 15-day trial version of 3D RAD. The minimum system requirements for 3DRAD are a Windows 9x or Windows 2000 machine with a 90 MHZ processor, 16 megabytes of RAM, DirectX 6 or greater and a Direct3D compatible video card.

NOTE

3DRAD will not alter your system settings in anyway and can be removed from your system by simply deleting the folder you installed 3drad in.

- **MilkShape 3D by Mete Ciragan (www.swissquake.ch/chumbalum-soft)**

The 'Ms3d' folder contains the file for MilkShape 3D, a shareware product and for a registration fee of $20 US Dollars you can't beat this product. You have 30 days to see just how awesome this product is! Go to http:www.swissquake.ch/chumbalum-soft and take a step up as a developer. The minimum system specs are a P200 32 MB RAM, Software OpenGL drivers and about 2MB HD space on a Win95 or higher machine.

- **GoldWave Sound Editing by Chris Craig (www.goldwave.com)**

In the 'GoldWave' folder you will find this shareware demo version of the Goldwave sound editor. It is shareware and requires you to register it if you keep it (about $40 US).

GoldWave requires a 486 or better CPU, a mouse, 16MB of RAM, 3MB of disk space, and a sound card. A coprocessor is recommended (but not required). For best performance, use a Pentium 200MHz or faster processor with 64MB of RAM or more.

- **Paint Shop Pro by Jasc, Inc. (www.jasc.com)**

In the 'PSP6-2' folder is a 30 day demo version of Paint Shop Pro.6. The minimum system requirements are a mouse, Pentium class computer. 32 MBS of RAM, 30 MBS hard drive space, and at least a 256 color display.

- **Sample Game Files**

In the 'sample games' folder of the ROM are all the files and assets used in the exercises in the book in part 2. Please note that all needed assets are within those files.

Sample Games folder

1. Defiler
   Spacedel2.gam
   Spacedel3.gam

2. Dragon
   dragon.gam

3. Ghost Hunter
   GhostHunter.gam

4. tgflibs
   Dragon.gam
   GhostHunter.gam
   Spacedel2.gam
   Spacedel3.gam

INDEX